The End of Employer-Provided Health Insurance

The **End** of **Employer-Provided Health Insurance**

WHY IT'S GOOD FOR YOU, YOUR FAMILY, and YOUR COMPANY

PAUL ZANE PILZER and
RICK LINDQUIST

WILEY

Published by John Wiley & Sons, Inc., Hoboken, New Jersey.
Published simultaneously in Canada.

For general information about our other products and services, please contact our Customer Care Department within the United States at (800) 762-2974, outside the United States at (317) 572-3993 or fax.(317) 572-4002.

Wiley publishes in a variety of print and electronic formats and by print-on-demand. Some material included with standard print versions of this book may not be included in e-books or in print-on-demand. If this book refers to media such as a CD or DVD that is not included in the version you purchased, you may download this material at http://booksupport.wiley.com. For more information about Wiley products, visit www.wiley.com.

Library of Congress Cataloging-in-Publication Data

Pilzer, Paul Zane.
  The end of employer-provided health insurance : why it's good for you, your family, and your company / Paul Zane Pilzer, Richard Lindquist.
     pages cm
  Includes bibliographical references and index.
  ISBN 978-1-119-01211-5 (hardback); ISBN 978-1-119-01213-9 (ebk); ISBN 978-1-119-01212-2 (ebk)
  1. Health insurance—Self-insurance—United States. 2. Healthcare reform—United States. I. Lindquist, Richard. II. Title.
  HG9396.P5498 2014
  368.38'200973—dc23

                                                                                          2014029362

Printed in the United States of America
10 9 8 7 6 5 4 3 2 1

CONTENTS

PREFACE

In 1999, I (Paul Zane Pilzer) was elated to learn that my wife Lisa was pregnant, but my joy turned to panic when my family lost our employer-provided health insurance due to our moving from Texas to Utah. In addition to potentially losing access to our medical providers, if our baby was born prematurely it could cost up to $60,000 a day for four months. And this amount didn't include care that a preterm child might need afterward or any medical care for Lisa. No wonder failed employer-provided health insurance is the number one cause of personal bankruptcy in the United States!

Fortunately, our baby was born healthy, and afterwards I found a solution to get affordable health insurance for my family. My solution was an individual health insurance policy purchased directly from the Blue Cross Blue Shield insurance carrier in our state. But there was a catch: The policy did not cover any pre-existing conditions (such as pregnancy), and every member of our family had to be healthy in order to be accepted by the insurance carrier. So, while my solution worked for three subsequent pregnancies, it wouldn't have helped us if our first child had not been born healthy.

As a serial entrepreneur, I view each negative consumer experience as a business opportunity. When you are a dissatisfied consumer of a product or service, you can either get angry, or get wealthy by starting a company providing the same product or service to other similarly dissatisfied consumers.

In 1999, I started a company, Extend Health, Inc., to provide employees of large companies individual health insurance policies paid for by their employer. (Extend Health was originally called Wellness Services and changed its name in 2004 to Extend Benefits and in 2008 to Extend Health. Extend Health was 100 percent acquired in May 2012 by Towers Watson for $435 million cash.) Our solution wasn't for everyone because—in 45 states at that time—every member of your family had to be healthy to be accepted for individual health insurance. In the five states that didn't require you to be healthy, the cost of individual health insurance was higher than the cost of employer-provided health insurance.

Despite not being able to serve all U.S. employees, the demand by employers was enormous for an affordable solution to the problem of providing their employees' health insurance. By 2007, Extend Health had grown to be one of the largest providers of individual health insurance policies funded by employers to U.S. employees and retirees. Extend Health focused almost exclusively on serving large employers, and my partners and I sold the company in 2012 to Towers Watson, one of the world's largest providers of traditional employer-provided health insurance.

The core competency behind Extend Health was technology and software we developed that allowed large employers to comply with a myriad of state and federal regulations when providing employees with individual health insurance policies funded by their employer. We helped more than 700,000 Americans get better health insurance. But I was disappointed; at that time our technology limited our customer base to mostly very large employers, whereas I've always preferred the excitement that comes from serving startups, small employers, and entrepreneurs.

So, in April 2006, I started Zane Benefits to affordably provide to small and medium-sized employers the same service that Extend Health provided to large employers—the ability to give their employees money to purchase their own individual health insurance policies. Zane Benefits, unlike Extend Health, does not sell health insurance, only software. We sell our software solution online either directly to employers or through insurance affiliates who then help each employee obtain their own individual health insurance policy.

Three important events occurred at Zane Benefits in the summer of 2007, our first full year in operation.

The first event occurred on July 30, 2007, when Zane Benefits was featured with my dog-eared caricature on the front page of *The Wall Street Journal*. Initially, when I heard earlier that *The Wall Street Journal* was running the story, I phoned the editor-in-chief and pleaded with him to wait until we had more employees and distribution in place to serve customers. I can still remember him telling me:

> *Professor Pilzer, we don't run stories to suit the timing of your business, we choose our stories by their relevance to our readers. And this story about allowing employees to choose their own individual health insurance policy funded by their employer is the biggest story affecting U.S. employers and employees that I've seen in my five years running* The Wall Street Journal.

By the end of 2007, Zane Benefits had distribution agreements in place for its software with the largest payroll providers and insurance carriers in the nation, including Paychex and United Healthcare. But, as highlighted in *The Wall Street Journal* story, our solution was controversial because not all employees qualified for individual health insurance at the same price, and at that time most individual health policies did not cover pre-existing medical conditions.

The second important event occurred on August 24, 2007, when I hired Rick Lindquist, a 22-year-old with a BS and BA in economics and computer science from Duke University. Over the next seven years Rick rose from being a trainee to director of sales and then president of the company. Rick keeps Zane Benefits focused on better ways to serve both our employer customers and their individual employees.

When I first interviewed Rick as a potential trainee, he asked about our company's health insurance plan, saying that his father had told him: "A good job comes with good (employer-provided) health insurance." His father's advice was challenged when Rick accepted our job offer and purchased an individual health insurance policy for $57 a month—a policy he still has today, seven years later, now costing $113 a month. Since Zane Benefits provides him with a $150 per month allowance for individual health insurance, Rick's effective out-of-pocket cost for health insurance has been $0 since he joined the company.

When the Affordable Care Act (Obamacare) was passed in 2010, Rick was among the first to realize that starting in 2014, when Obamacare would be implemented, it would no longer make financial, logical, or social sense for any U.S. employer to continue offering employer-provided health insurance to employees. He has spent the past four years preparing Zane Benefits for our explosive growth, and on June 4, 2014, Rick's picture appeared on the front page of *The New York Times* business section in a feature story about Zane Benefits and how we help employees transition to individual health insurance plans funded by their employer.

The third important event also occurred in August 2007 when I was joined on the board at Zane Benefits by two professional investors, Dave Eastman and Jim Tozer. Collectively, the three of us have more than 100 years of wisdom and senior management experience to help guide the brilliant operating team recruited and managed by our young president.

In 1976, when I was 22 years old (like Rick was in 2007), I was similarly recruited from the Wharton Business School to join Citibank by Jim Tozer, then a rising senior vice president at Citibank. Over the past 38 years, Jim has taught me that the most important rewards that come from working in business are the lifelong friends you make along the way.

At the time of the writing of this book, Zane Benefits has helped more than 3,000 employers transition their employees to individual health insurance plans, saving hundreds of millions of dollars each year. And now, due to the recent reforms to the individual market, Zane Benefits is expected to help more than 25,000 employers make a similar transition by 2017, providing their employees much better health insurance while saving employers and employees billions of dollars each year.

It is with great pleasure that I and my co-author Rick Lindquist present *The End of Employer-Provided Health Insurance*. We hope this book helps you, your family, and your employees get better, cheaper, and safer health insurance, while saving you and your employer thousands of dollars per person each year. We also hope this book helps you realize that the true rewards from working in business come from the lifelong friendships you build every day with your customers, suppliers, co-workers, and investors.

Sincerely,
Paul Zane Pilzer

EXECUTIVE SUMMARY—WHY YOU SHOULD READ THIS BOOK

H ealth insurance in the United States changed dramatically when President Obama signed the Affordable Care Act (popularly known as ACA or Obamacare) into law on March 23, 2010, and the U.S. Supreme Court rendered a final decision to affirm the law on June 28, 2012.

However, most Americans don't yet know this because many insurance brokers, insurance carriers, and larger employers don't want them to know.

This is because the $1.2 trillion employer-provided health insurance industry relies on most Americans under age 65 paying two to four times (200 to 400 percent) what they should be paying for health insurance under an outdated belief that the only way to get good health insurance is from an employer.

The facts are that since 2014, thanks to the Affordable Care Act:

1. Every American, regardless of their health, is entitled to get affordable individual health insurance from their state's ACA-mandated Health Insurance Marketplace (also known as an Exchange) that is better than employer-provided coverage for about one-half the price (50 percent) of an employer-provided plan.

2. Most American families earning less than $100,000 a year qualify to receive a 50 percent (on average) monthly federal subsidy (called a premium tax credit) towards the cost of their individual policy, but only if their employer does not offer them affordable employer-provided health insurance. This subsidy reduces the cost from one half (50 percent) to about one-quarter the price (25 percent) of their employer-provided plan.

3. Instead of offering their employees health insurance, employers are allowed to offer employees defined contribution, employer-funded individual health insurance where the employer contributes a fixed monthly amount toward the cost of each employee's individual health insurance policy.

Your employer may not want you to know this because:

1. Employers with more than 50 employees are required to pay a $2,000 to $3,000 per year non-deductible penalty for each of their employees

who obtain subsidized individual health insurance from their state's ACA-mandated Health Insurance Marketplace (or Exchange).

2. Employers don't want their employees, especially the healthy ones, to leave the employer-provided health insurance plan because employers need their participation and premiums to pay for the unhealthy employees, and because most insurance carriers require 75 percent participation from eligible employees to renew the company's employer-provided health insurance policy.

3. Employees who are offered affordable employer-provided health insurance are automatically disqualified from receiving their share of the federal subsidy on the Health Insurance Marketplace even if the employee rejects their employer's inferior coverage.

Insurance brokers may not want you to know this because they may not be qualified to sell affordable individual health insurance policies through the ACA-mandated Health Insurance Marketplaces now open in every U.S. state. Despite some early computer glitches when these Exchanges first opened in late 2013, every state now has a working state-run or federally-run Exchange (often called a Health Insurance Marketplace). These Health Insurance Marketplaces offer applicants affordable and subsidized individual policies regardless of their health or pre-existing medical conditions.

Your insurance company may not want you to know this because it only offers employer-provided health insurance coverage and/or it may not be participating in its state's ACA-mandated Health Insurance Marketplace which offers better coverage than employer-provided plans for about one-half (pre-subsidy) to one-fourth (after-subsidy) the cost.

As explained throughout this book:

1. Employer-provided health insurance is the greatest financial risk facing most American families.

2. Employer-provided health insurance is the greatest challenge facing U.S. employers, small and large, when it comes to recruiting and retaining top-quality employees.

3. Individual health insurance policies covering the same medical providers as employer-provided coverage are now available for Americans regardless of their health at one-half (pre-subsidy) to one-fourth (after-subsidy) the cost of employer-provided coverage.

4. Once you get a subsidized individual health insurance policy your monthly premium can almost never increase unless your income does— that's because the amount of your monthly federal subsidy is calculated so that you pay a fixed percent of your income for your individual health insurance.

5. New defined contribution healthcare solutions allow employers to reimburse employees for individual health insurance costs in lieu of offering traditional employer-provided health insurance. These defined contribution solutions save businesses and their employees 20 to 60 percent on health insurance costs annually.
6. All Americans, employers, and employees need to understand how the new federally-mandated Health Insurance Marketplace for individual health insurance works, what policies are available, how to choose one, how to sign up, and how to manage their lifetime individual health insurance and healthcare.

This book is written and organized for three types of readers:

1. **Employees of all U.S. companies.** You and your family need permanent, portable health insurance to get access to medical care, save money, and protect yourselves from our nation's failing employer-provided health insurance system. Lack of employer-provided health insurance is the biggest cause of personal bankruptcy for American families, and availability of health insurance is a major factor for every U.S. employee when choosing their next employer.
2. **Owners of small and medium-sized businesses.** If you are the owner or manager of a small to medium-sized business (1 to 999 employees), one of the biggest challenges you face in recruiting and retaining top quality employees is providing health insurance. Today, the majority of small to medium-sized businesses can no longer afford employer-provided coverage.
3. **Insurance agents, CPAs, and financial consultants.** You need to be able to advise your clients to help them and their employees get access to medical care, save money, and protect their families from the failing employer-provided health insurance system. Additionally, a new market of 50+ million individual health insurance consumers has emerged that will double in size to 100 million people over the next 10 years.

Employer-provided health insurance is the largest uncontrollable expense for many U.S. employers. Many employers have either eliminated employer-provided health insurance entirely or redesigned plans to require unaffordable cost-sharing by employees. Even the largest U.S. employers are challenged—in 2013 the Fortune 500 companies as a group spent more on employee health insurance than they earned in profits.

The U.S. employer-provided health insurance system is broken and it is getting worse each year. Since 2000, the percentage of Americans covered by employer-provided health insurance has steadily declined, and more than 10 million Americans have filed personal bankruptcy due to their employers' failed health insurance plan. But now there is a solution—employer-funded individual health insurance known as defined contribution health benefits.

Due to recent federal changes mandated by Obamacare to the U.S. individual health insurance market, individually-purchased health insurance is better and much less expensive for you, your family, and your company. The new individual Health Insurance Marketplaces in every state feature guaranteed acceptance at no extra cost for pre-existing medical conditions, a wide choice of plans, portability between employers, and provide coverage equal to or better than the most generous employer-provided plans. Moreover, for most employees earning less than $100,000 a year, the cost for each family member is heavily subsidized by the federal government. In 2014, 70 percent of the seven million people who enrolled their families through the federally-run Health Insurance Marketplaces paid less than $100 per month in out-of-pocket premiums for their entire family.

These benefits for consumers exist because of:

1. Trillions of dollars in federal subsidies to consumers who purchase individual health insurance plans.
2. Hundreds of billions of dollars in federal subsidies to insurance carriers to artificially reduce the cost of individual health insurance—all at taxpayer expense.

This book is written to ensure that you, your family, and your company get your fair share of the trillions of dollars the U.S. government will spend subsidizing individual health insurance plans between now and 2025.

We are at the beginning of a paradigm shift in the way businesses offer employee health benefits and the way Americans get health insurance—a shift from an employer-driven defined benefit model to an individual-driven defined contribution model. This parallels a similar shift in employer-provided retirement benefits that took place two to three decades ago from defined benefit to defined contribution retirement plans. Over the next 10 years, 100 million Americans will move from employer-provided health insurance to individually-purchased health insurance.

The purpose of *The End of Employer-Provided Health Insurance* is to show you how to profit from this paradigm shift while helping you, your family, and your employees get better, cheaper, and safer health insurance. It will help you save thousands of dollars per person each year and protect you from the greatest threat to your financial future—our nation's broken employer-provided health insurance system.

Using the techniques outlined in this book, you and your employer will save money on health insurance by migrating from employer-provided health insurance coverage to employer-funded individual plans at a total cost that is 20 percent to 60 percent lower for the same coverage. That's $4,000 to $12,000 in savings per year for a family of four for the same hospitals, same doctors, and same prescriptions.

INTRODUCTION—THE END OF EMPLOYER-PROVIDED HEALTH INSURANCE

S ince 2000, the percentage of Americans covered by employer-provided health insurance has steadily declined. Facing double-digit growth in health insurance premiums, many businesses have either eliminated health benefits or redesigned the plans to include higher deductibles, larger co-payments, and greater premium sharing by employees.

This price pressure has created a paradigm shift in the way small businesses offer employee health benefits—a shift from an employer-driven *defined benefit* model to an individual-driven *defined contribution* model. While the transition from employer-provided health insurance to individual health insurance has been gradual since 2000, the post-2014 enhancements to the Individual Market have accelerated this shift.

As a result, the Individual Market is expected to expand from 30 million insureds in 2012 to more than 150 million insureds by 2025 (U.S. Census, 2012; Mandelbaum, 2014).

This book focuses on this shift, which will be led by small businesses. Adopting defined contribution healthcare and individual health insurance plans will allow business owners and their employees to save a combined 20 to 60 percent ($4,000 to $12,000 in savings per family per year) on health insurance. Due to the significant cost advantage for business owners and their employees in the individual market, we predict 60 percent of businesses will eliminate traditional employer-provided health insurance in favor of defined contribution healthcare and individual health plans over the next three years.

HISTORY OF U.S. EMPLOYER-PROVIDED HEALTH INSURANCE

Prior to World War II, most Americans paid for their own medical care. They either paid their chosen provider directly, or through the Blue Cross Blue Shield health insurance entities that were created to offer guaranteed service for a fixed fee.

At that time, health insurance really was insurance—providing coverage only for major items like hospitalizations that people could not afford to pay for themselves. Many employees purchased their own individual or family health insurance policies, just as they do today with homeowners, auto, and life insurance.

After World War II, having witnessed the effects of hyperinflation on Germany after World War I, U.S. leaders and economists were concerned about potential postwar inflation. The U.S. Congress and President Roosevelt instituted wage and price controls during World War II and were determined to maintain them after the war.

As the war came to a close, in order to grant a concession to labor without appearing to violate wage and price controls, the federal government exempted employer-paid health benefits from wage controls and income tax. In effect, this paved the way for wage increases in the form of nontaxable, employer-sponsored health benefits.

This unreported personal income in the form of health benefits created an enormous demand for employer-provided health benefits over individual health insurance policies and incidental medical expenses purchased by employees with their own after-tax dollars. Employers received a 100 percent federal, state, and city tax deduction for the cost, and health benefits received by employees were exempt from individual federal, state, and city taxation.

The potential 2-for-1 tax advantage (depending on the income tax bracket of the employee) for employer-provided health insurance shifted the market away from health insurance and medical care purchased by individuals directly from providers.

By the mid-1960s, employer-provided health benefits were almost universal. The employer model worked well while costs remained low and employees stayed with the same company for their entire career. However, as healthcare costs increased and employees began to change employers regularly, the system began to erode.

THE DECLINE OF EMPLOYER-PROVIDED HEALTH INSURANCE

Employer-provided health insurance has been hit by massive inflation in recent years, making it less affordable for employers and employees. From 1999 to 2013, the annual premium that U.S. health insurance companies charged for employer-provided health plans increased approximately 182 percent to roughly $16,350 per family. For single coverage, the cost has increased about 168 percent to $5,884 per single (Kaiser Family Foundation, 2013).

During this period, many employers stopped providing health benefits entirely. U.S. jobs offering health benefits fell to 57 percent of all jobs in 2013, down from 66 percent in 1999.

The future is not bright—the average cost of employer-provided health insurance is expected to reach approximately $20,000 per family and $8,000 per single employee in 2016. On average, employees will be paying more and getting less in terms of higher deductibles, higher co-pays, and higher out-of-pocket (OOP) maximums.

HOW THIS BOOK IS STRUCTURED

Part I lays the groundwork for Part II and Part III by explaining why the end of employer-provided health insurance is inevitable. Part I concludes that by 2025, the majority of businesses will shift to defined contribution healthcare and individual health insurance. Chapter 1 highlights the inherent disadvantages of traditional employer-provided health insurance while Chapter 2 discusses the advantages of individual health insurance. Part I concludes by outlining the optimal solution for companies and employees—employer-funded individual health insurance (or defined contribution), which is the focus of Chapter 3.

Part II is a consumer's guide to navigating the new individual health insurance market. It begins in Chapter 4 by defining individual health insurance and reviews how much individual health insurance costs in Chapter 5. Chapter 6 walks the reader through the calculation of new federal subsidies—or premium tax credits—that cap the cost of a family's individual health insurance plan as a percent of household income. Chapters 7 and 8 discuss when and where to buy individual health insurance, including a detailed discussion of the new annual and special enrollment periods, and a step-by-step guide to navigating the new state-based Health Insurance Marketplaces. Chapters 9, 10, and 11 walk through how to choose the right individual plan, including an explanation of metallic tiers, coverage types, and provider networks. Chapter 12 suggests several ways for individual policyholders to reduce their annual healthcare costs, including opening up a health savings account (HSA) and shopping annually for a new individual health plan.

Part III is a company's guide to transitioning to defined contribution healthcare and individual health plans. It begins in Chapter 13 by explaining defined contribution healthcare in detail, including the advantages of the approach to both employees and employers. In Chapter 14, readers are walked through the process of conducting a defined contribution financial analysis for their companies using templates and an example company. Chapter 15 discusses how to implement and design a defined contribution program. Chapter 16 provides tips on selecting a defined contribution solution provider and Chapter 17 highlights the importance of communicating with employees during the transition to defined contribution. Part III includes numerous case studies based on real clients of Zane Benefits.

Appendix A provides a directory of state-specific guides to the individual health insurance market. Each state page provides sample individual health insurance rates and coverage levels compared with average employer-provided health insurance plans specific to the state.

ADDITIONAL MATERIALS AVAILABLE AT HEALTHINSURANCEREVOLUTION.ORG

In addition to the tools, templates, and information provided in this book, we have published, and will continue to publish, numerous additional guides, tools, and templates on the book website www.healthinsurancerevolution.org.

Part I

THE PROBLEM AND THE SOLUTION

This section of the book explains how your traditional employer-provided health insurance is a major threat to your financial future and it outlines a solution: employer-funded individual health insurance.

Chapter 1

THE DISADVANTAGES OF EMPLOYER-PROVIDED HEALTH INSURANCE

*D*on't despair as you start to read this chapter about the problems with employer-provided health insurance. Beginning with Chapter 2, this book is about a solution that you can take advantage of immediately.

Employer-provided health insurance is insurance provided by employers and offered to employees and dependents of employees. The premium cost is typically split between the employer and employee, with the employee typically paying all or most of the cost to add their dependents to the employer plan. With employer-provided health insurance, the risk is spread over the employees in the company who participate in the employer-provided plan and the premiums typically increase every year based on the previous year's healthcare costs of the group.

Healthcare costs now consume almost one-sixth of America's economy, and, during your lifetime, medical and health insurance costs are likely to be your largest or second-largest expense after housing. Your employer-provided health insurance is arguably the number one threat to your financial future.

Most Americans get health insurance from their employers and never think too much about it until they or a family member develops a serious health problem. That's when they first learn the details of their health insurance benefits, which medical providers they can use, and what their out-of-pocket expenses will be. The term *insurance* in employer-provided health insurance is misleading since the insurance terminates when you lose your job—often the time when you are most financially vulnerable.

Did you know? The number one cause of personal bankruptcy filings in the United States is unpaid medical bills, outpacing bankruptcies due to unpaid credit card bills and unpaid mortgages. Amazingly, three-quarters of affected families had employer-provided health insurance when they first became ill.

Have you ever thought about what would happen if you became ill, lost your job and your health insurance, and couldn't get another job? Every year this happens to millions of Americans with dire consequences—and it doesn't have to be a major heart attack or cancer to lead you to the poorhouse. Have you or a loved one ever had a medical issue requiring multiple doctor visits, laboratory tests, or hospital stays? Then you already know that behind virtually every ill person is a second person needed to transport them to and from medical appointments, get them meals, and/or explain what is happening to their medical providers. Even if you don't become ill yourself, you could still be terminated by your employer while you are performing this service for a spouse, child, or parent.

Approximately 1 million mostly middle- and upper-middle-class families file bankruptcy each year due to medical bills they can't pay—yet amazingly, three-quarters of these families had health insurance from their employer when they first became ill. A family bankruptcy typically affects three individuals and lasts for seven years—meaning up to 21 million people, including children, are living in economic purgatory at any given time due to failed employer-provided health insurance.

 Tip: As discussed in Chapter 2, these financial threats do not exist with individual health insurance because individual plans are portable, meaning you can keep your plan independent of your employment.

Few employers can afford to keep paying absent employees for more than a few weeks after those employees have used up their available sick time and vacation. Such employees are then let go, and their financial problems, which are the leading cause of bankruptcy in the United States, begin.

What are the chances that something like this could happen to you? There are hundreds of circumstances in which you could exceed your allowable sick and vacation leave, and the chances of this happening at some point in your working life are greater than 50 percent.

- **Outdoor activities.** Do you play sports, ski, snowboard, go boating, or ride bicycles? Any one of these outdoor activities could cause an injury that would prevent you from being able to work. Even without a specific injury, many active people will require some type of knee or leg surgery during their working lifetime.
- **Home accidents.** Although most people feel safest at home, the home is actually the place where you are most likely to have an accident requiring medical treatment or one that could prevent you from being able to work. Common causes of home accidents include falls, choking, shootings, poisoning, and improper use of medications.
- **Commuting/driving.** Do you commute to work? More than 3 million people are hurt each year in auto accidents. Common injuries include fractures, broken bones, and spinal damage resulting in short- and long-term disability.
- **High blood pressure.** About 65 million Americans over age 20 have high blood pressure, a chronic disease requiring medication and one that dramatically increases the chances of having heart disease during your working lifetime.
- **The overweight/obese.** Almost two-thirds of Americans are overweight or obese. This has contributed to more than 18 million Americans having diabetes and another 41 million over age 40 having prediabetes. Most people with prediabetes develop type 2 diabetes in 10 years. Diabetes virtually guarantees that you will have health issues requiring time away from work at some point in your life, and 65 percent of people with diabetes die from heart disease or stroke.
- **Cancer, heart attack, or stroke.** One in four men and one in five women will develop one of these debilitating diseases before age 65.

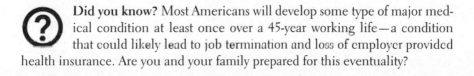 **Did you know?** Most Americans will develop some type of major medical condition at least once over a 45-year working life—a condition that could likely lead to job termination and loss of employer provided health insurance. Are you and your family prepared for this eventuality?

WHAT HAPPENS AFTER YOU LOSE YOUR JOB WITH EMPLOYER-PROVIDED HEALTH INSURANCE

Once you lose your job, you lose your employer-provided health insurance unless you elect to go on COBRA. COBRA is not a snake, although many people who have been on COBRA might disagree. COBRA, which stands for Consolidated Omnibus Budget Reconciliation Act of 1985, is the acronym for the name of the 1985 legislation that requires most employers with 20 or more employees to offer former employees the short-term opportunity to remain on the company's employer-provided health insurance plan at the employee's own cost.

COBRA allows you to continue your employer-provided health insurance for up to 18 months as long as you pay 100 percent of the cost of your former employer's plan plus a 2 percent administration fee (102 percent total).

Before COBRA, when employees are on their employer's health plan, employers typically charge each employee something between 10 and 20 percent of the pro-rata cost—if the employer-provided health plan total cost is $500 per month per person, the employee typically pays between $50 and $100 to include (just) themselves in the plan. When the same employee goes on COBRA, the employee's monthly cost typically rises 200 to 1,000 percent (two to 10 times) to up to $510 ($500 plus a 2 percent administration fee) of what they were paying when they were employed. The average annual cost in 2013 for COBRA was about $6,002 for singles and $16,678 for families (Kaiser Family Foundation, 2013).

If you can afford COBRA, and it is offered by your employer, it's only good for up to 18 months of coverage for you (the employee) and up to 36 months for dependents.

If you cannot afford COBRA, or if your illness requires treatment for more than the 18 to 36 months that COBRA is available, you will be forced to switch health plans. If you are in the middle of a health issue, this could be devastating because:

1. When you switch plans midyear, your deductibles and out-of-pocket maximums will be reset. Depending on your new plan, this could expose you to up to $12,000 in additional healthcare costs per year.
2. Your new plan may not cover your current doctor and hospitals, forcing you to transfer to new medical providers or pay out-of-network for your current providers—which could be almost the same in cost as having no health insurance.
3. Transferring to new medical providers who are not familiar with your recent medical history could be dangerous to your health or the health of a loved one.

The good news is that COBRA will be going away for most people because, thanks to the Affordable Care Act, most ex-employees can now get individual coverage for a small fraction of the cost of COBRA.

The good news is that COBRA will be going away for most people because, thanks to the Affordable Care Act, most ex-employees can now get individual coverage for a small fraction of the cost of COBRA. Generally, only people who cannot find an individual health insurance policy covering a critically-needed medical provider should consider staying on COBRA.

Each year between 1 and 2 million American families file personal bankruptcy. Until recently, the causes of these bankruptcies were unknown, and most people assumed credit card spending, divorce, and loss of employment to be among the major reasons. In February 2005, Harvard University released the results of its study, "Illness and Injury as Contributors to Bankruptcy."

The study interviewed Americans in bankruptcy courts and determined that about half were "medically bankrupt"—driven to bankruptcy by medical bills not covered by health insurance. Equally surprising, the study concluded:

- Three-fourths of the medically bankrupt had health insurance at the beginning of their illness.
- The majority of the medically bankrupt owned their own homes and had attended college.
- Many people filing medical bankruptcy were middle-class workers with health insurance who were unable to pay their copayments, deductibles, and exclusions in the employer-provided health insurance plan.

 This book teaches you how to avoid the insurance gaps that drive millions of Americans into medical bankruptcy.

10 REASONS EMPLOYER-PROVIDED HEALTH INSURANCE IS BAD FOR YOU, YOUR FAMILY, AND YOUR COMPANY

1. It's temporary—You lose your health insurance if you or your loved one gets sick.
2. It's overpriced—You pay $4,000 to $12,000 more than individual health insurance for the same coverage.
3. It's risky—Your coverage may be canceled at any time without notice.

4. It's limited—You don't get to pick your doctors and hospitals.
5. It's one-size-fits-all—You don't get to choose your deductible or copays.
6. It's unfair—You are disqualified from receiving your $2,000 to $12,000 per year share of the trillion-dollar federal subsidy.
7. It's unstable—Your cost could double due to one employee with a million-dollar claim.
8. It's bad for your career—People stay in jobs that don't let them realize their full potential.
9. It's bad for your business—Management spends time on health insurance that should be spent on customers and products.
10. It's bad for America—Employer-provided health insurance is the top reason U.S. healthcare costs are almost $4 trillion, approaching one-fifth the size of the U.S. economy.

1. It's Temporary—You Lose Your Health Insurance If You or Your Loved One Gets Sick

This is the biggest problem with employer-provided health insurance—it only covers you when you or a loved one is healthy enough for you to remain at work.

Sadly, most people don't realize this until they become too ill to come to work and get terminated, or they can't come to work because they are needed full-time to take care of a sick child or spouse.

Few employees with employer-provided health plans are aware that their health insurance terminates when they lose their job, and that COBRA, if it is offered, only covers them for up to 18 months at an exorbitant cost.

In 1985, when I (Paul Zane Pilzer) was giving a lecture at Moscow State University, a Soviet economist stood up and chastised me for working for "a cruel disheartening nation [the United States]" where "if you lose your job, you and even your children lose your health insurance." I remember denying his accusation and being shocked when I later found out that he was correct.

---

2. It's Overpriced—You Pay $4,000 to $12,000 More for the Same Coverage

The average cost to cover an employee with employer-provided health insurance has increased from $2,196 per year in 1999 to $5,884 per year in 2013. For family coverage, the cost has increased from $5,791 per year in 1999 to $16,351 per year in 2013. This is not sustainable for employers or employees. Prior to 2014, the annual cost of individual health insurance was about $2,500 a person—but there was a catch. Everyone medically qualified for employer-provided coverage but, in 45 states, only healthy people and their healthy families medically qualified for individual health insurance.

Did you know? The average cost to cover an employee with employer-provided health insurance has increased from $2,196 per year in 1999 to $5,884 per year in 2013. For family coverage, the cost has increased from $5,791 per year in 1999 to $16,351 per year in 2013. This is not sustainable for employers or employees.

Then, the Affordable Care Act (known as ACA or Obamacare) was passed in 2010. The ACA mandated that the price, benefits, and qualifications for individual health insurance be roughly the same or better than most employer-provided coverage. Starting in 2014, the ACA requires all individual health insurance policies to cover a list of essential health benefits (see Chapter 9) without any monthly, annual, or lifetime limitations.

Tip: Most Americans think that employer-provided coverage is better and/or cheaper than individual coverage that you purchase on your own. This used to be true; however, the full implementation of the Affordable Care Act in 2014 (Obamacare) has turned this paradigm upside down.

Even if you work for a company that pays 100 percent of the cost for you to participate in the employer-provided health insurance plan, you are probably paying between 50 and 100 percent of the cost to add your spouse and children to your employer-provided plan. Most people don't realize the cost of their family is typically deducted from their net wages via their paychecks.

Back in the 1960s, most employers paid the entire premium for employees and their dependents—with no employee contributions, copays, or other cost-sharing devices. Over the next three decades medical costs dramatically increased, and many spouses began receiving their own benefits by joining the workforce. In response, employers started paying only a portion or none of the premium for the employee's spouse and dependents. Today, employers offering employee health benefits typically pay only 25 to 75 percent of the cost for an employee's spouse and dependents. Only very few employers today still pay 100 percent of the cost for spouses and dependents.

Tip: Many employees are paying 50 to 100 percent of the cost of including their spouse and dependents on their employer's health plan without realizing it since it is automatically deducted from their paycheck.

Employer-provided health insurance has been hit by soaring costs in recent years, making it less affordable for employers and employees. As shown in Figure 1.1, from 1999 to 2013, the annual premium that U.S. health insurance companies charged for employer-provided health benefits plans increased approximately 182 percent to roughly $16,350 per family. For single coverage, the cost has increased about 168 percent to $5,884 per single (Kaiser Family Foundation 2013).

During this period, many employers stopped providing health benefits entirely. The percent of jobs that included health benefits fell to 57 percent—9 percent fewer U.S. jobs provided health benefits in 2013 versus 1999. The average cost of employer-provided health benefits is expected to reach approximately $20,000 per family and $8,000 per single in 2016. On average, employees on employer-provided health insurance will be paying more and getting less in terms of higher deductibles, higher copays, and higher out-of-pocket maximums.

3. It's Risky—Your Coverage May Be Canceled at Any Time without Notice

One of the scariest things about employer-provided health insurance is that you do not control the policy. Your employer may cancel the entire plan or change the benefits at any time with little or no notice to you, and there is no COBRA available when the entire plan is canceled.

Once your current plan is canceled, you lose access to it—there is no COBRA available on a canceled plan.

	1999	2013	Increase
Total annual family premium	$5,791	$16,351	+182%
Total annual single premium	$2,196	$5,884	+168%
Average monthly employee contribution (family)	$1,548	$4,560	+195%

Figure 1.1   Employer-Provided Health Insurance (1999 to 2013)

There are numerous reasons your employer may cancel your coverage:

- **Switching to a new health insurance company.** Every year (and some-times in the middle of the year), thousands of employers switch health insurance companies (and cancel the current coverage) due to the savings it presents to the business, or because the insurance company refused to renew the policy.
- **Failing to meet insurance company requirements.** If the health insur-ance provider audits your plan and finds that your company is out of com-pliance with the plan terms, such as a 75 percent minimum participation requirement, the insurance company can cancel coverage for the entire company.
- **Failing to make payment.** Retroactive termination for nonpayment of premium is permissible, and there is no requirement that a premium be accepted after the original due date.
- **Going out of business.** 10 to 12 percent of employers close each year—that's almost 1 million business closures per year.

Your employer-provided health insurance plan could be modified or canceled at any time without your consent.

Once your current plan is canceled, you lose access to it—there is no COBRA available on a canceled plan. Note also that if you are no longer employed and already on COBRA, and your former employer cancels their entire plan, you also lose your health insurance.

Fortunately, as explained in Chapter 7, having an employer or former employer cancel your plan is a *qualifying event* that makes you instantly eligible to purchase individual coverage on your state's Health Insurance Marketplace at any time, even outside the traditional annual *open enrollment* period. However, should this happen to you, you will still have to switch to a new health insurance policy and possibly even a new insurance company.

When you have to switch health insurance companies, as explained earlier, if you are in the middle of a health issue, it could be financially devastating and/or you could lose contact with your existing medical providers. Your new plan may not cover your current doctor and hospitals. If your new plan does not cover your current medical providers, you will be required to make a choice between (A) transferring to a new provider whom you may not trust or (B) paying out-of-network for your current provider which could be as expensive as having no health insurance at all.

Tip: As discussed in Chapter 2, these financial threats do not exist with individual health insurance because individual plans are controlled by you and not your employer.

4. It's Limited—You Don't Get to Pick Your Doctors and Hospitals

 Did you know? Most medical providers charge patients who don't belong to their health insurance network much higher prices (sometimes 10 times higher) than they charge to those in their network for the exact same service.

A major limitation of employer-provided health insurance is that you and your family do not get to pick the provider network. The provider network refers to the medical providers (e.g., doctors and hospitals) covered by the plan. See Chapter 10 for more on provider networks.

With provider networks, health insurance companies contract with medical providers in local areas to provide service to their policyholders or members for either a flat monthly fee or a discounted rate. Employer-provided health insurance plans will typically provide access to a provider network. If you seek care outside of this network of providers, your insurance may not pay for the services or pay a lower amount. Today, most medical providers, from local pediatricians to big-city hospitals, charge patients who don't belong to their health insurance network much higher prices (sometimes 10 times higher) than they charge those in their network for the exact same service.

If your preferred doctor or hospital providers are not in your employer plan's network, the plan may not cover you if you continue to receive services from those doctors. Even worse, the only way to manage this problem is to either (1) switch medical providers or (2) switch employers.

 Tip: As discussed in Chapter 2, individual health insurance allows you to choose your doctor and hospital network when you choose your policy.

5. It's One-Size-Fits-All—You Don't Get to Choose Your Deductible, Copays, or Coinsurance

When it comes to health insurance, employees have very different needs. However, your employer-provided health insurance plan takes a one-size-fits-all approach. With employer-provided health insurance, most employees do not get to choose from a wide range of deductibles or copays. As result, most employees are paired with coverage that does not fit their family's needs.

Annual deductible—This is the annual amount of your medical expenses that you must pay before your health insurance company begins paying providers or reimbursing you for claims. Traditional plans have deductibles of up to $1,500, as well as copays for doctor visits and prescriptions. High deductible plans have deductibles from $1,000 to $10,000, but much lower premiums.

Copay—This is the amount that you pay each time you visit the doctor, pharmacy, or other medical provider. If you have children and visit the doctor often, you are typically better off with a higher premium plan that charges you a fixed amount (copay) for each doctor visit regardless of what is done during the visit.

Coinsurance—This is the amount, typically about 20 to 30 percent, that most insurance companies expect you to pay on your annual medical expenses after you have met your deductible. Fortunately, most coinsurance clauses have an upper limit of about $4,000 to $10,000. Your maximum coinsurance obligation plus your annual deductible is called your *out-of-pocket maximums*—referring to the maximum out-of-pocket annual expense you could incur under the policy. Some newer high-deductible plans, including many HSA plans, do not charge you coinsurance; they pay 100 percent of your medical expenses once you have met the deductible (see Chapter 9 for more on out-of-pocket maximums).

A mismatch of coverage with your needs can cost you thousands of dollars per year unnecessarily. How? Health insurance plans that cover more of your medical expenses (i.e., health plans with lower deductibles) usually have a higher monthly payment. As a result, you pay more up front in the form of higher premiums in exchange for getting to pay less when you receive medical care.

For example, a plan with a low deductible would probably work best for a family expecting to visit the doctor and pharmacy regularly. However, the same plan might be a poor choice for a young, single adult male who only expects to go the doctor once per year for his annual physical. Since the young, single employee will not use the coverage he is paying up front for, he is being charged up to 100 percent more than he actually needs. By contrast, if he were able to select a high deductible HSA plan (see Chapter 12 for more on HSAs), he could be saving thousands of dollars in an account for future medical expenses.

	Bronze	Silver	Gold	Platinum
Monthly premium (with subsidies applied)	$0	$164	$321	$402
Deductible (family)	$10,000	$4,000	$0	$0
Coinsurance	30%	20%	20%	10%
Doctor copay	$60	$45	$30	$20
Out-of-pocket maximum (family)	$12,700	$12,700	$12,700	$8,000

Figure 1.2   Example Rates for an Employee Earning $40,000/Year (Family of Four, Adults Age 40)

Source: Covered California 2014.

Tip: The majority of employees only go the doctor one to two times per year. Most employees with employer-provided health insurance are overpaying up front in the form of higher insurance premiums for coverage they will probably never use.

In contrast, the Affordable Care Act mandates that individual plans sold on the marketplaces be offered at five levels — Bronze, Silver, Gold, Platinum, and Catastrophic. These levels have nothing to do with the care you get, just the deductible, copays, and coverage you receive from the insurance company. (See Figure 1.2.)

Tip: Individual health insurance allows you to choose your health insurance plan deductibles and copays.

6. It's Unfair—You Are Disqualified from Receiving Your $2,000 to $12,000 Per Year Share of the Trillion-Dollar Federal Subsidy

As crazy as it might sound at first, you should be asking your employer, "Could you please cancel our employer-provided health insurance plan?" Why? Because if you are offered qualified affordable employer-provided health insurance by your employer, you and your family are disqualified from receiving the federal subsidy, even if you are eligible based on your income.

Let's say you live in Dallas, Texas, earn $60,000 per year, and have a family of five. Your employer may offer you an employer-provided plan where your employer pays the full $500 per month cost per person for you, and you pay for your four family members at a monthly cost of $1,200 a month. That's $14,400 per year out of your pocket to have your entire family of five covered by the employer-provided health insurance plan.

Alternatively, on the Texas Health Insurance Marketplace (available via www.healthcare.gov), you could purchase better coverage with an individual Blue Cross Blue Shield Silver plan for all five family members including you without any government subsidy for $899 per month—that's for permanent health insurance, $30 copays for doctor visits, and $0 for generic prescriptions. That's $10,788 ($899 × 12) a year before the federal subsidy for better coverage than the $14,400 per year you would pay just to add your family to the employer-provided group plan.

 Tip: Most U.S. families will find themselves thousands of dollars per year better off if their employer canceled their employer-provided health insurance coverage, and that's before asking their employer to reimburse them for part of the cost of an individual health insurance policy.

But, if your employer didn't offer you qualified affordable employer-provided coverage, you would receive a $580 per month federal subsidy towards paying the $899 per month cost, reducing your monthly premium to $319 per month for all five members of your family. This $580 per month subsidy is effectively a $6,960 tax-free cash gift for you and your family from the federal government.

As explained in Chapter 3, if your employer has less than 50 employees, there is no charge or penalty to your employer for you to receive this subsidy. But, if your employer has more than 50 employees, the employer would have to pay a penalty of up to $3,000 per year for each employee that receives subsidized coverage (up to a maximum penalty of $2,000/year for all employees after a 30 employee credit). When debating the Affordable Care Act in 2010, the Senate originally wanted this $2,000 per employee maximum penalty to be $20,000 per employee. However, Congress reduced it to $2,000 per employee when many employers threatened to close their doors entirely rather than pay $20,000 per year in penalties for an $8 per hour employee earning as little as $16,000 per year.

As shown in Figure 1.3, it gets even better if you earn $38,000 per year and your employer doesn't offer an employer-provided plan—you would get free coverage for your entire family under Medicaid.

If you earned $80,000 per year versus $60,000 per year, your federal subsidy would fall from $580 per month to $312 per month, causing your $899 per month premium before subsidy to fall to $587 per month. Even if you earned $80,000 per

| | Annual Income | | |
	$38,000	$60,000	$80,000
Monthly premium	Free	$899/month	$899/month
Federal subsidy	Medicaid	$580/month	$312/month
Net cost	Free	$319/month	$587/month

Figure 1.3 Dallas, Texas, Couple, Age 35, Three Children—Blue Advantage Silver HMO

year, your annual cost for much better, permanent individual coverage would be $7,044 per year ($587 × 12) for all five members of your family versus your employer charging you $14,400 per year just to add your family members to their employer-provided group plan.

 A massive tax subsidy is now available to help individuals buy individual health insurance coverage through the new state-based Health Insurance Marketplaces. The subsidy caps the cost of an individual's health insurance at 2 to 9.5 percent of their household income if their household income is less than 400 percent above the federal poverty line (that's about $100,000 per year for a family of four in 2014).

7. It's Unstable—Your Cost Could Double Due to One Employee with a Million-Dollar Claim

If you work for a small or medium-sized employer with employer-provided health insurance, if one employee has a baby, a surgery, or is diagnosed with a chronic illness, you are likely to see a large premium rate increase at renewal time. That's because the insurance company needs to recover their losses from a relatively small group of people.

Employer-provided health insurance is misleading because insurance means spreading the risk among a large group of people or organizations so that no single entity bears the cost of a catastrophic illness. However, that's not how employer-provided health insurance works. Each time an insured employee in your organization runs up large medical bills, your organization ends up paying these costs the following year via an increase in its annual health insurance premium. The insurance employers pay for is actually little more than a delayed bill-paying mechanism.

Tip: As discussed in Chapter 2, individual health insurance pools diversify the risk across a much larger population.

In 1985, I (Paul Zane Pilzer) testified to the U.S. Congress about the problems facing small businesses with employer-provided health insurance. I explained:

> *A typical owner of a small business probably knows the first name of each child of an employee who has diabetes—even though they are not supposed to know. A small employer with a $35,000-a-year employee should not be burdened with the $75,000-a-year medical cost for a child of that employee who has diabetes—or have to face the terrible choice between staying in business versus taking care of the sick child of an employee.*
> Paul Zane Pilzer testifying before the Committee on
> Government Operations, U.S. Congress, October 1985

Many employers wish all they had to worry about was paying $75,000 a year for the medical costs of a diabetic child. Some medical situations today, from preterm births to cancer, can cost hundreds of thousands or millions of dollars—making the entire employee health plan unaffordable, or potentially even driving the employer out of business.

Suppose you work for a 51-person company where one participant develops a health condition costing $200,000 a year or more. Next year, the health insurance premium paid by your company will go up by $200,000. The cost of your employer-provided medical plan would increase more than $500 a month per employee, forcing your employer to cut benefits or possibly terminate the plan. What would happen if two people developed such a condition? Employer-provided group health insurance plans are ticking time bombs as their workforce ages.

These annual benefit reductions and/or increased outlays by employees inevitably lead to an ongoing version of adverse selection—a perpetual process referred to as the "employer health insurance death spiral."

The death spiral starts when an employee's cost to participate in the employer-provided plan exceeds the employee's willingness to pay. When this happens, the healthiest employees begin to drop off the employer plan in favor of individual policies. This causes the remaining employer risk pool to become proportionately sicker, resulting in even higher insurance premiums on renewal the following year. Then, the process repeats itself—the employer reduces benefits to maintain costs, more healthy employees drop off, and the rate goes up even more the following year.

This employer-provided health insurance death spiral perpetuates until the business either: (1) cancels the plan itself or (2) is unable to get enough employees to stay in the employer pool and the plan is cancelled by the insurance company for low participation. Virtually all small employer policies require participation of 75 percent or more of eligible employees in order to be renewed.

8. It's Bad for Careers—People Stay in Jobs That Don't Let Them Realize Their Full Potential

Millions of Americans today are modern-day slaves either unable to retire early, working in jobs they don't really want, or working in jobs that don't actualize their full potential—all because they need their employer-provided health insurance to take care of themselves, a spouse, or a child with a chronic medical condition.

Patients with chronic medical conditions like depression, cancer, or diabetes typically require care by the same medical provider over a long period of time, and changing doctors can be very detrimental to their care as well as to their wallet.

While the Affordable Care Act (ACA) has made affordable individual health insurance accessible to millions of Americans, when employees switch from employer-provided coverage to an individual policy, it is unlikely that their new health insurance company has a network that covers all of their existing providers.

Even if an employee finds an individual health insurance company network that covers their existing medical providers or equivalent substitutes, it will typically be very expensive to switch their insurance company and network of providers as previously described.

Although the ACA has helped millions of Americans get individual health insurance, millions more Americans still remain virtual slaves to their employer's health insurance plan because they don't know that cheaper, better individual health insurance is available in the federally-mandated Health Insurance Marketplaces.

---

9. It's Bad for Business—Management Spends Time on Health Insurance That Should Be Spent on Customers and Products

In our specialized economy today, success in business requires that managers and owners focus on better ways to serve their customers. This ranges from continually improving your products and services to finding better ways for your customers to obtain and pay for your products and services. No stone can be left unturned when it comes to improving the customer experience.

! Health insurance is an economic crisis for employers as well as individuals. The cost of health benefits now exceeds profits for most of the Fortune 500 companies. GM is in trouble because health insurance adds $1,550 to the cost of every car it sells.

Unless your company is large enough to have dedicated, full-time employees managing your employer-provided health insurance program, the money and time you and your managers spend getting your employees covered is one of the greatest threats to your business. That's because every hour you spend managing your employer-provided health insurance is another hour you are not spending managing and improving your product or service. Even if your company is large enough to justify having dedicated full-time managers of your employer-provided health insurance plan, with health insurance costs today exceeding profits for many companies, it's rare that the CEO and CFO of a Fortune 500 company doesn't spend many hours managing their health benefits program.

Although they don't know it, many employers are not competent at managing their employer-provided health insurance benefits. Just as you see some of your customers are relatively uneducated about how to properly buy and save money on your product or service, you and your managers are similarly uneducated when it comes to knowing how much employer-provided health insurance coverage to purchase and how to pay for it. This is because there is virtually no transparency for employers when it comes to managing their employer health benefits program. Everything is disguised—from how much their health insurance broker makes in commissions and overrides on the different policies they recommend, to the performance and efficiency of each medical provider in the plans' networks.

10. It's Bad for America—Employer-Provided Health Insurance Is the Top Reason U.S. Healthcare Costs Are Almost $4 Trillion, Approaching One-Fifth the Size of the U.S. Economy

When you drive to work today look around at the people, cars, and buildings you pass by. Between one-sixth and one-fifth of the people you pass on their way to work, representing 17.5 percent of our gross domestic product, work producing a product or service nobody really wants to buy—healthcare, or more accurately sickness care, since what most Americans call healthcare has very little to do with health.

Despite the fact that the U.S. spends two-and-a-half to three times per person what other developed nations spend on healthcare, the United States is the unhealthiest developed nation on earth. There are many reasons proposed for why this is so.

For example, 95 percent of the pharmaceutical prescriptions filled each year in the United States are for drugs you are expected to take for the rest of your life—because drug companies find it much more profitable to create customers for life by producing maintenance drugs that treat the symptoms of diseases versus drugs that cure diseases.

Medical providers from the individual doctor to the largest hospital are paid for their procedures and time spent versus their outcomes or health of their patients.

However, the major reason that the U.S. healthcare industry costs so much is because the employers who pay for most U.S. healthcare do not have a financial stake in the long-term health of their employees.

Employees used to stay with one company for 25 years or more. Today, the average employee is projected to change jobs more than 10 times over his or her 45-year working life. Most of the major illnesses on which you can spend $1 today to save $100 tomorrow (like heart disease from obesity or cancer from poor nutrition) will not show up until an employee is long gone or retired, at which time the $100 cost is picked up by another employer or by taxpayers through Medicare.

As medical costs have escalated, employers have, in effect, told their medical providers to pay for only those expenses related to keeping or getting the insured back to work—and this does not include paying for the prevention of a disease that will not manifest itself during the expected tenure of the employee with the company.

Despite a new federal mandate in the ACA that employers must cover preventive care, the federal definition of preventive care includes tests like mammograms and prostrate exams that merely screen for diseases rather than help prevent them (see Chapter 9). Significant weight reduction, nutritional advice, vitamins, minerals, smoking cessation, and hundreds of other wellness-related treatments are excluded from most employer-provided and most individual health insurance plans. Although at least with individual health insurance plans you can choose to apply the savings to your wellness care.

Did you know? More than one-sixth of the U.S. economy is devoted to healthcare spending and that percentage continues to rise every year. Our employer-based health insurance system is not delivering value equal to the roughly $3.5 trillion we spend annually on healthcare. Experts agree that an estimated 20 to 30 percent of that spending—up to $1 trillion a year—goes to care that is wasteful, redundant, or inefficient.

We could go on and on about why healthcare costs so much in the United States. But this is not a book about healthcare; it's a book about health insurance and how to finance healthcare—the number one financial challenge facing America, American employers, and American families. The exorbitant cost of U.S. healthcare is one of the major reasons the United States has so large a federal deficit and federal debt.

The number one reason U.S. healthcare costs so much is because the overwhelming majority of U.S. nongeriatric care is paid for indirectly through third-party employers versus directly by consumers themselves.

The U.S. healthcare marketplace has been discouraged from developing innovative healthcare solutions for consumers at affordable prices because it has focused only on solutions that could be sold to employers' human resource and insurance company executives. This is in contrast to the dramatic innovation in every other part of the U.S. economy such as automobiles, restaurants, personal computers, telecommunications, and so forth, which are focused on solutions sold directly to consumers.

America's employers have become the nation's healthcare gatekeepers, deciding, in advance, what type of medical care employees should receive—which by definition often means yesterday's treatments versus today's treatments. This also prevents entrepreneurial medical providers and alternative medical providers from developing better treatments, since they cannot get paid for them.

In summary, rising healthcare costs, driven mostly by employer-provided health insurance, punish our nation on multiple fronts:

- For you and your family, rising healthcare costs mean less money in your pockets and force hard choices about balancing your children's education, food, rent, and needed care.
- For your company, rising healthcare costs make it more expensive to add new employees and reduce budgets available for marketing, customer service, and product development.
- For the government, rising healthcare costs lead to reduced funding on other priorities such as infrastructure, education, and security.

As you will see throughout this book, all of this has recently changed thanks to new federal legislation and regulations that have leveled the playing field between employer provided health insurance and individual health insurance policies that you purchase yourself.

Chapter 2

THE ADVANTAGES OF INDIVIDUAL HEALTH INSURANCE

An individual or family health insurance policy is a policy purchased from an insurance company covering you and selected family members. The terms individual policy, family policy, individual and family policy, and individual or family policy all mean the same thing—a policy purchased by a consumer directly from an insurance company covering an individual or a family.

It works just like car insurance. With individual health insurance, the risk is spread over a large group of people—hundreds of thousands, even millions, depending on the plan and insurance company.

Today, individual coverage is almost always better and costs about half the price of comparable employer-provided coverage. Moreover, most American families earning less than $100,000 a year are eligible for a federal subsidy to pay for individual health insurance—but only if their employer does *not* offer employer-provided coverage. The amount of the subsidy depends on income and family size and pays monthly, on average, about half the price of individual coverage—making individual coverage after the subsidy about one-fourth the price of comparable employer-provided coverage.

Your employer's health insurance broker and your employer's health insurance company may not want you to know this.

Your employer may also not want you to know this for several reasons— employers need healthy employees to participate in their employer-provided plan, and employers with more than 50 employees may be charged a $2,000 to $3,000 penalty for each employee who purchases individual health insurance with the federal subsidy.

But, you must know this because, as pointed out throughout this book, your employer-provided health plan is the greatest threat to your financial future.

Since 2000, the percentage of Americans covered by employer-provided health insurance has steadily declined. Facing double-digit growth in health insurance premiums, employers have either eliminated health benefits or redesigned the plans to include higher deductibles, larger copayments, and greater premium sharing by employees.

Fortunately, a paradigm shift is occurring in the way businesses offer employee health benefits—a shift from an employer-provided health insurance to employer-funded individual health insurance. This shift from employer-provided health insurance to individual health insurance was taking place gradually from 2002 to 2014, until January 1, 2014, when the Affordable Care Act (often called ACA or Obamacare) mandated major changes to the market for individual health insurance. These changes include:

1. The requirement for every state to have a new Health Insurance Market-place (see Chapter 8) to buy individual insurance.
2. The requirement for all individual health insurance companies to accept all applicants regardless of their health.
3. The availability of new federal subsidies—known as *premium tax credits*—for American families earning less than 400 percent of the federal poverty line (or less than approximately $96,000 per year in 2014). See Chapter 6 for more on premium tax credits.

As a result, the market for individual insurance is expected to expand from 30 million insureds in 2012 to more than 150 million insureds by 2025.

Prior to 2014, the annual cost of individual health insurance was about $2,500 a person and comparable employer-provided health insurance cost was about $6,000 per person—but there was a catch. In 45 states, only healthy people and their healthy family members medically qualified for individual health insurance. Individual health insurance plans could deny coverage or charge more for coverage based on health conditions, whereas employer-provided health insurance had to cover any employee at the same price regardless of their health. The main reason companies offered employer-provided health insurance (despite the much higher price tag) was because it used to be difficult and expensive for employees with a family member with a pre existing condition to find health insurance on the individual market.

In 2010, the Affordable Care Act was passed by Congress which mandated that, starting in 2014, the benefits and eligibility requirements for individual health insurance be roughly the same or better than most employer-provided coverage.

Did you know? The Affordable Care Act also provides safeguards to insurance companies in the form of risk adjustment, reinsurance, and risk corridors (see Chapter 5) to keep premiums low on individual policies regardless of the health of the insureds.

Most importantly, the Affordable Care Act provides enormous federal subsidies to Americans earning less than $45,000 for singles and $100,000 for families who purchase individual health insurance—capping their after-subsidy monthly premium cost at a fixed percentage of their income regardless of the cost of their individual policy.

As explained throughout this book, the Affordable Care Act requires all individual health insurance policies to cover a list of *essential health benefits* (see Chapter 9) without any monthly, annual, or lifetime limitations.

Thus, other than the fact that employees lose their employer-provided health insurance when they lose their job, price is now the most important difference to consumers between employer-provided health plans and individual health plans.

In 2014, the price for an unsubsidized individual plan purchased on the Health Insurance Marketplace is about $3,000 per year, which is one-half the price of a similar benefit, employer-provided plan costing approximately $6,000 per year per person. And, most Americans earning less than $100,000 per year for a family or $45,000 per year for an individual will receive a federal subsidy for, on average, half the unsubsidized price of individual coverage. If your family is eligible, this subsidy reduces the average individual plan to about $1,500 per year per person in cost, which is approximately one-fourth the price of comparable employer-provided coverage.

Individual health insurance is now equal (and in most cases better) than employer-provided health insurance, for about half the price (pre-subsidy) and about one-quarter the price (post-subsidy). With individual health insurance, you get to:

1. Pick the plan that best fits your needs, including your doctors, for about half the cost of an equivalent employer-provided plan.
2. Keep your individual health insurance policy for as long as you want, completely independent of your employment.
3. Receive a federal subsidy for, on average, about half the cost if you are a family earning less than $100,000 per year or a single person earning less than $45,000 per year.

 Tip: The federal subsidy is based on your location, income, and family size—larger families with four or more children typically qualify for federal subsidies at income levels up to $100,000 or more per year.

10 REASONS INDIVIDUAL HEALTH INSURANCE IS GOOD FOR YOU, YOUR FAMILY, AND YOUR COMPANY

1. It's portable—You keep your health insurance if you or your loved one gets sick.
2. It's 20 to 60 percent less expensive—You and your employer pay $4,000 to $12,000 less for the same coverage.
3. It's permanent—Your coverage cannot be canceled as long as you pay your premium.
4. It's not limited—You get to pick your doctors and hospitals.
5. It's customizable—You choose your deductible and copays.
6. It's subsidized—You may be eligible for a $2,000 to $12,000 per year share of the trillion-dollar federal subsidy.
7. It's stable—You're in a large group and your after-subsidy cost can only increase with your income.
8. It's good for careers—People are free to change jobs based on what's best for their career vs. what's best for their healthcare.
9. It's good for business—Management spends more time focusing on customers and products.
10. It's good for America—It empowers Americans to manage their own healthcare and it makes American businesses more competitive.

1. It's Portable—You Keep Your Health Insurance If You or Your Loved One Gets Sick

Unlike employer-provided health insurance, individual health insurance is real insurance because you get to keep your health insurance if you get sick. Your policy remains the same as long as you pay the premium regardless of what happens to your employment. If fact, your employer typically doesn't even know whether you have individual health insurance.

With individual health insurance, there is no COBRA when you lose your job because your job has nothing to do with your health insurance.

Most people are surprised to find out that with individual health insurance they get to keep their policy as long as they pay the premium, regardless of what happens to their employment. That's because, since World War II, most Americans believed that the only way to qualify for health insurance was to get a job with a company that had an employer-provided plan. And, prior to 2014, they were partially correct—especially if they or a member of their family had a health issue or a pre-existing condition.

But now, thanks to the Affordable Care Act, everyone qualifies for individual health insurance regardless of their health or if they have a family member with a pre-existing condition. And, most Americans qualify for an enormous federal subsidy that sets the monthly cost of their individual policy at a fixed percentage of their income regardless of what happens to the cost of healthcare or their presubsidy monthly premium.

2. It's 20 to 60 Percent Less Expensive—You and Your Employer Pay $4,000 to $12,000 Less for the Same Coverage

Today, because everyone medically qualifies for individual health insurance with no extra charge for pre-existing conditions, the main difference to consumers between an employer-provided coverage and comparable individual coverage is the price. While the price in 2014 for an employer-provided plan is approximately $6,000 per year per person, the unsubsidized price for an individual plan purchased in the individual market is only about $3,000 per year per person.

 Tip: Unsubsidized individual health insurance today costs about half the cost of comparable employer-provided health insurance. But it gets better. Most individuals earning less than $100,000 a year qualify for a monthly federal subsidy which makes their after-subsidy individual health insurance cost about a quarter the cost of comparable employer-provided coverage.

For most employees—due to an enormous federal subsidy only granted to employees not offered qualified affordable employer-provided coverage—the cost of employer-provided coverage is actually, on average, four times (400 percent) the cost of comparable individual coverage. Depending on the cost of living in your state and city, if your family income is less than roughly $100,000, the ACA mandates a maximum monthly net price for individual health insurance based on family size and annual income.

For most employees, the presubsidy (unsubsidized) cost of individual health insurance is about one-half the cost of employer-provided health insurance, and the after-subsidy cost is about one-fourth the cost. But it gets even better. Since each taxpayer's subsidy amount is calculated so that they pay a fixed (by Congress) percent of their income for individual health insurance, once an employee gets an individual health insurance policy their premium can almost never go up unless their income increases. They are immune if their actual policy increases in price because their subsidy will increase by the same amount.

What's the catch? Only employees not offered affordable, qualified, employer-provided coverage at work are eligible for the federal subsidy. See #6, It's Subsidized, further on.

During the first three months of 2014, approximately 7 million people received individual health insurance from the federally mandated Health Insurance Marketplaces—the average cost for everyone after subsidies was

Annual Household Income (2014)	Monthly Premium (without subsidy)	Monthly Subsidy Amount	Your Monthly Cost
$30,000	$506	$356	$150
$40,000	$506	$230	$276
$50,000	$506	$111	$395
$60,000	$506	$31	$475
$70,000	$506	$0	$506

Figure 2.1 Individual Health Insurance Cost for Family of Two Adults in Dallas, Texas

approximately $82 per month ($984 per year) per person. The average cost for those not receiving subsidies was $346 per month ($4,152 per year) (Kaiser Family Foundation 2013).

For example, as shown in Figure 2.1, if you are a family of two in Dallas, Texas earning $40,000 a year in modified adjusted gross income, your price for a Blue Cross Blue Shield Silver plan on the individual exchange is about $506 per month before you receive a federal subsidy of $230 per month for a net cost of $276 per month. Notice how the subsidy scales down with increased income.

- If your modified adjusted gross income is $30,000 a year, your subsidy increases to $356/month, for a net cost of $150/month.
- If your modified adjusted gross income is $40,000 a year, your subsidy decreases to $230/month, for a net cost of $276/month.
- If your modified adjusted gross income is $50,000 a year, your subsidy decreases to $111/month, for a net cost of $395/month.
- If your modified adjusted gross income is $60,000 a year, your subsidy decreases to $31/month, for a net cost of $475/month.
- If your modified adjusted gross income is $70,000 a year, your subsidy decreases to $0/month, for a net cost of $506/month.

These subsidies change dramatically based on the size of your family. As you can see in Figure 2.2, if your family lived in Dallas, Texas, had three children (for a total family size of five), you would be eligible for a much larger subsidy even if your income rose to $110,000 or more.

During the first three months of 2014, approximately 7 million people received individual health insurance from the federally mandated Health Insurance Marketplaces—the average cost for everyone after subsidies was approximately $82 per month ($984 per year) per person.

Annual Household Income (2014)	Monthly Premium (without subsidy)	Monthly Subsidy Amount	Your Monthly Cost
$40,000	$926	$803	$123
$60,000	$926	$580	$346
$80,000	$926	$312	$614
$100,000	$926	$135	$791
$110,000	$926	$56	$870

Figure 2.2   Individual Health Insurance Cost for Family of Five in Dallas, Texas

Nationwide, the average individual policy sold in 2014 costs about half the cost of comparable unsubsidized employer-provided health insurance. But since most Americans qualify for a federal subsidy based on their income, the average individual policy sold in 2014 actually costs, on average, about one-fourth the cost of employer-provided coverage.

That's $4,000 to $12,000 in savings per year for a family of four for the same hospitals, same doctors, and same prescriptions.

Moreover, if your household income is less than $100,000/year per family or $45,000/year per single, the cost of individual health insurance is one-tenth to one-fourth the cost of employer-provided coverage.

You may even get your employer to fund your monthly premium (see Chapter 12).

 Tip: The Affordable Care Act subsidizes insurance companies to keep individual health insurance premiums low, especially during the first three years.

3. It's Permanent—Your Coverage Cannot Be Canceled As Long As You Pay Your Premium

One of the best things about individual health insurance versus employer-provided health insurance is that you control the policy. Your coverage cannot be canceled as long as you pay your premium. In contrast, as explained in Chapter 1, your employer may cancel employer-provided coverage or change the benefits at any time, with little or no notice to you, and there is no COBRA available when the plan is canceled.

4. It's Not Limited—You Get to Pick Your Doctors and Hospitals

When you choose your own individual health insurance policy, you get to choose which network of doctors and medical providers you wish to use for your family instead of having this choice made for you by your employer.

As you will learn in Chapter 10, the ability to choose your own medical providers and type of network is one of the best features of individual health insurance. Even if you have a high-deductible, individual policy where you pay most of your own medical expenses, you pay each medical provider only the discounted price it would otherwise have received from an insurance company or large employer if you didn't have a high-deductible policy.

5. It's Customizable—You Choose Your Deductible and Copays

When you select an individual health insurance policy, you choose your copay, annual deductible, and coinsurance (see Figure 2.3).

Annual deductible—This is the annual amount of your medical expenses that you must pay before your health insurance company begins paying providers or reimbursing you for claims. Traditional plans have deductibles of up to $1,500 as well as copays for doctor visits and prescriptions. High-deductible plans have deductibles from $1,000 to $10,000 but much lower premiums.

Copay—This is the amount that you pay each time you visit the doctor, pharmacy, or other medical provider. If you have children and visit the doctor often, you are typically better off with a higher premium plan that charges

	Bronze	Silver	Gold	Platinum
Monthly premium (with subsidies applied)	$0	$164	$321	$402
Deductible (family)	$10,000	$4,000	$0	$0
Coinsurance	30%	20%	20%	10%
Doctor copay	$60	$45	$30	$20
Out-of-pocket maximum (family)	$12,700	$12,700	$12,700	$8,000

Figure 2.3 Example Rates for an Employee Earning $40,000/Year (Family of Four, Adults Age 40)

you a fixed amount (copay) for each doctor visit regardless of what is done during the visit.

Coinsurance—This is the amount, typically 20 to 30 percent, that most insurance companies expect you to pay on your annual medical expenses after you have met your deductible. Fortunately, most coinsurance clauses have an upper limit of about $10,000. Your maximum coinsurance obligation, plus your annual deductible is called your out-of-pocket maximum—referring to the maximum out-of-pocket annual expense you could incur under the policy.

For some families who are relatively healthy, it makes sense to save a few thousand dollars a year on their premium by accepting a higher annual deductible or an out-of-pocket maximum of $10,000 or more. But for other families who don't have the cash, and/or have a family member with an ongoing medical issue, it often makes more sense to pay a higher premium to get a lower annual deductible or out-of-pocket maximum.

When you choose an individual health insurance policy, you get to choose from a seemingly unlimited array of amounts for copays, annual deductibles, and coinsurance. In contrast, you typically get only a few choices with employer-provided coverage.

The Affordable Care Act mandates that individual plans sold on the Exchanges be offered at five levels—Bronze, Silver, Gold, Platinum, and Catastrophic. These levels have nothing to do with the level of care you get, just the deductible, copays, and type of coverage you have access to.

 Tip: Individual health insurance allows you to customize your health insurance plan deductibles, copays, and coinsurance.

---

6. It's Subsidized—You May Be Eligible for a $2,000 to $12,000 Per Year Share of the Trillion Dollar Federal Subsidy

Since January 1, 2014, most individuals purchasing individual health insurance on their state's Health Insurance Marketplace are eligible for a federal subsidy when they purchase individual health insurance. The subsidy is administered as a tax credit but it is effectively a simple monthly discount for most consumers since you don't have to wait until you file your personal tax return to receive it. Here's how the federal subsidy works.

Let's say you live in Dallas, Texas, have a family of five, and earn $60,000 a year. You go to healthcare.gov to shop for a Blue Cross Blue Shield Silver plan that is roughly equivalent to a typical employer-provided plan with a $30 copay per doctor visit, $0 copay for generic prescriptions, and a $500 deductible for an emergency room visit. You choose a Blue Advantage Silver HMO plan with a $2,500 annual deductible per person and an unsubsidized premium of $927/month.

When you enter in your annual modified adjusted gross income (MAGI) of $60,000 to purchase your $927/month premium individual policy, you are told you are eligible for a federal subsidy (technically called a tax credit) of $580/month for an after-subsidy monthly premium cost of $347/month ($927–$580 = $347). You then are given a choice between having the federal government pay monthly all or part of this $580/month subsidy amount to your insurance company towards your premium, or receive this $580/month as a refund on your income taxes when you file your personal income tax return the following year. Consumers are expected to overwhelmingly elect to have the federal subsidy applied each month to their premium. Now let's see what happens if your annual income was $65,000 versus $60,000.

When you enter in your annual income of $65,000 to purchase your $927/month premium individual policy, you get a federal subsidy (technically called a tax credit) of $517 a month for an after-subsidy monthly premium cost of $410/month ($927–$517 = $410). The federal government will start immediately paying your insurance company $517/month towards the premium of this policy.

Figure 2.4 summarizes the subsidy at these and a few other levels of annual income.

Since the federal subsidy is administered as a tax credit, at the end of the year your MAGI must be $60,000 or less. If not, you will owe the federal government a refund of part of the federal subsidy you received up to $580/month ($6,960/year). For example, if you got an unexpected $5,000 bonus on January 1 and your annual income rose to $65,000, your retroactive federal subsidy (tax credit) would be

Annual Income	Unsubsidized Cost	Federal Subsidy	After-Subsidy Cost
$58,000	$927/month	$604/month	$323/month
$60,000	$927/month	$580/month	$347/month
$65,000	$927/month	$517/month	$410/month
$75,000	$927/month	$383/month	$544/month
$90,000	$927/month	$214/month	$713/month
$100,000	$927/month	$130/month	$797/month

Figure 2.4 Silver Blue Cross Blue Shield Policy for Family of Five in Dallas, Texas

$517/month versus the $580/month you received—and thus you would owe the federal government $63/month or $756 for 12 months. Conversely, if your annual income fell to $58,000, you would get a tax refund of $288 ($24/month times 12 months).

Eligibility for the federal subsidy is limited to Americans who meet certain income and family size requirements, and who do not have access to qualified affordable health insurance through an employer or another government program. Eligibility is based on a standard called the federal poverty level (FPL). The tax credits cap the cost of health insurance between 2 and 9.5 percent of annual household income, on a sliding scale based on income, for individuals and families who earn up to 400 percent of FPL. This translates to an individual earning up to $45,960 in 2013 and a family of four earning up to $94,200 in 2013. Families with more than four persons receive subsidies even with annual incomes of $120,000 or more.

When the HealthCare.gov website was first released in October 2013, the only way to get rates and information on plans was to go through a cumbersome registration and verification process. However, this was recently changed, and now healthcare.gov provides consumers with free, easy access to rates, plans, and the amount of their federal subsidy without even giving their name.

7. It's Stable—You're in a Large Group and Your After-Subsidy Cost Can Only Increase with Your Income

When you purchase an individual health insurance policy, you become a member of an insurance group. But it's not the relatively small group limited to the employees of one company—it's the large group of people in your state who purchased a similar policy from the same insurance company in a given time frame. Monthly premiums paid for individual policies typically increase annually with the level of inflation or overall medical costs. The insurance company is allowed to ask their state insurance regulator for a rate increase based on the actual prior year's health costs for everyone in your group.

However, unlike with employer-provided health insurance policies, these groups of individuals are so large that even the catastrophic illness of hundreds of members would not result in a significant increase in your monthly premium. In contrast, in a small company, if one of the employees gets an expensive illness like diabetes or cancer, the following year the insurance company could double the cost that employer is paying for health insurance. Many employers are forced to pass increased costs on to employees or drop health insurance coverage because of catastrophic employee illnesses. Huge, sudden increases in health insurance costs generally don't happen with individual health insurance because your group is so much larger.

There are also laws and regulations requiring individual health insurance policies to be renewable—meaning you can't be dropped by your insurance company for any reason except nonpayment of your premium.

State regulations also protect you from significant increases in your individual health plan's monthly premium. Insurance companies are generally prohibited from raising premiums on existing members above the levels paid by new people choosing to join.

But even if a large number of people in your group incur catastrophic health expenses, it is unlikely that the insurance company will increase your monthly premium by a pro rata amount. That's because a large rate increase will cause consumers, particularly healthy ones who are not afraid to change networks, to go on the Health Insurance Marketplace during their next enrollment period and choose a cheaper policy.

Thanks to the Affordable Care Act, even this potential for rising premiums based on the rising cost of healthcare does not apply to most people who purchase individual health insurance on a Marketplace and are eligible for the federal subsidy.

If you are eligible for the federal subsidy, in most cases your premium can only increase when your annual income increases—you are basically immune from increases in the unsubsidized cost of your individual insurance policy due to rising healthcare costs. That's because the size of your federal subsidy automatically changes so you pay a fixed percentage of your annual income for health insurance, and this percentage depends mostly on your income, your family size, and where you live.

For example, in 2015, let's assume you earn $60,000 per year and purchase a Silver policy for your family on your state's Marketplace with an unsubsidized price of $900 per month. The Affordable Care Act says that you should pay 6 percent of your income after subsidy, $3,600 per year or $300 per month, for your family's basic individual health insurance. Thus, you would receive a federal subsidy of $600 per month, so that the after-subsidy cost of your policy is $300 per month ($900 unsubsidized cost minus $300 after-subsidy cost equals $600 per month federal subsidy).

Now, assume that in 2016 the unsubsidized cost of your policy rises from $900 per month to $1,050 per month, but your income of $60,000 per year remains the same. Your after-subsidy cost is fixed by ACA at 6 percent of your income (based on $60,000 per year) and thus your federal subsidy would increase from $600 per month to $750 per month ($1,050 unsubsidized cost minus $300 after-subsidy cost equals $750 per month federal subsidy).

It's a little more complicated than this and explained in more detail in Chapter 6. This is because once you figure out the amount of your federal subsidy, which is based on the second lowest-cost Silver plan, you can then increase or decrease your after-subsidy cost by choosing a higher (Gold) or lower (Bronze) benefit policy. In the example above, in 2015 you could apply your fixed $600 per month subsidy to a $750 per month unsubsidized Bronze plan for an after-subsidy cost of $150 per month. Or you could buy up to a $1,000 per month Gold plan and pay $400 per month after-subsidy cost.

 Tip: After-Subsidy Individual Health Insurance Premiums Can't Increase with the Cost of Healthcare—The Affordable Care Act sets a maximum percent of income each family or single should pay for basic individual health insurance (defined as the second lowest-cost Silver plan in their area). This percentage of income is based on their annual income, the size of their family, and where they live—not on the rising cost of their individual health insurance policy.

Separately from this price protection for consumers against rising healthcare costs, the Affordable Care Act is subsidizing insurance companies to keep individual health insurance premiums low permanently and especially during the first three years of Obamacare.

8. It's Good for Careers—People Are Free to Change Jobs Based on What's Best for Their Career versus What's Best for Their Health Insurance

Changes that used to take place in 50 years or more now take place in five years or less. While employers would like their employees to think that their employer is helping them keep up with technology, few employers can afford to spend the money it takes to train and retrain existing employees, versus hire new employees with the skills the employer needs. Similarly, the primary way for many employees to actualize their full potential is to change jobs and/or careers every three to five years.

Employees who have individual health insurance versus employer-provided coverage find it easier to change jobs because their job change has minimal or virtually no impact on their family.

Every employee should get individual health insurance separate from their employer in order to be poised to maximize their potential and take full advantage of every opportunity they have to advance in their careers.

9. It's Good for Business—Management Spends More Time Focusing On Their Customers and Products versus Employee Health Benefits

While every employer complains about the cost of employer-provided health insurance, the main economic reason why individual health insurance is better for employers is that it keeps management focused on improving their products and services versus improving their employer-provided health insurance.

In our highly specialized economy, vertical integration is a thing of the past. The more a company relies on third party, specialized, outside suppliers to help produce its products or services, the faster the company can adapt to changes and keep its own product or service on the cutting edge of technology. This is also true as companies help their employees get the best individual health insurance for themselves and their families. Why? Because employer-provided coverage disqualifies employees from getting better subsidized individual coverage on their state's Marketplace.

10. It's Good for America—It Empowers Americans to Manage Their Own Healthcare and It Makes American Businesses More Competitive

Ultimately, individual health insurance is not just cheaper than employer-provided coverage, it's much healthier. Today, the Affordable Care Act, by mandating essential health benefits for both types of coverage, has made price the major difference between individual health insurance and employer-provided health insurance. But tomorrow, the major difference will be quality of care and preventive or wellness care.

Once consumers get used to purchasing their own individual policies through online exchanges, consumers will seek out what they really need—better medical providers, transparency regarding providers, and preventive/wellness care. In every area of our economy where consumers have choice—from more affordable restaurants to managing retirement benefits to purchasing retail products— technology has allowed our economy to deliver more for less. This will be true of healthcare once consumers are allowed to make their own decisions on their health insurance and, ultimately, their healthcare providers.

Additionally, compared to their overseas competitors who do not offer employer-provided coverage to employees, some U.S. companies today are no longer price competitive. Particularly in manufacturing, many employers can no longer afford the enormous cost, in both management time and money, of providing employer-provided coverage. Switching their employees to individual coverage will make many of these companies competitive again, as well as greatly improve the health of their employees.

THE OBVIOUS SOLUTION—EMPLOYER-FUNDED INDIVIDUAL HEALTH INSURANCE

As Chapter 1 and Chapter 2 have explained, individual health insurance is now better than employer-provided health insurance for you, your family, and your company because:

1. Individual health insurance is less expensive.
2. Individual health insurance enables choice.
3. Individual health insurance stays with you when you switch jobs.

This begs the question: Can you choose your own individual health insurance and get your employer to cover the cost?

The answer is an emphatic, "Yes!" Your company may cancel its employer-provided health plan and give all or part of the savings to employees to reimburse them for all or a portion of their individual health insurance premiums.

This concept is commonly referred to as *defined contribution healthcare*, which we discuss in the next chapter.

Chapter 3

THE SOLUTION—EMPLOYER-FUNDED INDIVIDUAL HEALTH INSURANCE

M illions of working Americans believe that the only way they can get health insurance is from an employer. Until recently, their belief was accurate. However, in the past few years, a quiet revolution has changed the health insurance options available to employees and businesses:

- Individual health insurance has become cheaper and better than traditional employer-provided health insurance.
- Most Americans are now eligible for monthly federal tax subsidies (called premium tax credits) for individual health insurance if their employers do not offer employer-provided health insurance.
- New defined contribution programs allow employers to reimburse employees for individual health insurance costs.

These changes mean that your company can get out of its health insurance conundrum while still (1) enabling employees to obtain high quality health insurance, and (2) providing a defined contribution health benefits program that helps recruit and retain the best employees.

THE COMING REVOLUTION—DEFINED CONTRIBUTION HEALTH BENEFITS

The health insurance market is undergoing a paradigm shift from an employer-driven defined benefit model to an individual-driven defined contribution model. The number of small and medium businesses (with less than 200 employees) offering coverage is down from 68 percent in 2000 to 57 percent in 2013 (see Figure 3.1). While the transition from employer-provided health insurance to individual health insurance has been gradual since 2000, the post-2014 enhancements to the individual market have accelerated this shift.

The post-2014 individual market's features of guaranteed acceptance, choice, portability, and tax credits have made individual health policies much more attractive to employees than employer plans. As a result, the number of policyholders in the individual market is projected to increase to more than 150 million by 2025. Additionally, new defined contribution programs allow your company to reimburse employees for their individual health insurance costs—enabling your company to offer employee health benefits for recruiting and retention purposes without absorbing the premium and administrative costs of sponsoring traditional employer-provided health insurance.

60 Percent of Small Businesses Will Switch to Defined Contribution by 2018

Due to the advantages of the post-2014 individual market and the availability of new defined contribution programs, we predict 60 percent of small businesses will eliminate traditional employer-provided health insurance in favor of defined contribution healthcare and individual health plans over the next three years. And, by 2025, the majority of U.S. businesses of all sizes will terminate employer-provided plans in favor of individual health insurance.

Employer Size	1999	2013
3–9 employees	55%	45%
10–24 employees	74%	68%
25–49 employees	88%	85%
50–199 employees	97%	91%
All small and medium employers (3–199 employees)	65%	57%
All large employers (200+ employees)	99%	99%
All firms	66%	57%

Figure 3.1 Percentage of Employers Offering Health Benefits 1999 to 2013

Source: Kaiser Family Foundation 2013.

To better understand this paradigm shift, let's take a look at the different ways employers provide health benefits to employees. Today, employers provide employees with access to health insurance in one of the following three ways:

1. Self-insured employer-provided healthcare.
2. Fully-insured employer-provided healthcare.
3. Defined contribution healthcare.

1. Self-Insured Employer-Provided Healthcare

This is how large employers (1,000-plus employees) typically provide tax-free healthcare to their employees. Employers contract with a health insurance company, such as Blue Cross Blue Shield, to provide employees medical care and receive direct reimbursement from the employer for the actual cost of care used by employees. Today, although most employees think a health insurance company actually pays for their medical providers, approximately two-thirds of Americans receiving employer-provided healthcare participate in a self-insured plan versus a traditional fully-insured plan. These plans are known as defined benefit plans since the employer defines the terms of the health benefits it offers its employees.

2. Fully-Insured Employer-Provided Healthcare

This is how small and medium-sized employers (2 to 999 employees) typically provide tax-free healthcare to their employees. Employers annually purchase an employer-provided health insurance policy from an insurance company that pays for their employees' healthcare no matter what the cost—but each year the premium is increased to cover (and/or recover) the medical expenses of the employee group based on the previous year's expenses. Today, approximately one-fourth of Americans receiving employer-provided health insurance participate in a fully-insured plan. This figure has been rapidly declining for two reasons: (1) Rising premiums make it more difficult each year to maintain the insurer-required minimum participation levels of 75 percent or more of eligible employees; and (2) the Affordable Care Act now makes individual health insurance equal to or better than fully-insured employer-provided health insurance plans for effectively one-fourth to one-half the cost. These plans are also known as defined benefit plans since the employer, in choosing the plan it buys from the insurance company, defines the health benefits it offers its employees.

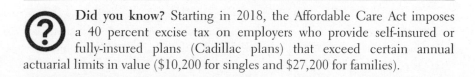 **Did you know?** Starting in 2018, the Affordable Care Act imposes a 40 percent excise tax on employers who provide self-insured or fully-insured plans (Cadillac plans) that exceed certain annual actuarial limits in value ($10,200 for singles and $27,200 for families).

---

3. Defined Contribution Healthcare

This is how approximately 5 percent of U.S. employers provide money, either tax-free or taxable, to employees who purchase their own individual health insurance policy. This is the fastest growing way employers provide healthcare to employees, especially since 2014 when the Affordable Care Act made all Americans eligible for individual health insurance regardless of their health or pre-existing conditions. These plans are known as defined contribution plans because the employer defines only its monetary contribution amount and allows each employee to choose their own benefit (the individual health insurance plan).

TAX-FREE VERSUS TAXABLE DEFINED CONTRIBUTION PROGRAMS

As explained in more detail in Chapter 13, employers currently offer defined contribution healthcare using one of the following three methods:

1. **Taxable stipend**—All similarly situated employees receive a fixed, taxable stipend to purchase individual health insurance, say $100 to $400 per month, whether or not they actually purchase health insurance. The employee's monthly contributions are typically added to his or her paycheck. At the end of the year, employees receive a form showing the amount of their stipend that they should report as income on their personal income tax return.

2. **Taxable reimbursement**—All similarly situated employees are granted a fixed, taxable defined contribution amount to purchase individual health insurance, say the same $100 to $400 per month, but only receive the money if they actually purchase health insurance. Employees purchase their own individual health insurance policy and submit proof to their employer (or the employer's third-party provider). The employee receives monthly reimbursements up to the employer's defined contribution amount that are typically added to their paycheck. At the end of the year each employee receives a form showing the amount of his or her reimbursements which should be reported as taxable income on personal income tax forms.

3. **Tax-free reimbursement**—All similarly situated employees are granted a fixed, tax-free defined contribution amount to purchase individual health insurance, say the same $100 to $400 per month, but only receive money if they actually purchase health insurance. Employees purchase their own individual health insurance policy and submit proof to their employer (or the employer's third-party provider). Employees receive monthly reimbursements up to their defined contribution amount that are typically added to their paycheck tax-free.

As we will examine shortly, providing reimbursements of individual health insurance premiums requires companies to comply with certain federal rules and regulations. Due to these requirements, many companies choose to work with a third-party solution provider to ensure compliance (see Chapter 16).

Overview—How Tax-Free Defined Contribution Works

With the tax-free defined contribution approach, an employer establishes a formal self-insured medical reimbursement plan that meets tax code guidelines to reimburse employees for their specific documented individual health insurance costs on a pre-tax basis—this arrangement is often referred to as a health reimbursement plan (HRP).

When providing tax-free reimbursement of individual health insurance policies through an HRP, the employer must ensure compliance with federal regulations, including but not limited to legal plan documents, summary plan descriptions, and new market reforms required by the Affordable Care Act.

For example, in order to comply with the rules outlined in IRS Notice 2013-54, the HRP must be structured to reimburse employees for only: (a) health insurance premiums up to a specified monthly healthcare allowance, and (b) unlimited basic preventive health services as required by the Public Health Services (PHS) Act Section 2713.

Compliance with changing federal guidelines may not be a do-it-yourself task for most employers, but it is crucial to ensure that employers structure tax-free and/or taxable reimbursement arrangements that work today and in the future. Although almost all employees would prefer receiving tax-free reimbursement for their individual health insurance premium, if the federal government began to tax such reimbursements, employees would still prefer receiving taxable reimbursements versus no reimbursements at all.

At Zane Benefits, many of our clients prefer to set up a formal tax-free reimbursement plan for the following reasons:

1. **Control**—Reimbursement plans ensure employees use the money on health insurance. If employees do not purchase health insurance, they do not get your defined contribution.
2. **Preferred employer tax treatment option**—Setting up a tax-free reimbursement plan will allow your company to save 7.65 percent in payroll taxes on your defined contributions, versus paying the same amount to employees as taxable income.
3. **Preferred employee tax treatment option**—Setting up a tax-free reimbursement plan will allow your employees to save 20 to 40 percent in state and federal income and payroll taxes.

History of Tax-Free Reimbursement of Individual Health Insurance

Since the origin of the United States, U.S. employers have been allowed to give money to their employees for almost any purpose, from buying a house to paying for medical care to contributing to retirement. Period. Your employer may give you money to purchase Christmas presents for your family or to rent a car when traveling to visit customers. The only consideration of the state and federal government is whether money given by employers to employees is taxable income, like wages, or nontaxable income, like qualified contributions to their retirement plan.

Thus, in the simplest case the money for Christmas presents is most likely taxable income and the money for retirement is nontaxable.

In general, money paid to employees by employers is taxable income except for:

1. Qualified contributions to insurance premiums.
2. Qualified distributions (or reimbursements) from self-insured plans for healthcare, including premiums.
3. Qualified contributions to retirement plans such as 401(k)s.
4. Qualified contributions to healthcare accounts such as health savings accounts.
5. Qualified reimbursement to employees of legitimate third-party business expenses.

The key word in all cases is *qualified*. Employers and employees must make sure that money given to employees tax-free qualifies under specific federal regulations that are generally enforced by the IRS.

Moreover, when money given to an employee does not qualify as a tax-free payment to an employee, either because the regulations have not been carefully followed or because too much money was given, the most common penalty is that the money (or excess money) is retroactively considered to be taxable income to the employee.

As an example, assume a single U.S. employee has an adjusted gross income (AGI) in 2014 of $50,000 and receives an additional $2,000 in 2014 of qualified contributions to his health benefits plan. According to the IRS.gov website, his federal taxable income rate would be about 12 percent or $6,000 per year. Now, assume this employee's $2,000 in 2014 tax-free contributions was, in 2015, deemed by the IRS to be nonqualified. The employee would have to retroactively pay about 12 percent of the $2,000 in income taxes ($240) plus approximately $100 in interest and penalties on the $2,000 in healthcare contributions that he thought were qualified. In effect, the IRS would ask him to refile his 2014 tax return as if he earned $52,000 versus $50,000.

This is the most commonly misunderstood item about the Internal Revenue Service (IRS) and its enforcement of the U.S. tax code. When taxpayers make an honest mistake about their income, their penalty is not that they are sent to jail. Most often, the penalty is to refile the tax return that contained the mistake, paying any additional taxes, plus penalty and interest on the revised additional taxed amount. A payment by an employer that is later deemed not to be qualifying would be subject to an administrative correction and re-filing, along with the attendant interest and minor penalties.

Traditionally, only employees participating in qualified employer-provided health benefit programs were allowed to receive their benefits tax free. To qualify for tax-free status, the employer was required to offer equivalent health benefits to all similarly situated employees—say, all cashiers or all store managers—and the plan administration had to follow very technical federal regulations for employee welfare benefit plans. These regulations are detailed in ERISA (Employee Retirement Income Security Act of 1974) and its two major amendments, popularly known as COBRA (Consolidated Omnibus Budget Reconciliation Act of 1985) and HIPAA (Health Insurance Portability and Accountability Act of 1996).

When author Paul Zane Pilzer worked at Citibank in the 1970s, the bank had 300 people devoted to keeping Citibank's self-insured, self-managed, employee health insurance plan in compliance with state and federal regulations. In the 2000s, Zane Benefits developed web-based software, ZaneHealth, which effectively did the same work of those 300 people for a fixed price to employers of $12 per month per employee.

As the U.S. economy moved from being composed of large employers to more small employers and self-employed entrepreneurs, the smaller firms began adopting medical reimbursement plans to reimburse employees for their own individual health insurance plans. While the tax code has supported this approach since the 1950s, the practice was uncommon until the 1990s. As federal regulators and policymakers became aware of these new medical reimbursement plans, they began drafting updated rules and regulations in support of them. Specifically, in order to remove confusion and level the playing field for all U.S. taxpayers, the federal government did the following in the 1990s and 2000s to clarify and support the tax equality of individual health insurance under the U.S. tax code:

1. **Self-employed health insurance premium deduction**—In 1993, Congress passed a bill to become effective in 2003 that makes individual health insurance premiums tax-deductible for self-employed individuals.

2. **Health reimbursement arrangements**—In 2002, the IRS published Notice 2002-45 that codified and spelled out the rules for employers to reimburse employees tax free for medical-care expenses and individual health insurance premiums via medical reimbursement plans referred to as HRAs, or health reimbursement arrangements.

As of this writing, Congress has not altered the United States tax code as it relates to tax-free reimbursements of individual health insurance premiums. Self-employed persons receive a 100 percent tax deduction for their individual health insurance policy premiums, and employers are allowed to reimburse employees for the cost of their individual health insurance premiums tax free via a medical reimbursement plan under Section 105 of the Internal Revenue Code (Internal Revenue Code, 1954).

Federal versus State Law Controversy

During the period following IRS Notice 2002-45, from 2002 to 2013, the IRS promoted employers reimbursing employees for individual health insurance premiums tax free, and small- and medium-sized employers began cancelling (or not starting) employer-provided health insurance plans. Despite this, there was initially some state versus federal law controversy regarding an employer's reimbursement of individual health insurance. Some state insurance departments argued that individual health insurance policies reimbursed by employers were effectively small group plans—and thus the insurance companies had to offer such individual coverage to all employees regardless of pre-existing conditions.

These state insurance departments had a not-so-hidden agenda. Under the 1996 HIPAA legislation, beginning in 2006 every U.S. state was required to offer affordable individual health insurance (i.e., risk pool coverage) to individuals in their state who were denied individual coverage for pre-existing conditions. These state insurance departments bullied employers into maintaining their employer-provided group plans to avoid financing expensive insurance for a flood of otherwise uninsurable employees in accordance with their state's federal legal obligation to provide affordable health insurance for their neediest citizens with a sick child or a chronic illness.

This controversy between federal and state regulations was featured in a front-page story about Zane Benefits, Inc. in *The Wall Street Journal* on July 30, 2007. In this article, the newspaper mentioned that our methods were being followed by Walmart, United Healthcare, and others—but still quoted an associate professor from Georgetown University as saying "I think this is blatantly illegal" (Terhune 2007).

Now, more than seven years later, Zane Benefits appears to have been correct. There has not been a single case where a state insurance department succeeded in getting an employer reimbursing an employee for an individual policy to be considered an employer-provided health insurance policy—and thus requiring the insurance company to offer such an individual policy to other employees regardless of pre-existing conditions.

From 2002 to 2013, some state insurance departments unsuccessfully argued that an individual health insurance policy being reimbursed by an employer through an HRA created a de facto small group plan.

Fortunately, as of January 1, 2014, this entire issue is moot because the Affordable Care Act requires that every individual health insurance policy be guaranteed-accepted regardless of the health or pre-existing medical conditions of the applicant. Even if a state insurance department succeeds in getting an individual policy reimbursed by an employer to be considered an employer-provided health insurance plan, it doesn't matter because effective January 1, 2014, all individual policies are available to all Americans regardless of their health or pre-existing conditions.

THE REGULATORY CRISIS OF 2013 OVER REIMBURSEMENT PLANS FOR INDIVIDUAL HEALTH INSURANCE

In September 2013, as the federal government prepared to implement the key provisions of the Affordable Care Act, certain officials in the Obama Administration realized the depth of the financial crisis that Congress had created with the ACA.

When President Obama took office on January 20, 2009, the primary purpose of his proposals for healthcare reform was to make affordable healthcare available for the 45 million uninsured Americans who either could not afford health insurance or who did not qualify for individual health insurance because they had a family member with a pre-existing condition. In drafting the original ACA legislation, the Obama Administration carefully made sure that affordable individual health insurance would be made available to everyone, but excluded from the definition of everyone the 160 million Americans who got their health insurance through an employer-provided health insurance plan. No one in the Administration wanted to see employers stop contributing $1.2 trillion a year to their employees' healthcare. This status quo was upended in the negotiations leading to the final passage of the Affordable Care Act in 2010.

In 2009, Obama Administration officials knew that U.S. employers would drop their employer-provided plans if their employees were able to purchase better, safer, and cheaper subsidized individual health insurance policies. To stop this from happening, the original Obama Administration proposals mandated: (1) that all employers offer their employees employer-provided health insurance, and (2) that employers who did not offer a health insurance benefit would incur a non-deductible fine of $20,000 per employee for each of their employees who purchased subsidized individual health insurance on an Exchange (now called the Health Insurance Marketplace, as discussed in Chapter 8).

Obama Administration officials also called this fine the penalty or the employer *shared responsibility payment*, and expected that this $20,000 per employee penalty would be much larger than the cost of employer-provided health insurance—which was then approximately $5,000 per person per year. They were almost correct. The original version of Obamacare, passed in late 2009 by the U.S. Senate, set the non-deductible fine at $20,000 per employee per year—four times more the 2010 estimated tax-deductible $5,000 per year cost of employer-provided health insurance.

Did you know? The original version of the Affordable Care Act passed by the U.S. Senate called for employers to pay a $20,000 per year non-deductible fine for each of their employees who obtained subsidized individual health insurance on an Exchange. Surely every employer would rather pay the then $5,000 per year tax-deductible cost for employee health insurance versus risk incurring a $20,000 per year per employee non-deductible fine for each employee who received a subsidy.

Then, in February 2010, as the debate over the ACA became heated in the U.S. House of Representatives (Congress), the U.S. unemployment rate skyrocketed to its highest level since the Great Depression. Suddenly, the focus of the nation shifted from healthcare reform to unemployment. Employers testified in Washington that they would close even more stores and factories, and move millions more jobs overseas if they had to pay a non-deductible $20,000 penalty for each employee without employer-provided health insurance.

The end result was that employment trumped healthcare. The final version of the Affordable Care Act was signed by President Obama into law on March 23, 2010. It contained a reduced employer fine of only $2,000 (versus $20,000) per employee when an employee obtained subsidized individual coverage on the Health Insurance Marketplace, and a fine of $0 for smaller employers with less than 50 employees who were exempted entirely from the fine.

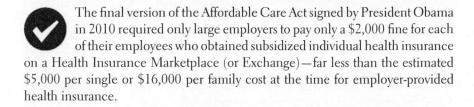

The final version of the Affordable Care Act signed by President Obama in 2010 required only large employers to pay only a $2,000 fine for each of their employees who obtained subsidized individual health insurance on a Health Insurance Marketplace (or Exchange)—far less than the estimated $5,000 per single or $16,000 per family cost at the time for employer-provided health insurance.

Thus, there were concerns in 2010, that when Obamacare was implemented in 2014, it would cause many employers to drop employer-provided coverage entirely and pay the fine. *The Wall Street Journal* reported on May 21, 2010, that AT&T paid $2.4 billion in 2009 for health insurance for its 283,000 employees and would only have to pay $600 million in penalties if it dropped coverage (Goodman 2010).

The final version of the Affordable Care Act signed by President Obama in 2010 exempts small businesses with fewer than 50 employees from fines for not offering coverage.

But, for the most part, these concerns subsided when it appeared that the Supreme Court might rule the ACA to be unconstitutional. After passage in 2010, the Affordable Care Act became tied up in the courts until the U.S. Supreme Court ruled the Affordable Care Act to be constitutional on June 28, 2012.

Tip: While the Affordable Care Act in 2010 mandated that larger employers not offering affordable health insurance to employees would have to pay a $2,000 per employee penalty starting on January 1, 2014, on July 9, 2013, the Obama Administration subsequently delayed the implementation of this penalty until January 1, 2015, for employers with 100 or more employees, and until January 1, 2016 for employers with 50 to 99 employees.

Thus, in September 2013, regulatory officials in Washington were facing the following dilemma:

Starting January 1, 2014, individual health insurance would be better, cheaper, and safer than traditional employer-provided health insurance, and subsidized individual policies would be available to every

American at one-half to one-fourth the cost of employer-provided coverage. How could the Administration stop employers from dropping employer-provided health insurance en masse and costing the federal government up to $1.2 trillion per year?

The situation looked even worse in September 2013 than it did back in 2010. Why? Because in 2012, the Obama Administration delayed enforcement of the $2,000 per employee fine for employers until 2015 and 2016. Thus in 2014, there wasn't a $2,000 per year fine for any employers shifting the cost of their employee's health insurance from the employer to the federal government via the Health Insurance Marketplace.

By 2014, U.S. employers were paying approximately $8,000 per employee towards the cost of health insurance for approximately 160 million employees and their dependents—that's more than $1.2 trillion per year in cost that could be shifted from private businesses to the federal government if employers dropped employer-provided health insurance. To put this $1.2 trillion in perspective, the entire U.S. federal deficit in 2014 is projected to be about $500 billion.

More realistically, employers wouldn't simply want to drop employer-provided health insurance entirely—they would want to take part of the money they were spending on employer-provided health insurance and give it to employees to purchase individual policies for about one-fourth to one-half the cost (depending on their income) of their employer-provided coverage.

The challenge then facing the federal regulators in September 2013 was: How do we slow down this transition by employers from employer-provided health insurance to employer-funded individual health insurance?

As much as the regulators wanted to rewrite the Affordable Care Act to prevent employers from switching their employees to cheaper and better individual health insurance policies, there was little they could do:

1. **Taxable stipend**—Regulators could not stop or even limit employers from giving their employees a fully taxable stipend to spend on individual health insurance.
2. **Taxable reimbursement**—Regulators could not stop or even limit employers from giving their employees taxable compensation in the amount they spent on individual health insurance.
3. **Tax-free reimbursement**—Regulators could slow down employers from switching employees to individual health insurance policies by manipulating a provision of the Affordable Care Act so as to make it more difficult for employers to reimburse employees tax-free for individual health insurance premiums—even though such an action would conflict with 13 years of federal policy to level the playing field for all U.S. employees

and make it simpler for employers to reimburse employees for individual health insurance.

September 13, 2013—IRS Notice 2013-54 Attempts to Slow Transition to Employer-Funded Individual Health Insurance

On September 13, 2013, the Internal Revenue Service, the U.S. Department of Health and Human Services, and the U.S. Department of Labor released guidance addressing the issue of tax-free employer contributions towards individual health insurance policies (U.S. Department of Labor, 2013). The effect of this guidance was to make it more cumbersome, but not impossible, for employers to give employees tax-free reimbursement of premiums paid for individual health insurance. Here's a summary of the impact of this guidance.

1. Since 2002, the IRS has promoted the use of Health Reimbursement Arrangements (HRAs) where employers reimburse employees tax-free for the cost of premiums for individual health insurance up to a fixed, maximum monthly allowance. Typically, an employer gives employees a monthly allowance of $100 to $400 to spend on IRS-approved medical items, which includes individual health insurance premiums.
2. The Affordable Care Act defines most benefits like doctor visits and pharmaceuticals provided by health plans to be "essential health benefits." Other items, such as acupuncture or adult dental care, are not considered essential health benefits. The Affordable Care Act requires most health insurance plans to cover essential health benefits without annual or lifetime limits.
3. The Affordable Care Act also requires all health plans to cover a list of preventive care items, such as mammograms and prostrate screenings, which typically cost up to $1,000 per year per person.
4. The 2013 Guidance states that a medical reimbursement plan, such as an HRA, even if it provides only $1 per month in benefits, is essentially itself a health plan and is thus subject to the unlimited lifetime benefits rules and preventive care coverage rules of the Affordable Care Act. The guidance claims this applies to the medical reimbursement plan even if the beneficiary of the plan purchases an individual health insurance policy which, by definition, must already cover unlimited essential health benefits and preventive care.

Note that the federal regulators issued this new information as guidance rather as new law or regulations. This is because the regulators are over-stepping their statutory authority and don't have the legal authority to expand ACA as they see fit—they must follow the actual law passed by Congress.

WHAT SHOULD EMPLOYERS DO NOW TO REIMBURSE EMPLOYEES TAX-FREE FOR INDIVIDUAL HEALTH INSURANCE?

Despite the position of the authors that the IRS guidance is overreaching and will be superseded or repealed, the authors recommend that all employers follow the guidance. Employers seeking to give their employees tax-free reimbursement for individual health insurance premiums should do the following:

1. Set up a Section 105 Health Reimbursement Plan (HRP) to give their employees a monthly allowance to purchase (only) individual health insurance and nothing else. Individual health insurance premiums are not an essential health benefit under ACA and thus an employer is not required to offer unlimited annual and lifetime amounts for employees to purchase individual health insurance.
2. Specify in the HRP plan documents the coverage of unlimited basic preventive care services required by the ACA.
3. Require in the HRP plan documents that employees who choose to participate must purchase an individual health insurance policy that meets all ACA requirements for unlimited essential health benefits and for preventive care.
4. Require in the HRP plan documents that employees seeking preventive care must first look to their (required) individual health insurance policy and only seek preventive care coverage required by ACA if their health insurance policy defaulted on its obligation to provide preventive care.

This simple workaround has two drawbacks for employers and their employees:

1. It limits employers from using HRPs (or HRAs) to offer creative, customized benefits tailored to their workforce. For example, employers employing workers in hazardous occupations sometimes offered these workers extra tax-free drug and alcohol counseling in the past as a component of their medical reimbursement plans, something they can't do with a one-benefit (individual health insurance premium) HRP.
2. It technically (although not practically) puts the employer at risk for up to approximately $1,000 per year in preventive care expenses per employee in the unlikely event that the employee's chosen individual health insurance company defaults on its preventive care obligation. Employers can limit this liability by having an employee's defined contribution amount for health insurance be reduced by any preventive reimbursements requested by the employee.

! The authors believe that IRS Notice 2013-54 is an overreaching attempt by some government bureaucrats to slow down the transition from employer-provided health insurance to employer-funded individual health insurance. These shortsighted bureaucrats will not succeed because tens of millions of Americans are shifting to subsidized individual health insurance even without tax-free reimbursements for their premiums.

CONCLUSION

Since 2000, the percentage of Americans covered by job-based health insurance has steadily declined. Facing double-digit annual percentage growth in health insurance premiums, businesses have either eliminated health benefits or redesigned the plans to include higher deductibles, larger copayments, and greater premium sharing by employees.

This price pressure has created a paradigm shift in the way businesses offer employee health benefits—a shift from employer-provided health insurance to employer-funded individual health insurance. While the transition from employer-provided health insurance to individual health insurance has been gradual since 2000, recent enhancements to the individual market have accelerated this shift.

As a result, the individual market is expected to expand from 30 million insureds in 2012 to more than 150 million insureds by 2025. During this transition, many Americans (most likely including you) will be required to shop for and purchase an individual health insurance policy. Part II will help you navigate this new world.

Part I Appendix—How Employer-Provided Healthcare Created the Overpriced, Bloated $4 Trillion U.S. Healthcare Industry

Prior to World War I, Americans paid directly for their own medical care and most babies were born at home. In the period between World War I and World War II, the medical industry developed new life-saving procedures, and births moved from the home to the hospital. This increased

(continued)

Part I Appendix—How Employer-Provided Healthcare Created the Overpriced, Bloated $4 Trillion U.S. Healthcare Industry (*Continued*)

demand for catastrophic and maternity care created a need to help patients finance that care. In 1929, Blue Cross hospital insurance entities began offering guaranteed hospital services for a fixed fee, and in 1930, Blue Shield entities began offering reimbursement for expensive physician services. As World War II ended and millions of Americans returned home to start a family, suddenly everyone wanted health insurance.

At that time, health insurance really was insurance. It provided coverage only for major and unusual items like emergency hospitalizations and births that people could not afford to pay for themselves, but not for regular items such as doctor visits and prescription drugs. This was similar to today's auto, life, and homeowners insurance where you only receive a benefit when you have an accident, a death, or a catastrophe—your insurance doesn't cover any regular maintenance items like oil changes, doing exercise, or fixing a leaking roof. Imagine what would happen to the cost of oil changes if customers didn't have to pay for them directly (no need to compare prices), but rather showed their auto insurance card and had the insurer pay for it—and then imagine what would happen to the cost of auto insurance as the increased cost of those oil changes was reflected in the auto insurance premiums. The same dynamic has driven U.S. healthcare spending since World War II.

During World War II, the U.S. federal government instituted wage and price controls on many goods and services. Having witnessed the effects of hyper-inflation on Germany post-World War I, U.S. leaders were concerned about potential post-World War II inflation and were determined to maintain wage and price controls after the war. But labor and U.S. labor unions had different ideas. They had seen their wages frozen while many business owners and government suppliers had made millions during the war, and labor was considering calling a general strike when the war ended.

In 1945, in order to grant a concession to labor without appearing to violate wage and price controls, the federal government exempted employer-provided and employer-paid health benefits from being reported as personal income by employees. In effect, the IRS allowed employers to pay employees off the books or under the table with healthcare. This paved the way for wage increases in the form of nontaxable, employer-sponsored health insurance or healthcare. Unions started demanding nontaxable health benefits to cover every conceivable medical product and service, including incidental items like doctor visits and prescription drugs that employees could have afforded to pay for themselves.

Almost overnight, employer-provided health insurance went from covering only items that patients could not afford themselves, to covering every conceivable medical product or service. Everything became covered—from the smallest prescription drug to an ever-expanding list of medical procedures, some with dubious patient benefits.

It's easy to see why employees preferred tax-free compensation to taxable wages. In 1952, the U.S. marginal federal personal income tax rate ranged from 42 percent on income over $10,000/year to 92 percent on income over $250,000/year—averaging 50 percent or more for most skilled workers or executives. Who wanted a wage increase when the federal government alone, before additional state and city income taxes, took 50 to 92 percent of your wage increase? Employees and executives bargained away wage increases for health benefits until they made sure every possible health-related item was covered. Employers didn't seem to mind because every $1 they gave employees in health benefits was financially equivalent to giving them the equivalent of $2 on average in taxable wages, and up to $10 if they were a high-income executive.

From 1950 to 2000, U.S. employers spent money on their employees' healthcare as if they were drunken sailors on shore leave—seemingly not caring about the cost or about the outcomes of each prescription or procedure. Led by employers' largesse and labor union concessions, annual U.S. healthcare spending rose from about $500 per person in 1950 to $5,000 per person in 2000. In 2000, when employers finally took notice, it was too late—U.S. healthcare spending exceeded $1 trillion and the cost to the largest employers as a group exceeded what they earned in profits, threatening their very existence.

Then, it got worse. From 2000 to 2014, U.S. healthcare spending rose from $1.25 trillion ($5,000 per person) to almost $4 trillion ($12,500 per person). In 2009, largely due to the costs of providing healthcare for their employees, both General Motors and Chrysler filed for Chapter 11 bankruptcy protection.

While today the U.S. marginal federal personal income tax rate is much lower, ranging from roughly 25 percent on income of $50,000/year (family) to 39.6 percent on income over $400,000/year, U.S. employers and

(*continued*)

Part I Appendix—How Employer-Provided Healthcare Created the Overpriced, Bloated $4 Trillion U.S. Healthcare Industry (*Continued*)

employees seem permanently addicted to paying for, and receiving, tax-free employer-provided healthcare.

More than anything else, this created the situation we have today where we pay the most and get the least. The United States spends two to three times more per person on healthcare than any other developed nation, and the United States is the unhealthiest developed nation on earth. Incredibly, approximately 50 percent of the medical procedures done in doctor's offices and hospitals do more harm than good.

Part II

HOW TO MAKE INDIVIDUAL HEALTH INSURANCE WORK FOR YOU AND YOUR FAMILY

T his section describes great new ways that can save you thousands of dollars each year while getting better coverage for your family.

Chapter 4

WHAT IS INDIVIDUAL HEALTH INSURANCE?

There is a new and better way to purchase health insurance for you and your family. It's called individual health insurance. Individual health insurance is a policy you purchase directly from the insurance company through a licensed health insurance broker or through the Health Insurance Marketplace in your state.

If you have never heard of individual health insurance before, you are not alone. Prior to 2014, less than 10 percent of the U.S. population (20 to 30 million Americans) had this type of insurance while most Americans (more than 160 million) relied on health insurance purchased through their employer. However, due to the advantages of the individual market (such as lower cost, choice, portability, and guaranteed acceptance), U.S. companies are terminating employer-provided health insurance in favor of employer-funded individual health insurance.

As a result, the number of Americans purchasing individual health insurance is expected to grow to 150 million by 2025. Soon, it will become commonplace for employees to purchase a plan on their own—just like car insurance

THE ADVANTAGES OF INDIVIDUAL HEALTH INSURANCE

There are four primary advantages of individual health insurance for you and your family: lower costs, choice, portability, and guaranteed acceptance. (See Figure 4.1.)

1. *Lower costs*. Individual health insurance plans cost 20 to 60 percent less than traditional employer-provided health insurance, on average, and special discounts (also called subsidies) are now available for plans

57

	Employer-Provided Health Insurance	Individual Health Insurance
Keep your plan when you switch jobs	No	Yes
You choose the coverage and doctors	No	Yes
Premium tax credits available	No	Yes
Coverage for pre-existing medical conditions	Yes	Yes
Coverage for essential health benefits	Yes	Yes
Average cost (2014)		
Single	$6,472/year	$3,048/year
Family	$17,986/year	$9,108/year
How is the plan paid for?	Your employer purchases the plan. You reimburse your employer via your paycheck.	You purchase the plan. Your employer may reimburse you via your paycheck.

Figure 4.1   Employer-Provided Health Insurance versus Individual Health Insurance

purchased in the Health Insurance Marketplaces. If you qualify, these discounts, called *premium tax credits*, will allow you and your family to buy individual plans at significantly reduced prices. Also, if you or your spouse is currently employed, you may be able to get 100 percent of your premium reimbursed by the company.

2. *Choice.* With individual health insurance, you choose the coverage and doctors that best fit your family's needs. Purchasing individual health insurance is now simple—there are no questions about your health and you will be asked a few additional financial questions to see if you qualify for a premium tax credit. Four standard levels of coverage, called metallic tiers, categorize individual health plans: (1) Platinum, (2) Gold, (3) Silver, and (4) Bronze. Within each tier, you choose your coverage by insurance company, doctor network, and coverage provided by the plan.

3. *Portability.* With individual health insurance, you and your family keep your health insurance when you switch jobs. Individual health policies

are permanent and portable, independent of your employment. This is especially valuable if you or a family member have pre-existing medical conditions.

4. *Guaranteed acceptance.* All individual market insurance companies must make individual health plans available on a guaranteed-issue basis. This means you and your family may not be denied coverage due to a pre-existing condition. There is one catch—you can only buy health insurance during the annual special enrollment periods described in Chapter 7.

Everyone uses the healthcare system at some point in life. You never know when an accident might happen or a family member will get sick and need to see a doctor. When that day comes, the expenses could be financially devastating. This part of the book will guide you through the process of purchasing health insurance in the individual market. Let's begin by walking through what health insurance really is.

WHAT IS HEALTH INSURANCE?

Health insurance is different from all other types of insurance. When you buy life insurance, automobile insurance, or homeowners insurance, you do not expect to have a claim in the near future. You purchase these types of insurance for financial protection against the occurrence of an unlikely event that you wish to avoid—like a death, an auto theft, or a fire. If such an event occurs, you generally receive money that you are free to spend any way you wish.

In contrast, with health insurance, you expect to have claims in the near future and you almost never receive money when you have a claim. Instead, your insurance company directly pays the medical providers that have taken care of you—typically paying them either a flat monthly fee or a small fraction of what they would charge you directly if you didn't have health insurance.

This is because what we call health insurance in the United States consists of two separate but related components:

1. *Insurance coverage*—Financial protection against the medical expenses of an accident or illness.
2. *Provider network*—Access to a network of physicians, hospitals, and other medical providers that provide services at greatly discounted rates.

We discuss these two components in detail in Chapters 9 and 10 respectively, but first, it is imperative that you become familiar with the most common insurance terms.

 Tip: Make sure you understand the most common insurance terms—this will give you the ability to shop and compare different options to find the best deals.

Your Annual Deductible—The Amount You Pay before Your Coinsurance Kicks In

Your *annual deductible* is the amount you must pay for covered care each year before your health insurance begins to pay. For example, a $1,000 deductible will require you to pay $1,000 out-of-pocket for covered services before the insurance company pays.

Your Coinsurance—The Amount You Pay after Your Deductible

Your *coinsurance* is the percentage of medical costs you are required to pay after your annual deductible is met. For example, the health insurance plan may cover 80 percent of charges for a covered surgery, leaving you responsible for the other 20 percent. The 20 percent you must pay is called the coinsurance.

Your Annual Out-of-Pocket Maximum—The Maximum Amount You Will Pay Each Year

Your *annual out-of-pocket maximum* is the absolute maximum amount of money you will pay for covered services during a year. Once you reach your annual out-of-pocket maximum, your health insurance plan covers your medical costs at 100 percent.

Your Copayment—The Cost of a Doctor Visit or Pharmacy Item

Your *copayments* (or *copays*) are set dollar amounts you pay to your medical providers for specific covered services. The most common types of copays are doctor visit copays and pharmacy copays. For example, you may make a $40 copay for each covered visit to your primary care provider. Often, copays are capped at a certain number of uses per year.

Your Premium—The Cost of Health Insurance

Your *premium* is the amount you pay to the insurance company for your individual health insurance plan, usually monthly. The monthly premium you are required to pay is determined based on the following factors: (1) your location, (2) your age, (3) your family size, (4) you and your family's tobacco use, (5) the insurance coverage provided by the plan, and (6) the size and quality of the provider network provided by the plan.

Five Key Insurance Terms
1. **Annual Deductible**—The amount you must pay for covered care each year before your health insurance begins to pay.
2. **Coinsurance**—The percentage of medical costs you are required to pay after your annual deductible is met.
3. **Annual Out-of-Pocket Maximum**—The maximum amount of money you will pay for covered services during a year.
4. **Copayments**—The set dollar amounts you pay to your medical providers for specific covered services.
5. **Premium**—The amount you pay to the insurance company for your individual health insurance plan, usually monthly.

Now that you are familiar with the basics of health insurance, let's move on to how much individual health insurance costs.

WHAT YOU LEARNED
- Individual health insurance is a policy you purchase through a licensed health insurance broker or through the Health Insurance Marketplace in your state.
- Individual health insurance plans cost 20 to 60 percent less than traditional employer-provided plans on average.
- Individual health insurance allows you to choose your coverage level and doctor networks.
- Individual health insurance is portable, meaning you keep the plan when you switch jobs.
- Individual health insurance companies must accept new members regardless of pre-existing conditions.
- Health insurance is made up of two separate, but related components: (1) insurance coverage, and (2) the provider network.

Chapter 5

HOW MUCH DOES INDIVIDUAL HEALTH INSURANCE COST?

O n average, individual health insurance coverage costs 20 to 60 percent less than comparable employer-provided coverage—that is $4,000 to $12,000 in savings per year for a family of four for the same hospitals, same doctors, and same prescriptions. Additionally, depending on your family size and income, you may be eligible for a federal subsidy (or premium tax credit) to further reduce your costs. In this chapter, we will walk through how your individual health insurance costs are determined.

Under the Affordable Care Act, the rates for individual health insurance are kept artificially low through three mechanisms—risk adjustment, reinsurance, and risk corridors—especially during the first three years of the ACA. Basically, the government is paying insurance carriers who take on higher-risk people by covering carriers for catastrophic cases through reinsurance, and collecting money from some carriers who insure primarily healthy individuals and giving it to carriers who take on high-risk cases (Kaiser Family Foundation 2014).

For families earning less than $100,000 a year, the cost for each individual is heavily subsidized by the federal government. In 2014, 70 percent of the 7 million people who enrolled their family through the federally-run Health Insurance Marketplaces paid less than $100 per month for their entire family.

HOW INDIVIDUAL HEALTH INSURANCE PREMIUMS ARE DETERMINED

The *premium* is the amount you pay to the insurance company for your individual health insurance plan, usually monthly. For each plan, the insurance company determines the initial premium based on the two core components of health insurance: (1) the insurance coverage provided by the plan, and (2) the size and quality of the provider network included with the plan.

1. The Insurance Coverage Provided by the Plan

Premiums are largely based on the health insurance coverage provided by the plan. However, the federal government has put standards in place to limit the variation of health insurance coverage between different plans in the individual market. The goal of these limits is to standardize the way insurance companies offer health insurance in order to make it easy for you and your family to make side-by-side comparisons of different plans.

Metallic Tiers for Coverage

Individual health insurance plans have been standardized into four primary metallic tiers: (1) Platinum, (2) Gold, (3) Silver, and (4) Bronze. Within each of these tiers, or plan categories, the plans must provide a certain level of insurance coverage (insurance companies refer to this as *actuarial value*). Generally speaking, the higher the metallic tier, the higher the premium, and the higher the actuarial value. (See Figure 5.1.) We discuss these plan categories in detail in Chapter 9.

For example, a family of four living in San Francisco, California would pay $682 per month for a Bronze-level plan and $1,389 per month for a Platinum-level health plan (see Figure 5.2). These rates do not include premium tax credits, which we discuss in detail in the next chapter. If that same family of four reported annual household income of $75,000 per year in 2014, they would only pay $181 per month for the same Bronze-level plan and $889 per month for the same Platinum-level health plan (see Figure 5.3).

Tier	Actuarial Value	Monthly Premium	Cost When You Get Care
Platinum	90%	$$$$	$
Gold	80%	$$$	$$
Silver	70%	$$	$$$
Bronze	60%	$	$$$$

Figure 5.1 Metallic Tiers for Coverage

Tier	Monthly Cost (no subsidies)	Type of Plan
Platinum	$1,389	HMO
Gold	$1,252	HMO
Silver	$935	HMO
Bronze	$682	HMO

Figure 5.2 Example Individual Health Plan Rates by Metallic Tiers for Coverage, without Subsidies, California 2014 (Family: Two Adults Age 35 with Two Children)
Source: Covered California 2014.

Tier	Monthly Cost (with subsidies)	Type of Plan
Platinum	$889	HMO
Gold	$752	HMO
Silver	$453	HMO
Bronze	$181	HMO

Figure 5.3 Example Individual Health Plan Rates by Metallic Tiers for Coverage, with Subsidies, California 2014 (Family: Two Adults Age 35 with Two Children, Annual Income $75,000/year)
Source: Covered California 2014.

Deductible and Out-of-Pocket Limits

All individual health plans are now subject to out-of-pocket limits. Specifically, an individual health plan's out-of-pocket maximum cannot exceed $6,600 for single coverage or $13,200 for family coverage in 2015 (see Figure 5.4). These limits will be adjusted in future years based on medical inflation. In general, the plans with lower deductibles and out-of-pocket maximums will have higher premiums.

For example, Figure 5.5 shows the deductibles, out-of-pocket maximums, and monthly premium costs for the same family of four living in San Francisco, California.

	Out-of-Pocket Max
Individual	$6,600
Family	$13,200

Figure 5.4 Out-of-Pocket Limits (2015)

Tier	Monthly Cost (no subsidies)	Deductible (single/family)	Out-of-Pocket Max (single/family)
Platinum	$1,389	$0 / $0	$4,000 / $8,000
Gold	$1,252	$0 / $0	$6,350 / $12,700
Silver	$935	$2,000 / $4,000	$6,350 / $12,700
Bronze	$682	$5,000 / $10,000	$6,350 / $12,700

Figure 5.5 Example Individual Health Plans with Premium Deductible and Out-of-Pocket Maximums by Metallic Tiers for Coverage, without Subsidies (Family: Two Adults Age 35 with Two Children)

Source: Covered California, 2014.

2. The Size and Quality of the Provider Network Included in the Plan

Premiums are also largely based on the size and quality of the provider network offered by the plan. The provider network is the group of doctors, clinics, hospitals, and other medical sites covered by your health insurance. If you seek care outside of this provider network, your insurance may not pay for the services or may pay a lower amount. In general, a larger and more robust network will lead to higher premiums than a network that is limited to a specific geographic region. As we will discuss in Chapter 10, it will be vital for you to take steps to ensure your preferred doctors and hospitals are covered by any individual health plan you consider for purchase.

PERSONAL FACTORS INFLUENCE YOUR INDIVIDUAL HEALTH INSURANCE PREMIUM

The actual premium you pay for an individual health insurance plan will be adjusted based on characteristics unique to you and your family's personal situation. Specifically, a plan's premium will be adjusted to account for you and your family's: (1) location, (2) age, (3) family size, and (4) tobacco use.

Personal Rating Factors Affecting Your Premium
  1. Location
  2. Age
  3. Family Size
  4. Tobacco Use

1. Location

Your individual health insurance premiums will vary depending on where you live. When you request a quote for an individual plan, one of the first pieces of information you will be asked to provide is your residential zip code. Health insurance companies set policy rates based on geographic locations called *rating areas*. Premiums for the same health insurance policy may vary drastically from one rating area to the next.

Tip: Moving to a different rating area within your state could save you and your family thousands of dollars per year.

---

2. Age

Premiums in the individual market may also vary based on your age on the date the policy is issued. However, there are limitations on how much a health insurance company can increase your price due to age. Specifically, the federal government limits how much an insurance company can increase your premium based on age—an older policyholder cannot be charged more than 300 percent the rate of a younger policyholder. See Figure 5.6 for a sample age-ratio chart for a hypothetical individual plan. In this example, if a 21 year old were to be charged $100, a 64-year-old could not be charged more than $300.

3. Family Size

Your individual health insurance premium will also be adjusted based on your family or household size. In most states, premiums for your family will be determined by adding the rate for each covered family member over 21 to rates for the oldest three covered children under age 21. Some states may choose to utilize standard family tiers (e.g., single versus family) for simplicity.

Age	Premium Ratio	Sample Premium
0–20	0.635	$63.50
21–24	1.000	$100.00
25–30	1.004–1.135	$106.95
31–40	1.159–1.278	$121.85
41–50	1.302–1.786	$154.40
51–63	1.865–2.952	$240.85
64 +	3.000	$300.00

Figure 5.6 Sample Age-Ratio Chart

4. Tobacco Use

Insurance companies may also adjust your premium based on you or your family's *tobacco use*. Tobacco use is defined as use of tobacco an average of four or more times per week within the past six months. The federal government limits premium variation based on tobacco use to a ratio of 1.5 to 1. If you provide false or incorrect information about you or your family's tobacco use, the insurance company has the ability to retroactively apply the appropriate tobacco use rating factor to your premium, but it is not allowed to cancel your coverage.

 Tip: If you or a family member uses tobacco, quitting could save you thousands of dollars per year.

SAMPLE INDIVIDUAL HEALTH INSURANCE RATES

Excluding premium tax credits (subsidies), the typical premium for an individual health plan in 2014 was $254 per month compared with an estimated average for employer-provided health insurance plan of $539 per month. To see the typical premium in your state, see Figure 5.7. *Note: these rates do not take into account federal subsidies.*

State	Sample Individual Premium
United States Average	$254
Alabama	$234
Alaska	$408
Arizona	$168
Arkansas	$271
California	$267
Colorado	$252
Connecticut	$244
Delaware	$289
District of Columbia	$294
Florida	$212
Georgia	$239
Hawaii	$183

Figure 5.7   Sample Individual Premiums by State for Single Adult Male, Age 40 (2014)

State	Sample Individual Premium
Idaho	$231
Illinois	$202
Indiana	$274
Iowa	$208
Kansas	$203
Kentucky	$274
Louisiana	$282
Maine	$295
Maryland	$214
Massachusetts	$349
Michigan	$200
Minnesota	$154
Mississippi	$276
Missouri	$238
Montana	$245
Nebraska	$219
Nevada	$246
New Hampshire	$289
New Jersey	$318
New Mexico	$218
New York	$418
North Carolina	$269
North Dakota	$271
Ohio	$228
Oklahoma	$191
Oregon	$214
Pennsylvania	$170
Rhode Island	$293
South Carolina	$230
South Dakota	$258
Tennessee	$180
Texas	$188
Utah	$207
Vermont	$426
Virginia	$250
Washington	$300
West Virginia	$248
Wisconsin	$244
Wyoming	$395

Figure 5.7 (Continued)

As we discuss in the next chapter, if your family earns less than $100,000 per year, or has three or more children, you are probably eligible for federal subsidies—called premium tax credits. These subsidies cap the amount of the premium you are responsible for each month as a percentage of your household income.

WHAT YOU LEARNED

- Individual health insurance premiums are largely based on the coverage and provider networks offered by the plan.
- New metallic tiers make it easy for you to compare different individual health plans.
- An individual health plan's out-of-pocket maximum cannot exceed $6,600 for single coverage or $13,200 for family coverage in 2015.
- The actual premium you pay for individual health insurance will be adjusted based on you and your family's location, age, family size, and tobacco use.
- The average premium for a Silver-level plan in 2014 was $254 per month for an individual compared with an estimated average employer-provided health insurance cost of $539 per month.

Chapter 6

PREMIUM TAX CREDITS: ARE YOU ELIGIBLE FOR THE SUBSIDY?

Depending on your family's size and income, you may be eligible for new federal subsidies—called *premium tax credits*—that cap your cost of health insurance as a percent of your household income. These tax credits will only be available for plans purchased through your state's Health Insurance Marketplace (also called the Exchange), which we discuss in Chapter 8. In this chapter, we will help you determine if you and your family are eligible for a premium tax credit.

Here are some quick facts about premium tax credits:

- Premium tax credits are only available to you and your family if you meet certain income and household size requirements.
- Premium tax credits are only available for plans purchased through the Health Insurance Marketplaces.
- Premium tax credits are advanceable and can be automatically sent monthly to the insurance company by the Health Insurance Marketplace—you do not need to wait until you file a tax return at the end of the year to receive your credit.
- Premium tax credits will be reconciled at the end of the year based on your actual income.

ARE YOU ELIGIBLE FOR PREMIUM TAX CREDITS?

Your family's eligibility for a premium tax credit is based on a standard, called the federal poverty level, or FPL. The FPL, which is set annually by the federal government, takes into account the number of people in your household and your annual household income (see Figures 6.1 and 6.2). Specifically, if you and your family make less than 400 percent of the FPL based on the number of people in your family, you will be eligible to receive a premium tax credit.

In 2014, this means that an individual making up to $46,680 and a family of four earning up to $95,400 may be eligible for a premium tax credit. See Figure 6.2 to determine if you are eligible based on your income.

Persons in Family	48 Contiguous States and D.C.	Alaska	Hawaii
1	$11,670	$14,580	$13,420
2	$15,730	$19,660	$18,090
3	$19,790	$24,740	$22,760
4	$23,850	$29,820	$27,430
5	$27,910	$34,900	$32,100
6	$31,970	$39,980	$36,770
7	$36,030	$45,060	$41,440
8	$40,090	$50,140	$46,110
For each additional person, add:	$4,060	$5,080	$4,670

Figure 6.1 2014 Federal Poverty Level by Household Size

Persons in Family	100% FPL	138% FPL	150% FPL	200% FPL	300% FPL	400% FPL
1	$11,670	$16,105	$17,505	$23,340	$35,010	$46,680
2	$15,730	$21,707	$23,595	$31,460	$47,190	$62,920
3	$19,790	$27,310	$29,685	$39,580	$59,370	$79,160
4	$23,850	$32,913	$35,775	$47,700	$71,550	$95,400
5	$27,910	$38,516	$41,865	$55,820	$83,730	$111,640
6	$31,970	$44,119	$47,955	$63,940	$95,910	$127,880
7	$36,030	$49,721	$54,045	$72,060	$108,090	$144,120
8	$40,090	$55,324	$60,135	$80,180	$120,270	$160,360

Figure 6.2 Income Ranges for 2014 by Household Size (48 Contiguous States and the District of Columbia)

You are only eligible for a premium tax credit if you meet all of the following requirements:

- Purchase coverage through the Marketplace.
- Have household income that falls between 100 and 400 percent of the FPL.
- Are not able to get affordable coverage through a qualified eligible employer-provided health insurance plan.
- Are not eligible for coverage through a government program, like Medicaid, Medicare, CHIP, or TRICARE.
- Do not file a Married Filing Separately tax return (unless you meet the criteria in Notice 2014-23, which allows certain victims of domestic abuse to claim the premium tax credit using the Married Filing Separately filing status for the 2014 calendar year).

Tip: If you are eligible for a tax credit, an online calculator will help you estimate your actual tax credit. This estimate will give you an idea of how much health insurance will cost you and your family.

DETERMINING THE AMOUNT OF YOUR PREMIUM TAX CREDIT

The amount of your premium tax credit is determined based on the premium for the second lowest-cost Silver plan (the benchmark plan) in your state's Health Insurance Marketplace. Specifically, the amount of your credit is equal to the total cost of the *benchmark plan* minus your family's *maximum contribution* for coverage.

Calculating Your Maximum Contribution

If you are eligible for a premium tax credit, your family's contribution is capped as a percent of your income—we refer to this as your family's *maximum contribution* to coverage. This maximum contribution is based on a sliding scale—families who earn less have a smaller maximum contribution and families who earn more have a larger maximum contribution as shown in Figure 6.3. Here are some examples.

- **Single 25-year-old.** Steve is 25 years old, is single, and has an annual income of $22,980, which equals 200 percent of the federal poverty line. Based on his income ($22,980) and household size (1), his maximum

If your income is:	Your expected contribution will be:
100% to 138% of poverty level	2% of your income
138% to 150% of poverty level	3% to 4% of your income
150% to 200% of poverty level	4% to 6.3% of your income
200% to 250% of poverty level	6.3% to 8.05% of your income
250% to 300% of poverty level	8.05% to 9.5% of your income
300% to 400% of poverty level	9.5% of your income

Figure 6.3 Table of Your Expected Contribution Toward Your Health Insurance Premiums

contribution is equal to 6.3 percent of his annual income, or $1,448 a year.
- **Family of 4.** John, Sally, and their two children have annual income of $58,875, which translates to 250 percent of the federal poverty line. Based on this income level ($58,875) and household size (4), the family's maximum contribution is 8.05 percent of their income, or $4,739 a year.

Figuring Out the Cost of Your Benchmark Plan

Your *benchmark plan* is the second lowest-cost Silver plan available to you and your family through your state's Health Insurance Marketplace. See Chapter 9 for more information on metallic tiers and plan categories. Your state's Health Insurance Marketplace will tell you which plan is your benchmark plan and how much it costs. Let's continue with our examples (see Figure 6.4):

- **Single 25-year-old.** Steve is eligible for a premium tax credit. The three lowest-cost Silver plans providing self-only coverage in Steve's area are

Annual Cost Before Premium Tax Credit	Silver Plan A	Silver Plan B	Silver Plan C
Steve (single 25-year-old)	$4,500	$5,000 *Benchmark*	$5,500
John, Sally, and 2 children (family of four, adults age 35)	$14,500	$15,000 *Benchmark*	15,500

Figure 6.4 Example Benchmark Plans

Plans A, B, and C, priced before the premium tax credit at $4,500, $5,000, and $5,500 per year, respectively. Plan B, which is the second lowest-cost Silver plan, will be Steve's benchmark plan.

- **Family of 4.** John, Sally, and their two children qualify for a premium tax credit. In the area where the family lives, the three lowest-cost silver plans that cover the entire family are Plans A, B, and C, which cost $14,500, $15,000, and $15,500, respectively. Plan B, which is the second lowest-cost Silver plan, will be the family's benchmark plan.

Calculating Your Premium Tax Credit

The amount of your premium tax credit is equal to the total cost of your benchmark plan minus your family's maximum contribution for coverage. For example, if your benchmark plan costs $300 per month and your maximum contribution is $200 per month, your premium tax credit would equal $100 per month, per the following formula:

Premium Tax Credit Calculation

Benchmark Plan – Maximum Contribution = Premium Tax Credit

Here's how it would work out for our two examples (see Figure 6.5):

- **Single 25-year-old.** Steve is 25 years old, is single, and has an annual income of $22,980 in 2014, which equals 200 percent of the poverty line. Based on his income ($22,980) and household size (1), his maximum contribution is equal to 6.3 percent of his annual income, or $1,448 per year ($121 per month). The benchmark plan available to Steve is priced at $5,000 per year ($417 per month). Therefore, Steve would be eligible for an annual premium tax credit equal to $3,552 per year ($5,000 minus $1,448) or $296 per month ($417 minus $121). Steve would pay only $121 per month of his $417 per month health insurance premium.
- **Family of four.** John, Sally, and their two children have an annual household income of $58,875, which translates to 250 percent of the federal poverty line. Based on this income level, the family's maximum contribution is 8.05 percent of their income, or $4,739 per year ($395 per month). In the area where John and Sally live, the total premiums for the benchmark plan that would cover all members of the family is $15,000 per year ($1,250 per month). The premium tax credit the family would be eligible for is $10,261 per year ($15,000 minus $4,739) or $855 per month ($1,250 minus $395). John and Sally's family would pay only $395 per month of their $1,250 per month health insurance premium.

| Income | | Expected Premium Contribution Remaining After Premium Credit | |
Percentage of Poverty Line	Household Income (2014)	Premium Contribution as Percentage of Income	Maximum Contribution (monthly)
Family of Four			
100–138%	$23,850–$32,913	2%	$40–$55
138–150%	$32,913–$35,775	3–4%	$82–$119
150–200%	$35,775–$47,700	4–6.3%	$119–$250
200–250%	$47,700–$59,625	6.3–8.05%	$250–$402
250–300%	$59,625–$71,550	8.05–9.5%	$402–$566
300–350%	$71,550–$83,475	9.5%	$566–$661
350–400%	$83,475–$95,400	9.5%	$661–$755
Individual			
100–138%	$11,670–$16,105	2%	$19–$27
138–150%	$16,105–$17,505	3–4%	$40–$58
150–200%	$17,505–$23,340	4–6.3%	$58–$123
200–250%	$23,340–$29,175	6.3–8.05%	$123–$197
250–300%	$29,175–$35,010	8.05–9.5%	$197–$277
300–350%	$35,010–$40,845	9.5%	$277–$323
350–400%	$40,845–$46,680	9.5%	$323–$370

Figure 6.5   Premium Tax Credits by Income (48 Contiguous States and the District of Columbia)

The cost of the benchmark will take into account family size, location, and age. For example, older people will get larger premium credits than younger people, and an individual who lives in a high-cost state would receive a larger premium credit than an individual with the same characteristics who lives in a low-cost state. However, the premium credit will not cover the portion of the premium that is due to a tobacco surcharge.

USING YOUR PREMIUM TAX CREDIT

The actual amount you will be required to pay for health insurance will depend on the plan you choose. Once your premium tax credit is calculated, you and your family can use the premium tax credit to buy any plan—whether it is Bronze, Silver, Gold, or Platinum. The amount of your premium tax credit will stay the same, regardless of which plan you choose.

Gold and Platinum plans will have higher premiums than the benchmark plan used to calculate the premium tax credit amount, so you may have to pay more out-of-pocket for these plans. On the other hand, Bronze plans will cost less than the benchmark plan. So, if you choose a Bronze plan, your out-of-pocket costs will be lower and, if the cost of the Bronze plan is less than or equal to the amount of your premium tax credit, your cost could be $0.

Here is an example:

- **Single 25-year-old.** Steve is 25 years old and is eligible for a premium tax credit equal to $3,552 for the year. The benchmark plan for Steve costs $5,000 per year. There is also a Bronze plan available that would cost $3,000 per year and a cheaper silver plan that costs $4,500. If Steve purchases the benchmark plan, he will have to contribute $1,448 for the year (the $5,000 premium minus the $3,552 premium credit). If Steve purchases the cheapest Silver plan which costs $4,500 a year, his contribution would go down to $948 for the year. If Steve purchases the Bronze plan that costs $3,500 a year, he would not have to pay any premiums because the premium tax credit would cover the cost of the entire premium. (See Figure 6.6.)

 Tip: If you have an income below 250 percent of the FPL, you might want to consider choosing a Silver plan—there may be additional cost-sharing subsidies available to your family if your income is below 250 percent of the FPL, and cost-sharing subsidies are only available on Silver plans.

	Benchmark Silver Plan	Lowest-Cost Silver Plan	Bronze Plan
Plan Premium	$5,000/year	$4,500/year	$3,500/year
Steve's Premium Tax Credit	$3,552/year	$3,552/year	$3,552/year
Steve's Annual Payment	$1,448/year	$948/year	$0/year
Steve's Out-of-Pocket Costs	$500 Deductible $2,250 Out-of-Pocket Max	$500 Deductible $2,250 Out-of-Pocket Max	$5,000 Deductible $6,350 Out-of-Pocket Max

Figure 6.6 Example Plan Options for Steve, with Tax Credit and Out-of-Pocket Costs

RECEIVING YOUR PREMIUM TAX CREDIT

When you apply for coverage in the Health Insurance Marketplace, the Marketplace will estimate the amount of the premium tax credit that you may be able to claim for the tax year, using the information you provide about your family size and income. Based on the estimate, you will decide whether (1) you want the estimated premium tax credit paid monthly in advance directly to your insurance company and applied to your monthly premiums, or (2) you want to receive the credit as a refund when you file your tax return for the year.

Receiving Your Premium Tax Credit in Advance

If you choose to receive your premium tax credit in advance, the Health Insurance Marketplace will send the premium tax credit directly to your health insurance company on your behalf, decreasing how much you will be required to pay each month. This is how it works.

- **Single 25-year-old.** Steve is eligible for a premium tax credit of $3,552 a year. During the open enrollment period in the fall, he chooses to purchase the second lowest-cost Silver plan for the upcoming year, which has an annual cost of $5,000. He decides to take the premium tax credit in advance, which means that the Health Insurance Marketplace will send a monthly payment of $296 ($3,552 divided by 12) directly to his health insurance company. This reduces Steve's out-of-pocket costs from $417 to $121 per month, which he will pay directly to the health insurance company. (See Figure 6.7.)

If you elect to receive advance payments of the premium tax credit, you will need to file taxes for the year in which you receive them. For example, if you received advance payments of the credit for the 2014 calendar year, you will need

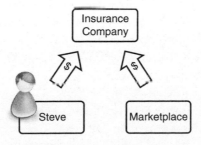

Figure 6.7   How Marketplace Premium Payments Work

to file a tax return for 2014 before the April 2015 deadline. Married couples who receive advance payments will need to file a joint return to qualify for the premium tax credit. Failure to file taxes may disqualify you and your family from receiving premium tax credits in subsequent years.

Notifying the Health Insurance Marketplace of Changes Affecting Your Advanced Premium Tax Credits

If you and your family experience a change in income or household size midyear, you should immediately notify your state's Health Insurance Marketplace—these changes will affect the amount of your premium tax credit. For example, if your income goes down, you may be able to get a higher advance payment of the premium tax credit for the rest of the year, which would lower your monthly premium payments. Alternatively, if your income increases, you will want to reduce your premium tax credits to avoid having to pay back excess advance payments when you file your taxes.

Also, if you are receiving a premium tax credit in advance and, in the middle of the year, you become newly eligible for other coverage, you should also report this change to the Health Insurance Marketplace. If you become eligible for Medicare, Medicaid, or employer-provided health insurance coverage midyear, you may lose your eligibility for your premium tax credit. See the following list of midyear changes for which you should notify the Marketplace.

NOTIFY MARKETPLACE OF THESE MIDYEAR CHANGES:

- Increases or decreases in your household income
- Marriage
- Divorce
- Birth or adoption of a child
- Other changes to your household composition
- Gaining or losing eligibility for Medicaid, Medicare, or employer-provided health insurance coverage

When the premium tax credit is paid in advance, the amount of the subsidy is based on an estimate of your income for the coming year. If the estimate is wrong, the subsidy amount will be incorrect. If you earn more than estimated, you will have to pay back part or all of the excess subsidy money when you file your taxes, which could total thousands of dollars.

Reconciling Your Advanced Premium Tax Credit at Tax Time

If you elect to receive your premium tax credit in advance, you will be required to reconcile the amount you received based on your estimated income with the amount that you should have received based on your actual income reported on your tax return. If your income for the year is higher than you previously estimated, you will be required pay the federal government the excess premium tax credit you received. Alternatively, if your actual income is lower than what you estimated, you will receive the difference in the form of a refund.

If you underestimate your income, there are limitations to the amount you would have to repay. Specifically, as long as your actual income is less than 400 percent of the FPL, the amount you can be required to pay back is capped at $1,250. See Figure 6.8 for the amount of the caps. Be aware that if your income for the year is greater than 400 percent of the FPL, you will be required to repay the entire premium tax credit you received in advance.

Receiving Your Premium Tax Credit as a Refund

Due to the risks of underestimating your income, you may want to elect to receive your premium tax credit at the end of the year as a refund. If you choose to get your premium tax credit when you file your income taxes rather than in advance, you will be sure to receive the correct premium tax credit amount because you will know exactly how much you earned that year. You should consider this option if:

- Your income is very close to 400 percent of the FPL.
- Your income varies from year to year, making it difficult to estimate accurately.

Percentage of Poverty Line	Annual Income for an Individual (2014)	Repayment Cap (single taxpayers)	Annual Income for a Family of Four (2014)	Repayment Cap (married taxpayers filing jointly)
Under 200%	Under $23,340	$300	Under $47,700	$600
200%–299%	$23,340– $35,009	$750	$47,700– $71,549	$1,500
300%–399%	$35,010– $46,679	$1,250	$71,550– $95,399	$2,500
400% and above	$46,680 and higher	Full amount	$95,400 and higher	Full amount

Figure 6.8 Repayment Cap by Household Income and Size

Tip: You should always accurately answer all questions when you apply to the Health Insurance Marketplace. That said, if you think you may get a raise in December, you might want to apply for your premium tax credit in November before you get the raise. At worst, your income will increase and you will have to pay back the excess premium tax credit you received. Or, your repayment amount will exceed the repayment cap and you will not be required to pay back the excess premium tax credit you received.

WHAT YOU LEARNED

- Premium tax credits are only available to you and your family if you meet certain income and household size requirements.
- Premium tax credits are only available for plans purchased through the Health Insurance Marketplaces.
- Premium tax credits are advanceable and can be automatically sent to the insurance company by the Health Insurance Marketplace—you do not need to wait until you file a tax return at the end of the year to receive your credit.
- Premium tax credits will be reconciled at the end of the year based on your actual income. If your income is still below four times FPL, you may not have to repay all the excess premium tax credit you received due to the repayment cap.
- Due to the risks of underestimating your income, you may want to elect to receive your premium tax credit at the end of the year as a refund.

Chapter 7

WHEN CAN YOU BUY INDIVIDUAL HEALTH INSURANCE?

H ealth insurance companies are now prohibited from denying coverage to people in the individual Health Insurance Marketplaces because of a pre-existing medical condition. But, there is a catch. You can only enroll in guaranteed-issue health insurance during limited *annual* or *special enrollment periods* defined by the federal government. The purpose of these enrollment periods is to control the cost to the government and insurance carriers—limiting the enrollment periods keeps you from waiting until you get sick to purchase health insurance.

Failure to purchase coverage during your enrollment period could result in you being forced to go without health insurance for a full year. Therefore, it is important that you understand how these enrollment periods work.

Specifically, there are two types of enrollment periods: (1) annual enrollment periods, and (2) special enrollment periods.

ANNUAL ENROLLMENT PERIOD

The annual enrollment period begins on October 15th and extends through December 7th each year. Figure 7.1 shows that the 2015 annual enrollment period has been changed to extend from November 15, 2014, to February 15th, 2015. During this time, you can purchase any health insurance plan available on the individual market. If you fail to purchase health insurance coverage during

Coverage Year	Annual Enrollment Period
2015	November 15, 2014–February 15, 2015
2016	October 15, 2015–December 7, 2015
2017	October 15, 2016–December 7, 2016
2018	October 15, 2017–December 7, 2017
2019	October 15, 2018–December 7, 2018
2020	October 15, 2019–December 7, 2019

Note: Actual dates are subject to change. Check with your state's Health Insurance Marketplace to confirm the actual dates for annual enrollment each year.

Figure 7.1   Annual Enrollment Periods (2015 to 2020)

the annual enrollment period, you will be unable to purchase coverage until the following year unless you qualify for a special enrollment period.

SPECIAL ENROLLMENT PERIODS

Under special circumstances, you may be able to purchase new individual health insurance coverage in the middle of the year via a special enrollment period. These special enrollment periods typically last for 60 days following the date of a triggering event. The most common types of triggering events are listed below (see Figure 7.2 for a comprehensive list).

 Tip: Remember, if you purchase a new individual health insurance plan midyear, you will need to meet the entire deductible and out-of-pocket limit as if you were enrolled in the health plan for a full 12 months.

You Lose Your Employer-Provided Health Insurance

- **You Lose Your Job**—If you had health insurance through your job and you lost your job (voluntarily or involuntarily), you are eligible for a 60-day special enrollment period.
- **Your Employer Cancels Coverage**—If you had health insurance through your job and your employer stops offering health insurance coverage, you are eligible for a 60-day special enrollment period.
- **You Become Ineligible for Coverage**—If you had health insurance through your job and you are no longer eligible, you are eligible for a 60-day special enrollment period.

Qualifying Event	Special Enrollment Period
Applicable to Both On-Marketplace and Off-Marketplace Policies	
Gaining/losing a dependent through birth/adoption/ foster care/placement for adoption.	60 days after the event.
Gaining a dependent through marriage.	60 days after the event.
Loss of eligible coverage from legal separation/ divorce, cessation of dependent status (aging out), death, or termination or reduction of working hours with employer.	60 days after the event.
Loss of coverage through an HMO due to relocation to a new service area.	60 days after the event.
Incurs claim that meets or exceeds lifetime limits on all benefits.	60 days after the event.
COBRA coverage ends.	60 days after the event.
Employer ceases contributions either to subscriber or dependents.	60 days after the event.
Permanent move (to a region where new plans are available).	60 days after the event.
Newly eligible/ineligible for advance payments of tax credits or change in eligibility from cost-sharing reductions.	60 days after the event.
Qualified Health Plan (QHP) substantially violates a material provision of its contract.	60 days after the event.
Enrollment in QHP is made in error.	60 days after the event.
Loss of minimum essential health coverage (Not including loss of coverage because of failure to make premium payment).	60 days before and after the event.
Applicable to Off-Marketplace Policies Only	
Enrollment in noncalendar year policy ends.	30 days prior to the end of the policy.
Applicable to On-Marketplace Policies Only	
Native American status.	60 days after the event.
Attaining citizenship.	60 days after the event.
Demonstration of exceptional circumstances, as determined by the Marketplace.	60 days after the event.

Figure 7.2 Special Enrollment Periods

You Add a Dependent

- **You get married**—If you get married, you are eligible for a 60-day special enrollment period starting on the date you get married.
- **You have a baby**—If you have a baby, you are eligible for a 60-day special enrollment period starting on your new child's birth date.
- **You adopt**—If you adopt a new dependent, you are eligible for a 60-day special enrollment period starting on the date you adopt.

You Lose Your Coverage Due to Divorce

- **You get divorced**—If you lose your coverage due to divorce, you are eligible for a 60-day special enrollment period starting on the date you get divorced.

You Become Newly Eligible or Ineligible for Premium Tax Credits

- **Reduction in salary/benefits**—If you had health insurance through your job and you become eligible for a premium tax credit due to a reduction in salary or benefits, you are eligible for a 60-day special enrollment period starting on the date you become eligible for premium tax credits.

You Permanently Move to a New Coverage Area with Access to New Individual Plans

- **You move to another state**—If you permanently move to another state, you are eligible for a 60-day special enrollment period starting on the date of your move.
- **You move to another county within your state**—If you permanently move from one county to another county within your state, you are eligible for a 60-day special enrollment period starting on the date of your move.

SPECIAL ENROLLMENT PERIODS—ACT FAST OR PAY

When you experience a triggering event for a special enrollment period, you should immediately decide where to buy health insurance (see Chapter 8) and begin the application process. Failure to purchase an individual plan by the end of your special enrollment period could force you to go without health insurance until the next annual enrollment period.

Tip: If you are already enrolled in a health plan and are eligible for a special enrollment period, you can change health plans, but you don't have to. You can choose to stay in your current plan.

If you fail to purchase health insurance by the end of your enrollment period, you may have missed your chance to buy health insurance for the year—unless you experience another triggering event. Going without coverage will expose you and your family to a tax penalty for each month you are uninsured.

YOU MUST BUY HEALTH INSURANCE—OR PAY A TAX PENALTY

Federal regulations now require you and your family to purchase health insurance coverage or else pay a tax penalty. Specifically, you are required to purchase a minimum level of health insurance called *minimum essential coverage*. Minimum essential coverage includes employer-provided insurance, individual health insurance, Medicare, and Medicaid.

If you fail to purchase minimum essential coverage for one or more months during a tax year, you must pay a tax penalty equal to 2.5 percent of your income once the penalty is fully phased in. (The minimum tax penalty is $695 for a single household and up to three times that amount for a family household.) Beginning in 2017, the penalties will be increased annually by the cost-of-living adjustment. See Figure 7.3.

Each year, the penalty is capped at an amount equal to the national average premium for Bronze-level health plans offered through Health Insurance Marketplaces. You can be exempted from the penalty for a month if during the month:

1. You have income below the filing threshold determined by the Secretary of Health and Human Services (HHS).
2. Your cost to purchase health insurance exceeds 8 percent of gross income.
3. You are a member of an Indian tribe.
4. The Secretary of HHS determines you qualify for a hardship that makes you incapable of obtaining health insurance.

WHAT TO DO IF YOU MISS YOUR ENROLLMENT PERIOD

If you miss your enrollment period, you have the following options: (1) Go uninsured until the next annual enrollment period, (2) purchase a short-term medical

Year	Tax Penalty
2014	The greater of: • $95 per person, up to a maximum of three times that amount for a family ($285) • 1% of household income
2015	The greater of: • $325 per person, up to a maximum of three times that amount for a family ($975) • 2% of household income
2016	The greater of: • $695 per person, up to a maximum of three times that amount for a family ($2,085) • 2.5% of household income
2017 and beyond	Penalties increased by cost-of-living adjustment

Figure 7.3 Penalties Phase-In Schedule

plan to bridge the gap until the next annual enrollment period, or (3) trigger a special enrollment period.

Option 1: Go Uninsured until the Next Annual Enrollment Period

Your first option is to remain uninsured until the next annual enrollment period. This is not recommended. Depending on your family's circumstances, going uninsured is a risky decision for two reasons. First, you will be required to pay any applicable tax penalties for not purchasing health insurance coverage. And, second, you are exposing you and your family to potentially serious financial liability in the event that you or one of your family members develops an illness or has an accident. Unexpected illnesses and accidents happen every day and the resulting medical bills can be disastrous.

Option 2: Purchase a Short-Term Medical Plan to Bridge the Gap until the Next Annual Enrollment Period

To help limit your potential liability for unexpected medical-care expenses, you may want to purchase a short-term medical plan.

Short-term medical plans provide you with coverage for a limited period of time, and can help you bridge the gap until the next annual enrollment period. Typically, these short-term plans provide coverage for 6 to 12 months (see Figures 7.4 and 7.5).

Age	Monthly Premium	Deductible	Type of Plan
25	$49.68	$1,000	Six-Month Short-Term Medical (20/1000)
35	$55.02	$1,000	Six-Month Short-Term Medical (20/1000)
45	$76.51	$1,000	Six-Month Short-Term Medical (20/1000)
55	$202.92	$1,000	Six-Month Short-Term Medical (20/1000)

Figure 7.4 Example Short-Term Medical Plan Costs (Individual)

Source: eHealthinsurance 2014.

Age of Adults	Monthly Premium	Deductible	Type of Plan
25	$180.48	$1,000	Six-Month Short-Term Medical (20/1000)
35	$222.12	$1,000	Six-Month Short-Term Medical (20/1000)
45	$406.10	$1,000	Six-Month Short-Term Medical (20/1000)
55	$616.46	$1,000	Six-Month Short-Term Medical (20/1000)

Figure 7.5 Example Short-Term Medical Plan Costs (Family of Four)

Source: eHealthinsurance 2014.

If you decide to purchase a short-term plan, make sure you understand all of the limitations and exclusions. Short-term medical plans are designed to protect you against unforeseen accidents or illnesses, and, therefore, typically do not include coverage for pre-existing conditions, preventive care, physicals, immunizations, dental, or vision care. It is also important to note that short-term plans are not considered to be *minimum essential coverage*, and even if you enroll in and maintain short-term coverage, you will still be subject to any applicable tax penalties for not purchasing qualified coverage.

 Tip: To learn more about short-term medical plans, go to www .healthinsurancerevolution.org/short-term-plans.

Option 3: Trigger a Special Enrollment Period

If you are in desperate need of individual health insurance coverage, your only option may be to trigger a special enrollment event. One way to do this is to make a permanent residential move. If you move to a new county or state, your move date will trigger a 60-day special enrollment period for you to purchase coverage.

WHAT YOU LEARNED

- You can only enroll in guaranteed issue health insurance during limited annual or special enrollment periods defined by the federal government.
- The annual enrollment period begins on October 15th and extends through December 7th each year. The 2015 annual enrollment period has been changed to extend from November 15, 2014 to February 15, 2015.
- Special enrollment periods typically last for 60 days following the date of a triggering event.
- Federal regulations now require you and your family to purchase health insurance coverage—called minimum essential coverage—or else pay the tax penalty.
- Minimum essential coverage includes employer-provided insurance, individual health insurance, Medicare, or Medicaid.
- If you fail to purchase minimum essential coverage for one or more months during a tax year, you must pay a tax penalty equal to 2.5 percent of your income once the penalty is fully phased in.

Chapter 8

WHERE CAN YOU BUY INDIVIDUAL HEALTH INSURANCE?

O ne of the primary purposes of the Affordable Care Act is to enhance the individual health insurance market. The law has eliminated discrimination based on health and gender, put standardized health plans into specific tiers of coverage, and created premium tax credits to help subsidize costs. In an effort to help you evaluate your options on the individual market in a single, unbiased place, the Affordable Care Act also created state-specific insurance exchanges, which are now called Health Insurance Marketplaces. These new Marketplaces are available in every state and make it easy for you to compare different plans and receive premium tax credits if you are eligible.

Health Insurance Marketplaces are not the only place to buy health insurance. An *off-marketplace* plan is a health insurance policy purchased directly from an insurance company or through an agent or broker, outside of your state's Health Insurance Marketplace (see Figure 8.1).

ON-MARKETPLACE OR OFF-MARKETPLACE—WHICH IS BETTER?

The consumer protections in the individual market apply to all individual health insurance policies, regardless of whether the coverage is purchased on-marketplace or off-marketplace. However, plans sold on-marketplace must be qualified health plans—meaning they have been certified by the Health Insurance Marketplace in your state and are eligible to be subsidized by your

On-Marketplace	Off-Marketplace
A health insurance policy purchased from your state's Health Insurance Marketplace (e.g., HealthCare.gov).	A health insurance policy purchased directly from an insurance company or through an agent or broker, outside of your state's Health Insurance Marketplace.

Figure 8.1 Definitions of On-Marketplace and Off-Marketplace

premium tax credit. If a plan is available on-marketplace *and* off-marketplace, the price and coverage will be the same regardless of where you purchase it. Keep in mind, some insurance companies offer plans that are only available off-marketplace, which may provide you and your family with additional coverage and price options.

 Did you know? All plans on the Health Insurance Marketplace must be qualified health plans. A qualified health plan is an insurance plan that is certified by the Health Insurance Marketplace, and meets ACA requirements such as coverage of essential health benefits.

If you are eligible for a premium tax credit, it is virtually always better for you to purchase an on-marketplace plan. This is because premium tax credits are only available for plans purchased via the Marketplace. Even if you and your family are not eligible for a premium tax credit today, purchasing an on-marketplace plan may be a safer option—if you purchase an off-marketplace plan and your income changes, you will be required to switch to an on-marketplace plan midyear to receive your subsidy, causing your deductible and out-of-pocket maximums to reset.

Did you know? Insurance companies have a huge incentive to sell their plans on the Marketplace because it gives them access to millions of Americans who will only be able to use their premium tax credits toward on-marketplace plans.

If you are not eligible for a premium tax credit and you are certain your income and household size will not change for the entire year, you may have more plan options off-marketplace. If you decide to shop off-marketplace, you have two options: (1) purchase a policy directly from a health insurance company, or (2) purchase a policy through a licensed health insurance broker. We discuss these options at the end of this chapter.

 Tip: If you are eligible or think you may become eligible for a premium tax credit midyear, purchase an on-marketplace plan. Most states allow health insurance brokers to participate in their Health Insurance Marketplace—thus you may still be able to use your favorite agent or broker if you qualify for a premium tax credit.

Even if you know you will not qualify for premium tax credits, it is a good idea to look at your Marketplace options to ensure you find the best policy for your needs. Be aware that the enrollment periods discussed in Chapter 7 apply to all individual health plans regardless of whether they are purchased on-marketplace or off-marketplace.

WHAT IS A HEALTH INSURANCE MARKETPLACE?

A Health Insurance Marketplace is an online marketplace in your state where you and your family can shop for individual health insurance using side-by-side price and benefit comparisons. One goal of the Health Insurance Marketplaces is to reduce the cost of health insurance by pooling the buying power of individual consumers. Additionally, if your family qualifies for a premium tax credit (discussed in Chapter 6), the Health Insurance Marketplace will facilitate the advance payment of your premium tax credit directly to your health insurance company—this means you do not need to wait until tax time to receive your subsidy. When you apply through your state's Marketplace you will also find out if you or a family member is eligible for free health insurance through Medicaid, CHIP, or Medicare.

 Did you know? Health Insurance Marketplaces were originally called Health Insurance Exchanges or just Exchanges. These terms may be used interchangeably.

By law, every U.S. state, including the District of Columbia, must establish a Health Insurance Marketplace for its citizens to purchase individual health

State	Marketplace Type	State	Marketplace Type
Alabama	Federally-Run	Montana	Federally-Run
Alaska	Federally-Run	Nebraska	Federally-Run
Arizona	Federally-Run	Nevada	State-Run
Arkansas	Federally-Run	New Hampshire	Federally-Run
California	State-Run	New Jersey	Federally-Run
Colorado	State-Run	New Mexico	State-Run
Connecticut	State-Run	New York	State-Run
Delaware	Federally-Run	North Carolina	Federally-Run
District of Columbia	State-Run	North Dakota	Federally-Run
Florida	Federally-Run	Ohio	Federally-Run
Georgia	Federally-Run	Oklahoma	Federally-Run
Hawaii	State-Run	Oregon	State-Run
Idaho	State-Run	Pennsylvania	Federally-Run
Illinois	Federally-Run	Rhode Island	State-Run
Indiana	Federally-Run	South Carolina	Federally-Run
Iowa	Federally-Run	South Dakota	Federally-Run
Kansas	Federally-Run	Tennessee	Federally-Run
Kentucky	State-Run	Texas	Federally-Run
Louisiana	Federally-Run	Utah	Federally-Run
Maine	Federally-Run	Vermont	State-Run
Maryland	State-Run	Virginia	Federally-Run
Massachusetts	State-Run	Washington	State-Run
Michigan	Federally-Run	West Virginia	Federally-Run
Minnesota	State-Run	Wisconsin	Federally-Run
Mississippi	Federally-Run	Wyoming	Federally-Run
Missouri	Federally-Run		

Figure 8.2 Chart of State Marketplace Types as of 2014

insurance policies and receive premium tax credits. Figure 8.2 lists all the states that have either implemented a state-run Marketplace or a federally-run Marketplace. (A state also has the option to run the Marketplace in partnership with the federal government. For purposes of this book, we consider these marketplaces to be federally-run.) Regardless of the approach your state has taken, the application process is virtually identical.

Your state's Health Insurance Marketplace website may have its own unique name. For example, California's Health Insurance Marketplace is called Covered California. See Figure 8.3 for other examples.

State	Marketplace Name	State	Marketplace Name
California	Covered California	Minnesota	MNSure
Colorado	Connect for Health Colorado	Nevada	Nevada Health Link
		New Mexico	BeWellNM
Connecticut	Access Health CT	New York	New York State of Health
District of Columbia	DC Health Link		
		Oregon	Cover Oregon
Hawaii	Hawaii Health Connector	Rhode Island	HealthSource RI
Idaho	Your Health Idaho	Vermont	Vermont Health Connect
Kentucky	kynect		
Maryland	Maryland Health Connection	Washington	Washington Healthplanfinder
Massachusetts	Massachusetts Health Exchange		

Figure 8.3   State-Based Marketplace Names

HOW TO USE YOUR STATE'S HEALTH INSURANCE MARKETPLACE WEBSITE

The easiest way to access your state's Health Insurance Marketplace is via the Internet (paper applications are also available at www.healthinsurance revolution.org/applications).

Every state is required to have a website providing online access to all available plans. Depending on whether your state's Marketplace is federally or state-run you will either use healthcare.gov or the website your state has created to access the Marketplace.

 Did you know? Since health insurance companies must compete for your business on the Health Insurance Marketplace, many may offer better and/or cheaper plans on your state's Marketplace than they will off-marketplace.

Figure 8.4 provides a list of state Health Insurance Marketplaces and their official websites as of the writing of this book. These websites may be updated in the future, so we have created a directory that will be updated regularly at

State	Marketplace Website	State	Marketplace Website
Alabama	www.healthcare.gov	Missouri	www.healthcare.gov
Alaska	www.healthcare.gov	Montana	www.healthcare.gov
Arizona	www.healthcare.gov	Nebraska	www.healthcare.gov
Arkansas	www.healthcare.gov	Nevada	www.nevadahealth
California	www.coveredca.com		link.com
Colorado	www.connectfor	New Hampshire	www.healthcare.gov
	healthco.com	New Jersey	www.healthcare.gov
Connecticut	www.accesshealth	New Mexico	www.bewellnm.com
	ct.com	New York	https://nystateof
Delaware	www.healthcare.gov		health.ny.gov
District of	www.dchealth	North Carolina	www.healthcare.gov
Columbia	link.com	North Dakota	www.healthcare.gov
Florida	www.healthcare.gov	Ohio	www.healthcare.gov
Georgia	www.healthcare.gov	Oklahoma	www.healthcare.gov
Hawaii	www.hawaiihealth	Oregon	www.coveroregon
	connector.com		.com
Idaho	www.yourhealth	Pennsylvania	www.healthcare.gov
	idaho.org	Rhode Island	www.healthsource
Illinois	www.healthcare.gov		ri.com
Indiana	www.healthcare.gov	South Carolina	www.healthcare.gov
Iowa	www.healthcare.gov	South Dakota	www.healthcare.gov
Kansas	www.healthcare.gov	Tennessee	www.healthcare.gov
Kentucky	https://kynect.ky.gov	Texas	www.healthcare.gov
Louisiana	www.healthcare.gov	Utah	www.healthcare.gov
Maine	www.healthcare.gov	Vermont	https://healthconnect
Maryland	www.marylandhealth		.vermont.gov
	connection.gov	Virginia	www.healthcare.gov
Massachusetts	www.mahealth	Washington	www.wahealthplan
	connector.org		finder.org
Michigan	www.healthcare.gov	West Virginia	www.healthcare.gov
Minnesota	www.mnsure.org	Wisconsin	www.healthcare.gov
Mississippi	www.healthcare.gov	Wyoming	www.healthcare.gov

Figure 8.4   List of Marketplace Websites

www.healthinsurancerevolution.org/marketplaces for you to use to access your state's Health Insurance Marketplace.

While each state has its own Marketplace, the overall experience is virtually identical. Every Marketplace provides the ability to review costs, complete side-by-side comparisons, and apply for premium tax credits. Using the Marketplace website is very similar to using a car insurance price comparison website like esurance.com. To begin the process, all you need to do is enter the URL of your state's Marketplace website into your Internet browser.

 Need help? If you need help finding your Marketplace website, visit www.healthinsurancerevolution.org/marketplaces for a state-by-state guide.

Once you are on the website, follow the online directions to begin the process. If you need assistance, phone and in-person support are available (see Figure 8.5). Generally, the Health Insurance Marketplace will require you to complete a three-step process: (1) Fill out the application, (2) Compare your options, and (3) Purchase a plan (see Figure 8.6).

Filling Out the Application

In order to view plan options, you will be required to provide personal information including your zip code, family size, age, tax information, and income. The following checklist provides a list of information you will need to provide during the application process. Be sure to provide accurate information to ensure you receive accurate results.

MARKETPLACE APPLICATION CHECKLIST

Be sure to have the following information available before you begin the Marketplace application process:

- Birth date and tobacco use for you and your family members.
- Your household's tax information for the previous year.

Phone support	The Marketplace help line is available for 24/7 assistance at (800) 318-2596
In-person help	You can find in-person help from a government appointed assister by going to LocalHelp.Healthcare.gov.
Broker help	Contact a local health insurance broker.

Figure 8.5 Getting Marketplace Assistance

Three-Step Application Process

1. Fill out the application: You'll provide information about you and your family, such as income, household size, current health coverage information, and more. This will help the Marketplace find options that meet your needs.
2. Compare your options: You'll be able to see all the options you qualify for, including private insurance plans and coverage through Medicaid and the Children's Health Insurance Program (CHIP). The Marketplace will also tell you if you qualify for premium tax credits on your monthly premiums.
3. Purchase a plan: After you choose a plan, you can enroll online and the Marketplace will facilitate your payment to the insurance company.

Figure 8.6 How to Apply for a Marketplace Plan

- Your household's projected income for the current year.
- Social Security numbers (SSNs) for you and your family members.
- Employer information for every member of your household who needs coverage.
- Employer-provided health insurance coverage information you or your family members are eligible for.
- Review a sample paper application to ensure you have all the information you need.

Comparing Different Plan Options

After submitting the application, you will be able to compare your plan options. Remember, not all plans are created equal — pricing will vary based on each plan's specific coverage level (see Chapter 9) and provider network (see Chapter 10). If you are eligible for a premium tax credit, the Marketplace will also automatically reduce your monthly premium by the amount of your premium tax credit.

 Tip: You can get an estimate of your expected health insurance cost on the Marketplace by going to www.healthinsurancerevolution.org/cost-estimator.

Selecting the Right Plan and Enrolling

Once you have evaluated your options and selected the right plan for you and your family, the Health Insurance Marketplace will facilitate your purchase and enrollment into the plan (see Chapter 11).

WORKING WITH HEALTH INSURANCE BROKERS

If you are a first-time purchaser of individual health insurance, you should strongly consider working with several health insurance brokers before buying coverage. Insurance companies are legally required to charge the same premium regardless of whether you purchase your policy directly from the carrier, through the Health Insurance Marketplace, or through a licensed health insurance broker. As a result, there are many advantages to working with a broker, including getting help filling out the applications, comparing off-marketplace plans and on-marketplace plans simultaneously, and evaluating the best coverage and network options for you and your family (see Figure 8.7).

To find a broker for your area, search online or ask friends or family members for recommendations. Many online brokers also have call center agents available to answer questions by phone.

 Tip: To search a database of health insurance brokers, see www.health insurancerevolution.org/brokers. You can find brokers who specialize in health insurance through the health insurance agent (directory).

Be careful when you shop online for health insurance, and watch the fine print. Most websites that offer online quotes request personal contact information and then don't deliver any online quotes—they sell your information to third parties along with your express permission to phone you. A good online insurance website should not ask for your name or contact information until you have seen quotes and are ready to choose a policy. When selecting a health insurance broker, make sure he or she meets the criteria in Figure 8.8.

Remember, brokers are compensated by insurance companies in the form of commissions for each health insurance policy they sell—this is typically calculated as a percentage of your premium. As a result, many brokers are incentivized to sell you the most expensive plan you are willing to buy. Watch out for biased advice.

Four reasons to use a broker:
1. Helps you fill out the application.
2. Helps you compare on-marketplace and off-marketplace plans at the same time.
3. Helps you evaluate coverage and network options.
4. Helps you manage your plan throughout the year.

Figure 8.7 Four Reasons to Use a Broker

✓ Check with your state regulator that an agent has a valid license and a
   clean record, and make sure health insurance isn't a sideline or a new
   specialty.
✓ Make sure to check for client reviews online before proceeding.
✓ Make sure the broker is certified to sell on-marketplace policies.
✓ Make sure the broker is appointed by the major insurance companies in
   your state.

Figure 8.8   Broker Evaluation Checklist

 Tip: Watch out for biased advice from entities that have a vested interest
in steering you in one direction.

You should expect your broker to continue advising and helping you after you
purchase a policy. If you become dissatisfied with your broker, you can always
switch to a new broker and redirect the commission to your new broker by inform-
ing the health insurance company.

BUYING DIRECTLY FROM THE HEALTH INSURANCE COMPANY

You can also contact any health insurance company directly to see plans available
in your area. Many insurance companies have websites that let you compare all
plans available from that company.

 Tip: To get a list of health insurance companies in your state, visit
www.healthinsurancerevolution.org/insurance-companies.

Remember, premium tax credits are only available for plans purchased
through a Health Insurance Marketplace. If you decide to buy directly from a
health insurance company or work with a health insurance broker, make sure
they are able (and willing) to help you purchase an on-marketplace plan if you
are eligible for a premium tax credit.

WHAT YOU LEARNED

- The Affordable Care Act created state-specific insurance exchanges, which are now called Health Insurance Marketplaces.
- A Health Insurance Marketplace is an online marketplace in your state where you and your family can shop for individual health insurance using side-by-side price and benefit comparisons.
- All plans on the Health Insurance Marketplace must be qualified health plans. A qualified health plan is an insurance plan that is certified by the Health Insurance Marketplace, and meets ACA requirements such as coverage of essential health benefits.
- Health Insurance Marketplaces are not the only place to buy health insurance. An off-marketplace plan is a health insurance policy purchased directly from an insurance company or through an agent or broker, outside of your state's Health Insurance Marketplace.
- If you are eligible or think you may become eligible for a premium tax credit midyear, you should purchase an on-marketplace plan.
- Even if you know you will not qualify for premium tax credits, it is a good idea to look at your Marketplace options to ensure you find the best policy for your needs.

Chapter 9

HOW TO CHOOSE YOUR COVERAGE—BRONZE, SILVER, GOLD, OR PLATINUM

I n the past, choosing the right individual health insurance coverage was complicated—it was nearly impossible to make side-by-side comparisons due to so many variations among different insurance plans. But, that is no longer the case. The Affordable Care Act has standardized the coverage provided by plans in the individual market. All individual health insurance plans must now be categorized into one of four standard levels of coverage: Bronze, Silver, Gold, or Platinum. (A fifth category, referred to as catastrophic coverage, may also be available in your state. Catastrophic plans pay less than 60 percent of the total average cost of care on average and are available only to people who are under 30 years old or have a hardship exemption.) Additionally, new benefit coverage requirements and out-of-pocket limits now apply to all individual health insurance plans. These standardizations have made it easy to compare and contrast the coverage provided by different individual health insurance plans and insurance companies.

When narrowing your choices to specific plans, you should evaluate the following coverage components for each option: (1) plan category, (2) out-of-pocket exposure, and (3) covered benefits.

CHOOSING A PLAN CATEGORY

The plan category you choose affects the average amount of money you will be required to spend on out-of-pocket costs in a year. Regardless of where you live, all plans in the individual market are separated into four metallic tiers—Bronze, Silver, Gold, and Platinum. These metallic tiers (or plan categories) have nothing to do with the quality or amount of care you get. The plan category determines how you and your plan share the costs of care. As the metallic tier increases in value, so does the percent of medical expenses, on average, that a health plan will cover. (See Figure 9.1.) Plans that cover more of your medical expenses will have a higher monthly premium, and plans with a lower monthly premium require that you pay more when you receive medical care.

Following is an explanation of the coverage provided by each plan category. In all categories, once you have met your plan's out-of-pocket maximum, the plan provides coverage at 100 percent.

- **Bronze.** Plans available in the Bronze category are designed to pay 60 percent of the average household's medical expenses. Bronze plans may seem attractive, but the exposure could mean higher out-of-pocket costs for you and your family if you or a family member were to develop an illness or have an accident.
- **Silver.** Plans available in the Silver category are designed to pay 70 percent of the average household's medical expenses. The Silver plan is the standard choice for most reasonably healthy families.
- **Gold.** Plans available in the Gold category are designed to pay 80 percent of the average household's medical expenses. Gold plans work well for families who see the doctor regularly and can afford the higher premium.

Category (Tier)	Average % of Expenses Paid by Health Plan	Average % of Expenses Paid by Individual	Your Monthly Premium Cost	Cost When You Receive Care
Platinum	90%	10%	$$$$	$
Gold	80%	20%	$$$	$$
Silver	70%	30%	$$	$$$
Bronze	60%	40%	$	$$$$

Figure 9.1   Health Plan Categories (Metallic Tiers)

- **Platinum.** Plans available in the Platinum category are designed to pay 90 percent of the average household's medical expenses. Platinum plans work well for families in poor health who see the doctors often and/or have family members with chronic medical conditions requiring regular care.

Did you know? Health insurance companies must offer at least one Silver plan and one Gold plan.

When choosing a plan category, you should consider you and your family's medical needs for the upcoming year (see Figure 9.2). If you expect to visit the doctor often and require regular prescriptions, you should consider plans in the Gold or Platinum categories—these plans generally have higher monthly premiums and pay more of your costs when you need care. On the other hand, if you don't expect to see the doctor more than once or twice per year, you should consider plans in the Bronze or Silver categories—these plans cost you less per month and pay less of your costs when you need care.

Tip: Although it may be tempting to purchase a low-end plan to save money on premiums, you should consider you and your family's medical history before proceeding.

	Platinum	Gold	Silver	Bronze
Monthly cost	$$$$	$$$	$$	$
Cost when you get care	$	$$	$$$	$$$$
A good option if you ...	Plan to use a lot of medical care services.	Want to save on the monthly premium, while keeping out-of-pocket costs low.	Need to balance your monthly cost with your out-of-pocket costs.	Don't plan on needing a lot of medical care services.

Figure 9.2 Selecting the Right Plan Category.

PICKING THE RIGHT OUT-OF-POCKET EXPOSURE

Once you have selected one or more plan categories to analyze, evaluate these six financial items for each plan within your selected category(ies):

1. Doctor visit copay
2. Prescription copay
3. Deductible
4. Coinsurance
5. Out-of-pocket maximum
6. HSA qualification

Reminder:

- Deductible—The amount you owe for covered services before insurance kicks in.
- Copayment (copay)—A fixed amount you pay for a covered healthcare service.
- Coinsurance—Your share of the costs of a covered healthcare service.
- Out-of-Pocket Maximum—The maximum amount of money you will pay for covered services during a year

---

Doctor Visit Copay

The doctor visit copay is the amount that you pay each time you visit the doctor. In a traditional low-deductible plan, this ranges from $10 to $35 per visit per patient. Most higher-deductible plans do not offer a doctor copay.

Prescription Copay

The prescription copay is the amount you will pay per prescription filled. Most healthcare plans offering pharmacy coverage break their coverage into three tiers: generic, formulary brand, and nonformulary. A typical plan for a 30-day prescription might charge a $10 copay for a generic drug, a $20 copay for a formulary-brand drug that is on a list maintained by the insurance company, and a discount from full retail for a drug that is neither generic nor on the formulary list.

Tip: If you are having doubts about whether to get pharmacy coverage, get it, then analyze your situation next year to see whether you want to keep it.

Tip: If you decline pharmacy coverage, most policies from major health insurance carriers still include free drug discount cards that offer you up to 15 percent off brand-name prescriptions and 50 percent off generic ones—see Chapter 12 for more on drug discount cards.

Deductible

Your deductible is the annual amount of your medical expenses that you must pay before your health insurance company begins paying providers or reimbursing you for claims. Traditional health insurance plans have deductibles of $1,000 or less, as well as copays for doctor visits and prescriptions. High-deductible plans have deductibles greater than $1,000—but much lower premiums.

Tip: Pay attention when calculating your medical payments to reach the deductible—doctor-visit copays and prescription copays are excluded. Also, the lower in-network price is used to calculate your deductible rather than the medical provider's full price.

Coinsurance

Your coinsurance is the percentage of medical costs you are required to pay after your annual deductible is met (see Figure 9.3). For example, the health insurance plan may cover 80 percent of charges for a covered surgery, leaving you responsible for the remaining 20 percent. The 20 percent you are required to pay is known as the coinsurance. Some high-deductible plans do not charge you

Coinsurance	Explanation
100/0	Once your annual deductible is met, your plan covers 100% of covered expenses.
90/10	Once your annual deductible is met, your plan covers 90% of covered expenses. You pay 10%.
80/20	Once your annual deductible is met, your plan covers 80% of covered expenses. You pay 20%.
70/30	Once your annual deductible is met, your plan covers 70% of covered expenses. You pay 30%.

Figure 9.3 Coinsurance Explained

	Out-of-Pocket Limits
Individual	$6,600
Family	$13,200

Figure 9.4 Out-of-Pocket Limits (2015)

coinsurance; they pay 100 percent of your medical expenses once you have met the deductible.

Out-of-Pocket Maximum

Your maximum coinsurance obligation plus your annual deductible is called your out-of-pocket maximum—referring to the maximum out-of-pocket expenses you could incur under the policy in a year (see Figure 9.4). All individual health plans are now subject to out-of-pocket limits. Specifically, a plan's out-of-pocket maximum cannot exceed $6,600 for single coverage or $13,200 for family coverage in 2015. These limits will be adjusted in future years based on medical inflation. Plans with lower out-of-pocket maximums will cost more than other plans with higher out-of-pocket limits.

 Tip: The industry term *out-of-pocket maximum* is confusing because it does not include doctor visit copays or prescription copays, nor does it often include payments to out-of-network medical providers.

HSA Qualification

A health savings account (HSA) allows you to save up tax-free dollars for future medical expenses or retirement. In order to qualify to open an HSA, you must first have high-deductible health insurance that meets the federal qualifications—this generally means the deductible must be above $2,600 per family or $1,300 per single and your out-of-pocket maximum must be less than $12,900 per family or $6,450 per single (2015) (see Figure 9.5). HSAs are discussed in detail in Chapter 12.

UNDERSTANDING THE BENEFITS COVERED

No matter what plan category or deductible you choose, many of the same benefits will be covered. Thanks to the healthcare reform legislation, comparing the

	Minimum Deductible	Maximum Out-of-Pocket
Individual	$1,300	$6,450
Family	$2,600	$12,900

Figure 9.5   HSA Qualification Requirements (2015)

benefits between different plans is now easy due to the following requirements that apply to all individual health plans:

1. Unlimited coverage for essential health benefits.
2. Free preventive care services.
3. Access to a Summary of Benefits and Coverage (SBC).

Unlimited Coverage for Essential Health Benefits

The Affordable Care Act requires all individual health plans to provide unlimited coverage for *essential health benefits*. Specifically, all individual plans must provide coverage for the following 10 categories of essential health benefits without any annual or lifetime limits.

1. Ambulatory patient services.
2. Emergency services.
3. Hospitalization.
4. Maternity and newborn care.
5. Mental health and substance use disorder services, including behavioral health treatment.
6. Prescription drugs.
7. Rehabilitative and habilitative services and devices.
8. Laboratory services.
9. Preventive and wellness services and chronic disease management.
10. Pediatric services, including oral and vision care.

The essential health benefits requirements in the Affordable Care Act have leveled the playing field between group coverage and individual coverage.

Free Preventive Care Coverage

All individual health plans must now provide free coverage for preventive care services. Specifically, all individual plans must cover the preventive services outlined in Figure 9.6 without charging you a copayment or coinsurance. This is true even if you have not met your annual deductible.

Summary of Benefits and Coverage

Make sure to review the Summary of Benefits and Coverage (SBC) for each plan (see Figure 9.7). This will allow you to compare and contrast the benefits offered by each plan you are considering. You can compare options based on specific benefits, and other features that may be important to you.

Once you have selected a few plans from different insurance companies that meet your financial and coverage needs, the next step will be to evaluate the provider network offered by the plan. The provider network is the group of

---

1. Abdominal aortic aneurysm one-time screening for men of specified ages who have ever smoked.
2. Alcohol misuse screening and counseling.
3. Aspirin use to prevent cardiovascular disease for men and women of certain ages.
4. Blood pressure screening for all adults.
5. Cholesterol screening for adults of certain ages or at higher risk.
6. Colorectal cancer screening for adults over 50.
7. Depression screening for adults.
8. Diabetes (Type 2) screening for adults with high blood pressure.
9. Diet counseling for adults at higher risk for chronic disease.
10. HIV screening for everyone ages 15 to 65, and other ages at increased risk.
11. Immunization vaccines for adults—doses, recommended ages, and recommended populations vary.
12. Obesity screening and counseling for all adults.
13. Sexually transmitted infection (STI) prevention counseling for adults at higher risk.
14. Syphilis screening for all adults at higher risk.
15. Tobacco use screening for all adults and cessation interventions for tobacco users.

Figure 9.6 Free Preventive Services

Insurance Company 1: Plan Option 1
Summary of Benefits and Coverage: What this Plan Covers & What it Costs

Coverage Period: 01/01/2014 – 12/31/2014
Coverage for: Individual + Spouse | Plan Type: PPO

⚠ **This is only a summary.** If you want more detail about your coverage and costs, you can get the complete terms in the policy or plan document at www.[insert] or by calling 1-800-[insert].

Important Questions	Answers	Why this Matters:
What is the overall deductible?	**$500** person / **$1,000** family Doesn't apply to preventive care	You must pay all the costs up to the **deductible** amount before this plan begins to pay for covered services you use. Check your policy or plan document to see when the **deductible** starts over (usually, but not always, January 1st). See the chart starting on page 2 for how much you pay for covered services after you meet the **deductible**.
Are there other deductibles for specific services?	Yes. **$300** for prescription drug coverage. There are no other specific deductibles.	You must pay all of the costs for these services up to the specific **deductible** amount before this plan begins to pay for these services.
Is there an out-of-pocket limit on my expenses?	Yes. For participating providers **$2,500** person / **$5,000** family For non-participating providers **$4,000** person / **$8,000** family	The **out-of-pocket limit** is the most you could pay during a coverage period (usually one year) for your share of the cost of covered services. This limit helps you plan for health care expenses.
What is not included in the out-of-pocket limit?	Premiums, balance-billed charges, and health care this plan doesn't cover.	Even though you pay these expenses, they don't count toward the **out-of-pocket limit**.
Is there an overall annual limit on what the plan pays?	No.	The chart starting on page 2 describes any limits on what the plan will pay for *specific* covered services, such as office visits.
Does this plan use a network of providers?	Yes. See www.[insert].com or call 1-800-[insert] for a list of participating providers.	If you use an in-network doctor or other health care **provider**, this plan will pay some or all of the costs of covered services. Be aware, your in-network doctor or hospital may use an out-of-network **provider** for some services. Plans use the term in-network, **preferred**, or participating for **providers** in their **network**. See the chart starting on page 2 for how this plan pays different kinds of **providers**.
Do I need a referral to see a specialist?	No. You don't need a referral to see a specialist.	You can see the **specialist** you choose without permission from this plan.
Are there services this plan doesn't cover?	Yes.	Some of the services this plan doesn't cover are listed on page 4. See your policy or plan document for additional information about **excluded services**.

Questions: Call 1-800-[insert] or visit us at www.[insert].
If you aren't clear about any of the underlined terms used in this form, see the Glossary. You can view the Glossary at www.[insert] or call 1-800-[insert] to request a copy.

OMB Control Numbers 1545-2229, 1210-0147, and 0938-1146   **1 of 8**

Released on April 23, 2013 (corrected)

Figure 9.7   Sample Summary of Benefits and Coverage
Source: www.healthcare.gov.

doctors, clinics, hospitals, and other medical sites covered by the plan. As we will discuss in Chapter 10, it will be vital for you to take steps to ensure your preferred doctors and hospitals are covered by any individual health plan you consider for purchase.

WHAT YOU LEARNED

- When narrowing your choices to specific plans, you should evaluate the following coverage components for each option: (1) plan category, (2) out-of-pocket exposure, and (3) covered benefits.
- The plan category you choose affects the average amount of money you will be required to spend on out-of-pocket costs in a year.
- All plans in the individual market are separated into four metallic tiers—Bronze, Silver, Gold, and Platinum.
- The Silver plan is the standard choice for most reasonably healthy families.
- Gold plans work well for healthy families who see the doctor regularly and can afford the higher premium.

- Platinum plans work well for families in poor health who see the doctor regularly.
- All individual health plans must now provide unlimited coverage for essential health benefits and free coverage for preventive care services.
- Make sure to review the Summary of Benefits and Coverage (SBC) for each plan. This will allow you to compare and contrast the benefits offered by each plan you are considering.

Chapter 10

NETWORKS—CHOOSING YOUR DOCTORS AND MEDICAL PROVIDERS

Today's health insurance plans are dominated by the managed care model—for each plan, insurance companies maintain a list of doctors and facilities from which you can choose. This list is called the *provider network*. The provider network is the group of doctors, clinics, hospitals, and other medical sites covered by your health insurance. Different individual health insurance plans will provide you with different levels of coverage depending on whether you receive medical care inside or outside of the plan's provider network. For example, if you seek care outside of this provider network, your insurance may not pay for the services or may pay a lower amount. Health insurance companies want you to use the healthcare providers in their network for two reasons: (1) the providers meet the health plan's quality standards, and (2) the providers charge the health insurance company discounted rates for services provided to policyholders.

 Did you know? A provider network is a group of physicians, hospitals, and other medical providers that have agreed with a health plan to provide medical services at prenegotiated prices and rates.

In general, a larger and more robust network will cost you more than a network that is limited to a smaller number of providers or a specific geographic region. It is vital for you to take steps to ensure your family's preferred doctors and hospitals are covered by the plans you consider for purchase. In this chapter, we will walk through the following:

1. How provider networks started.
2. Different types of plans.
3. Deciding between an HMO and a PPO.
4. Choosing your provider network.

HOW PROVIDER NETWORKS STARTED

Health insurance began in the United States during the Great Depression, when local hospitals began adopting the Blue Cross plans—providing groups of individuals with hospital care in return for a fixed monthly fee. Around the same time, employers began contracting with individual doctors to provide care to their workers for a fixed monthly fee—these were called Blue Shield plans. Over the subsequent decades, thousands of these plans were merged and consolidated into the independent Blue Cross Blue Shield health insurance companies that exist today. These companies, collectively known as "the Blues," maintain their own networks of independent doctors and hospitals to provide benefits at discounted prices to their policyholders.

Hundreds of other health insurance companies and independent network companies also developed their own networks—contracting with medical providers in their local areas to provide service to their policyholders or members for either a flat monthly fee or a discounted rate.

As new medical providers entered the marketplace, from ordinary physicians to specialized blood-testing laboratories, the only way for them to get patients was to offer great discounts to the largest purchasers of healthcare—the insurance companies and the medical-provider networks.

(?) **Did you know?** As medical providers lowered their prices to these large purchasing networks, the same medical providers raised their prices to patients outside the network—sometimes just to show the networks that they were giving them increasing discounts off the prices they charged others. Today, most medical providers, from local pediatricians to big-city hospitals, charge patients who don't belong to their health insurance network far higher prices (sometimes 10 times, or 1000 percent, higher) than they charge to those in their network for the exact same service.

Health insurance companies often determine which providers to contract with based on the size of the provider's discount and the availability of the provider's services to policyholders. Additionally, most insurance companies consider the quality of the provider, including educational background and board certification.

While virtually all individual health insurance plans supply a provider network, the type of plan you have will determine how you and your family can access and receive medical care from the available providers.

DIFFERENT TYPES OF HEALTH PLANS

When comparing your options in the individual market on the Health Insurance Marketplace, you will be able to see the details of each health plan. Make sure to note the type of each plan you're considering because different types of plans meet different needs. The plan type you choose will determine how you and your family gain access to and receive care inside and outside of the plan's network of doctors, hospitals, pharmacies, and other medical service providers. (See Figure 10.1.)

Preferred Provider Organizations (PPOs)—Fewer Restrictions, Higher Cost

A preferred provider organization (PPO) is a network of private, independent medical providers that have contracted with the PPO to supply services at either a fixed or discounted rate for each specific service—with the same medical providers also providing services to non-PPO members or other networks at different prices.

PPO health insurance plans typically charge higher monthly premiums than other plan types, but offer you a larger choice of physicians and medical providers.

Type of Plan	Summary
Preferred Provider Organizations (PPOs)	Fewer restrictions, higher cost
Health Maintenance Organizations (HMOs)	More restrictions, lower cost
Point of Service (POS) plans	A combination of PPOs and HMOs
Exclusive Provider Organizations (EPOs)	Coverage only from in-network providers
Indemnity Plans	Reimbursement-based coverage

Figure 10.1 Summary of Health Plan Types

PPO policyholders pay a discounted or flat copay fee for seeing a provider in the network, and they typically pay just the $20 to $30 copay (or perhaps nothing) after they have met their annual deductible.

PPO policyholders typically may also choose any out-of-network medical provider they wish by paying a greater percentage of the charges.

Tip: A PPO may be a good option for you and your family if you:

- Need flexibility when choosing physicians and other providers.
- Don't want the burden of obtaining a referral to see a specialist.
- Like the balance of greater provider choice versus lower premiums.

Health Maintenance Organizations (HMOs)—More Restrictions, Lower Cost

A health maintenance organization (HMO) is a group of medical providers who are often permanent full-time employees of the HMO. They collectively provide service to HMO members for a flat monthly fee or salary. HMOs often own their own hospitals. HMOs can be independent entities, like Kaiser Permanente in California, or virtual HMOs run by insurance companies that contract with independent medical providers to provide unlimited service for a flat monthly fee.

Most HMOs are fairly restrictive—you typically can see only those medical providers who are members of the HMO, and you must see your assigned or chosen HMO primary care doctor first to get a referral to a specialist. Some HMOs give their doctors daily patient quotas—limiting the time they can spend with each patient.

In return, the premium for an HMO health insurance policy is sometimes less than a PPO, and the out-of-pocket expenses—copays and prescription costs—are far less since many HMOs have their own pharmacy on the premises. In addition, HMO members rarely have to fill out claim forms.

Tip: An HMO may be a good option for you and your family if you:

- Prefer lower premiums.
- Like the tradeoff of in-network services.
- Desire good preventive services such as coverage for checkups and immunizations.

Other Types—POS Plans, EPOs, and Indemnity Plans

Point of Service (POS) Plans

Point of service (POS) plans are like PPOs, with some of the cost-saving features of HMOs (e.g., you must see your assigned or chosen primary care doctor first to get a referral to a specialist). They are a good choice for healthy people who want to save money on a PPO but don't mind having to go through a gatekeeper physician to see a specialist.

Tip: A POS may be a good option for you and your family if you:

- Need flexibility when choosing physicians and other providers.
- Desire primary care physicians to coordinate care.
- Like the balance of greater provider choice versus lower premiums.

Exclusive Provider Organizations (EPOs)

Exclusive provider organizations (EPOs) are similar to PPOs except that no coverage is offered to policyholders for out-of-network medical providers. EPOs are not popular because most people want to be able to see any doctor they want when they have a medical crisis. You should choose an EPO only if you are confident you will not want to see a specialist out of the network.

Tip: An EPO may be a good option for you and your family if you:

- Like the balance of less provider choice in exchange for lower rates.
- Can find the right services with a smaller panel of providers.
- Can afford potentially higher costs for unplanned events.

Indemnity Plans

Indemnity plans look more like other types of insurance—you can choose any medical provider you wish at any time, pay the provider yourself, and submit the receipt to your insurance carrier for reimbursement. However, your insurance carrier will typically reimburse you or pay your claims only at a percentage of the "usual, customary, and reasonable" rate for the service you received. Moreover, indemnity plans often have very high deductibles and are very expensive, so few people choose them over an HMO or a PPO. If you use primarily alternative medicine providers or if you live in an area where the doctors you prefer are not in a network accessible to you, you might be better off with an indemnity plan.

The only way to know is to phone your medical providers and ask whether they are covered by the network. You should also find out how much an indemnity plan would cover for each service.

 Tip: An indemnity plan may be a good option for you and your family if you:

- Seek high levels of flexibility and choice for doctors and hospitals.
- Are fine with the balance of higher rates in exchange for more service control.
- Can accept the burden of potentially increased administrative activity for referral and claims paperwork.

CHOOSING BETWEEN A PPO AND AN HMO

HMOs cost less, and PPOs offer more medical provider options, but there is no general way to compare the differences between an HMO and a PPO health insurance policy. You can analyze all the financial components regardless of whether the provider is a PPO or an HMO. But trying to compare them side by side would be like trying to compare a Lincoln to a Cadillac—it is a matter of personal preference.

Moreover, each HMO and PPO is very different, so the best way to choose is to locate members of a specific HMO and/or PPO in your area and ask how satisfied they are with their health insurance. Interestingly, surveys have found that there is very little difference between HMOs and PPOs in levels of satisfaction among people with chronic conditions; however, billing and customer service problems are more common to PPOs (see Figure 10.2).

HOW TO CHOOSE A MEDICAL PROVIDER NETWORK

You should pay more attention to choosing the right network than to whether the plan is an HMO or a PPO. Here are some suggestions for how to choose the right network.

Make a list of all the good physicians you know of in your area. Then, when you first select a specific health insurance policy and network to analyze, check to see if these physicians are in that network. You can do this online or by phoning the physician or the insurance company. Be sure to also ask how much you will be paying per doctor visit, because different networks have very different pricing discounts for each medical provider.

	HMO	PPO
Do I need to get a referral before I can see an in-network specialist?	Yes, usually.	No.
Can I go to a doctor or hospital that is not in the plan's network?	No, unless you need urgent or emergency care or if you have a point of service (POS) option that allows you to use non-network providers.	Yes, but you will pay more unless it is an emergency.

Figure 10.2 HMO versus PPO

Tip: If you are new to the area or don't have time to prepare a list of doctors, just look to see which major hospitals are in a specific network. The best doctors are usually in the network with the best hospitals.

Should you or a family member have a specific condition, like diabetes, you might ask around for names of good endocrinologists and pick your network based on them.

Tip: Most doctors today practice with other professionals in their own specialty, like a group pediatric practice. Although only one doctor in the group technically joins a network, all doctors in the group can provide network service. Never assume that a doctor is not in the network just because he or she is not listed—call and ask.

If staying with your current doctors is important to you, check to see if they are included in the provider directory before choosing a plan. Many tools are available to help you search, compare, and assess providers, hospitals, and other care facilities so you can make better decisions. See www.healthinsurancerevolution.org/tools for a list of such tools.

Tip: Do you travel often? If so, you should probably consider a policy from a national insurance company, such as UnitedHealthOne, with a robust national network.

BEWARE OF PRODUCTS THAT ARE NOT HEALTH INSURANCE

As you locate specific insurance companies and policies off-marketplace, you should be aware that many products sold outside of the Health Insurance Marketplace are disguised to look like health insurance but do not qualify as such. Real health insurance is both (1) access to a network of medical providers at discounted rates and (2) financial protection from medical bills.

Some products that look like health coverage policies are actually nothing more than poor network discount cards. Their marketing materials make them sound like guaranteed-issue, no-questions-asked health insurance, but they pay nothing for medical expenses.

The easiest way to spot these fake insurance policies is to ask for the state insurance license number of the person trying to sell them to you—these products are not insurance and are rarely sold by legitimate, state-licensed insurance agents or brokers. Another easy way to spot these fake policies is to look carefully for the word *insurance* in their written sales materials—they rarely use this term because they wish to evade the scrutiny of state insurance regulators.

When it comes to network access, the companies behind medical discount cards sometimes contract with legitimate medical provider networks, but at much lower discounts than those received by major insurance companies like the Blues.

 Tip: If a salesperson or website for one of these discount cards tells you to see whether your doctor is listed, check it out. Call the doctor's office manager and ask how much of a discount you would actually be receiving with this plan versus with the local Blue Cross Blue Shield plan.

WHAT YOU LEARNED

- A provider network is a group of physicians, hospitals, and other medical providers that have agreed with a health plan to provide medical services at prenegotiated prices and rates.
- In general, a larger and more robust network will cost you more than a network that is limited to a specific geographic region.
- It is vital for you to take steps to ensure your family's preferred doctors and hospitals are covered by the plans you consider for purchase.
- While virtually all individual health insurance plans supply a provider network, the type of plan you have will determine how you and your family can access and receive medical care from the available providers.

- HMOs cost less, and PPOs offer more medical provider options, but there is no general way to compare the differences between an HMO and a PPO health insurance policy.
- You should pay more attention to choosing the right network than to whether it is an HMO or a PPO.
- Beware of products that are not health insurance—real health insurance is both (1) access to a network of medical providers at discounted rates and (2) financial protection from medical bills.

Chapter 11

HOW TO SELECT THE RIGHT PLAN FOR YOU AND YOUR FAMILY

O nce you have narrowed your list of plan choices based on coverage level, plan type, and provider network, it is time to pick the right plan to purchase. The most useful way to pick a plan is to estimate your future healthcare needs and then review the major features of each policy.

Before you complete the analysis, make sure you have done the following:

- Calculated your premium tax credit amount.
- Narrowed your options to plans within one or two metallic tiers.
- Narrowed your options to plans with specific coverage levels.
- Narrowed your options to plans with your preferred plan type and providers.

ESTIMATING YOUR FUTURE HEALTHCARE SPENDING

To compare different health insurance policies, you have to first make assumptions about your future healthcare needs, as shown in Figure 11.1. If you have not had a major illness recently, the best way to do this is to look at what you spent on medical care last year. After you have prepared this list, think carefully about the health of each family member and estimate what you might spend next year.

You should be able to come up with your exact out-of-pocket expenses for healthcare last year (including your health insurance premium) and an estimate of next year's spending.

119

Questions to Ask Yourself	This Year's Spending	Next Year's Spending
Pharmacy How many prescriptions filled? Total dollars spent? What will be different versus last year?	$	$
Doctor Visits How many visits? Total dollars spent? What will be different versus last year?	$	$
Therapists (Physical/Emotional) How many visits? Total dollars spent? What will be different versus last year?	$	$
Hospitalizations How many hospitalizations? Total dollars spent? What were the causes? Are there any major items pending? What will be different versus last year?	$	$
Other Medical Items Total dollars spent on other items (crutches, etc.). Are there any major items pending?	$	$
Health Premiums Paid Last Year Are there any major insurance items pending?	$	$
Total Costs	$	$

Figure 11.1   Current and Future Healthcare Estimate Worksheet

COMPARING POLICY FEATURES

Once you have estimated what you may spend next year, you need to collect the following basic information for each policy you are considering. All of this information should be readily available in any brochure or website describing an individual policy. Once you have the information, make up your own worksheet similar to the one in Figure 11.2.

Using the two worksheets, figure out what your total healthcare costs will be next year under each different policy you are considering.

 Tip: There are virtually unlimited ways to analyze this data, and no single correct way to do so. A good health insurance broker can help you by asking the right questions, but ultimately you will have to make the final decision on which policy feels right for you.

Name of Policy	Monthly Premium	Annual Deductible	Annual OOP Max.	Doctor-Visit Copay	Coinsurance
Policy 1	$268	$5,000	$6,350	$60/visit	70/30
Policy 2	$364	$2,000	$6,350	$45/visit	80/20
Policy 3	$402	$0	$6,350	$30/visit	90/10

Note: Numbers have been chosen for illustrative purposes only.

Figure 11.2 Insurance Policy Analysis Worksheet

SELECTING THE PLAN AND BUYING

Once you've chosen the policy that best meets your requirements and budget, you are ready to submit your application along with a check or bank debit authorization for the first month's premium. When you fill out your application for health insurance, be clear and concise and do not leave anything out. If you do not understand a question, call and ask—do not leave it blank. It typically takes two to four weeks to receive a formal response to your application from the time you submit it.

WHAT YOU LEARNED

- The most useful way to pick a plan is to estimate your future healthcare needs and then review the major features of each policy item by item.
- Once you've chosen the policy that best meets your requirements and budget, you are ready to submit your application along with a check or bank debit authorization for the first month's premium.
- When you fill out your application for health insurance, be clear and concise and do not leave anything out.
- It typically takes two to four weeks to receive a formal response to your application from the time you submit it.

Chapter 12

HOW TO REDUCE YOUR INDIVIDUAL HEALTHCARE COSTS

B y now, you have most likely discovered you can save thousands of dollars each year by purchasing your own individual health insurance plan. Once you switch to individual health insurance your healthcare paradigm shifts:

- You now want to cut down on your healthcare spending since each dollar you save you get to keep—and over the years these dollars could add up to hundreds of thousands of dollars.
- You must learn to balance your new financial incentive to save on healthcare costs against the legitimate healthcare needs of your family.
- You have a new incentive to eat better, exercise more, and invest in wellness care to improve your health—since staying healthy is the best way to save on your healthcare costs.

In this chapter, we will examine six things you can do to save on your healthcare costs:

1. Ask your employer to reimburse your individual insurance premium.
2. Shop for a new health insurance plan annually.
3. Open a health savings account (HSA).
4. Ask your doctors to spend your money as if it were their money.
5. Save on pharmacy costs.
6. Change your lifestyle (diet and exercise).

1. ASK YOUR EMPLOYER TO REIMBURSE YOUR INDIVIDUAL PREMIUM

If you or your spouse is employed, you should contact your company's HR department to request they adopt a defined contribution healthcare program. With this approach, instead of providing a one-size-fits-all employer-provided health insurance plan (a defined benefit), your company reimburses you for your individual health insurance policy cost up to a monthly healthcare allowance (or defined contribution) set by the company. Here is a basic overview of how your defined contribution program will work once it is implemented. As pictured in Figure 12.1, the concept is simple. With a defined contribution program, your company offers you and your coworkers a monthly healthcare allowance to use on individual health insurance. You and your coworkers purchase their own individual health plan, and are reimbursed up to the defined contributions the company has made available.

If your company is among the 50 percent of employers with an employer-provided health insurance plan, your company can save 20 to 60 percent by switching to defined contribution healthcare. Alternatively, if your company is among the 50 percent of companies that have already terminated employer-provided health insurance due to costs, your company can reestablish an employee benefits program. Your company should not switch to a defined contribution program for just the obvious financial reasons. In addition to saving thousands of dollars, all of your co-workers will also receive the numerous benefits of individual policies described throughout this book. See Part III for more information on defined contribution healthcare.

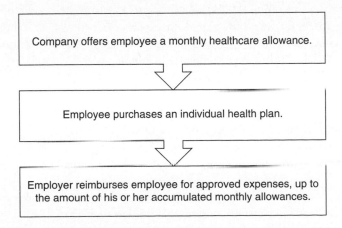

Figure 12.1 How Defined Contribution Works

Tip: If you want your company to reimburse you for your individual health insurance costs, give your HR leader and CEO a copy of this book. Summaries are also available on the book website— www.healthinsurancerevolution.org.

2. SHOP FOR A NEW HEALTH INSURANCE PLAN ANNUALLY

You should reevaluate your health insurance options annually to ensure you are covered by the best plan for the lowest possible cost. During the annual enrollment period every year, you should revisit your state's Health Insurance Marketplace to get updated health insurance rates and coverage options for the upcoming year. If you find a new plan that either (1) provides better coverage at the same cost, or (2) provides the same coverage at a lower cost, you should switch health plans.

 Tip: During the annual enrollment period every year, you should revisit your state's Health Insurance Marketplace to get updated health insurance rates and coverage options for the upcoming year.

3. OPEN A HEALTH SAVINGS ACCOUNT (HSA)

Health savings accounts (HSAs) allow you to save hundreds of thousands of dollars, tax free, for your future medical expenses or retirement. When people say they have a health savings account, they typically mean that they have a high-deductible, HSA-qualified health insurance policy, combined with an IRA-type savings account called an HSA.

HSAs have triple tax advantages:

1. Contributions are tax deductible going in.
2. Appreciations are tax free.
3. Withdrawals are tax free (when used for qualifying medical expenses).

Federal regulations allow HSAs to be offered by insured banks and credit unions, insurance companies, and any institution that offers IRAs. Depending on the state in which you live, the bank or financial institution offering the HSA may be called either a custodian or trustee.

You may feel most comfortable opening your HSA at a local bank or credit union, but there is no need to do so. Unlike with a checking or savings account, you may never make frequent cash deposits or cash withdrawals from your HSA. Moreover, once the balance in your HSA has grown to more than a few thousand dollars, you will probably want to move most of your HSA funds to a money market fund, a financial advisory firm, or a brokerage firm that can help you invest for the maximum long-term return. Many financial institutions offer the same options for investing high-balance HSAs that they offer for IRAs.

You should choose an HSA provider the same way you choose any other IRA or financial service account—paying particular attention to annual or monthly maintenance fees, withdrawal fees, debit card fees, and so on.

Tip: Fees you pay to your financial institution are typically automatically deducted from your HSA—but you don't want them to be. You should contribute the maximum amount allowed each year to your HSA, and you are allowed to exclude from contributions reasonable banking-type fees paid with non-HSA funds. Some financial institutions allow you to pay your HSA fees with a check from a separate account—ask if you can do this.

Contrary to what many people think, you may have an unlimited number of different health savings accounts at an unlimited number of financial institutions—provided the total contributions and withdrawals to all of them combined do not exceed the IRS regulations for a single HSA.

Tip: Most financial institutions today charge annual fees of $3 to $5 per month ($36 to $60 per year) to maintain an HSA, and some waive this fee and pay higher interest if your HSA balance is above $5,000 or $10,000—thus you may want to keep just one HSA until your HSA balance reaches the level to qualify for free service or higher interest rates.

You may freely transfer balances directly from one HSA account to another—but you should never transfer money from an HSA to a non-HSA account because such transfers could be deemed taxable withdrawals for nonmedical purposes.

Your HSA is the best investment vehicle to save you money on taxes today and earn tax-free interest and appreciation for tomorrow—even better than an IRA or 401(k). You will not have to pay taxes on HSA withdrawals after retirement if you use your HSA funds for qualified medical expenses for you, your spouse, or your dependents. You should contribute the maximum amount of money into your HSA each year as soon as possible. You may make a self-contribution anytime during the calendar year or up until April 15 (or whenever you file your tax return) of the following year. When you file your income tax return, you get an above-the-line deduction for 100 percent of your self-contributions—even if you do not itemize your deductions. If a relative makes the contribution for you, you (not your relative) get the income tax deduction, even if you take the money out and spend it the next day (on qualified medical expenses).

Although there is an exhaustive list of qualified medical expenses for which you can use your HSA funds, in most cases the correct financial decision is to not touch the funds in your HSA until you reach retirement.

You receive all of your HSA tax benefits by making contributions to your HSA, and you receive no additional tax benefits by withdrawing funds to pay for qualified medical expenses. Moreover, the funds withdrawn from your HSA no longer accumulate tax-free interest and appreciation. Just as you should fully fund your HSA before putting $1 into your IRA or 401(k), you should also spend any non-retirement funds you have available for medical expenses before taking out even $1 of your HSA before retirement.

Assume you have both an HSA and a normal savings or brokerage account (and assume an 8 percent long-term interest rate, age 35, and a 40 percent combined federal and state income tax bracket). Your family spends $2,000 a year on qualified medical expenses, which you could pay with either your HSA or your ordinary savings account. You could use your HSA and leave $2,000 in your savings account, where it would earn compound interest at the rate of 5.2 percent after taxes (8 percent less 40 percent in income taxes). After 30 years, this extra $2,000 a year would have appreciated to $139,016. However, if you left this same $2,000 in your HSA earning 8 percent without having to pay income taxes, in 30 years it would be worth $259,290, almost twice as much.

Here's the best deal of all when it comes to leaving money in your HSA. There is no time limit on how long you can wait to reimburse yourself with funds from your HSA as long as the medical expense was incurred after you opened your HSA. If you spent $2,000 of non-HSA money for qualified medical expenses for 30 years, and left this $60,000 in your HSA accumulating tax-free interest, in year 30, or anytime you wish, you could still reimburse yourself up to $60,000 tax-free—and spend this money on anything, including nonmedical items.

Tip: Each year, make a list of your qualified medical expenses and receipts, but don't reimburse yourself from your HSA. If you ever want money from your HSA for a nonmedical expense, you can then make tax-free withdrawals for unreimbursed expenses all the way back to the first day you opened your HSA—even if it's 30 years or more later.

Sometimes you may not have the money available to pay your medical expenses without touching your HSA, or you may not have enough money to make an annual contribution to your HSA. In such cases, you should still pay all of your qualified medical expenses outside of your HSA and then pass the reimbursement through your HSA to maximize your income tax savings.

For example, say you cannot afford to make any new HSA contributions this year. Let's assume that at the end of the year, or before April 15 when you file your tax return, you calculate that you have spent $3,800 for qualified out-of-pocket medical expenses. You should make a contribution of $3,800 to your HSA and simultaneously make a qualified withdrawal of $3,800 to reimburse yourself for these expenses. This way, you get a $3,800 above-the-line deduction from your income taxes for your medical expenses, even if you do not itemize your deductions, thus saving yourself $1,330 in income taxes (assuming a 35 percent combined state and federal tax bracket).

You are your own administrator of your HSA. The bank or financial institution where you keep your HSA will typically not ask you about contributions or withdrawals—you are solely responsible to the IRS to comply with HSA rules and regulations. If you make a mistake by withdrawing funds for a nonqualified expense, and have evidence that it was a mistake, you are allowed to return these funds to your HSA without penalty up until April 15 of the following year. If you make a permanent withdrawal for nonqualified expenses, you must report such a withdrawal as taxable income and pay an additional penalty on the withdrawn amount.

Similarly, if you contribute more than the legal annual maximum to your HSA, you are allowed to withdraw and return the excess contribution and any earnings on it without penalty up until April 15 of the following year. If you do not, you must pay an excise tax on the excess contribution and its earnings and lower your contribution the following year by the amount of the excess contribution.

HSA-Qualified Medical Expenses

You are allowed tax-free withdrawals from HSAs at any time for qualified medical expenses. Before retirement, the best HSA strategy is to leave as much as possible inside your HSA, since you can take reimbursement at any time. You are allowed to withdraw money, tax free, from your HSA for a long list of qualified medical expenses, including:

- Prescriptions (including copays)
- Doctor visits (including copays)
- Dental
- Chiropractic

- X-rays and other medical procedures
- Over-the-counter medications
- Eyeglasses, contacts, LASIK, and other vision care
- Hearing aids
- Transportation to and from medical providers
- Weight-loss programs (medically supervised)
- Smoking cessation
- Medicare premiums
- Long-term care expenditures

4. SPEAK TO YOUR DOCTOR ABOUT SPENDING YOUR MONEY AS IF IT WERE HIS OR HER OWN MONEY

Most doctors already know how to spend your money as if it were their money. They are just too busy to take the time to do so, or they may be prohibited from doing so by the owners of their medical practice or by their malpractice insurance carriers. Here's how to get them to do it.

Prescriptions

When a doctor writes out a prescription, say: "We have high-deductible insurance." Be prepared for the doctor to rip up the prescription and write a new one stating, "This drug is cheaper and is really the same thing anyway."

 Tip: Don't wait for your doctor to prescribe something and then ask for a cheaper equivalent—tell your doctor up front that you have a health savings account and high-deductible health insurance. You'll be surprised how many doctors already know about HSAs and how to save money on healthcare.

One reason doctors don't prescribe cheaper equivalent drugs is that doctors and their medical practices have financial incentives to prescribe certain brands of drugs. The pharmaceutical companies keep figuring out the latest legal way to compensate medical doctors who prescribe their brand-name products.

Sometimes doctors don't prescribe cheaper equivalent generics or therapeutic substitutes out of ignorance. There are equivalent generics or therapeutic substitutes for almost all popular drugs. When you politely tell them, most doctors are pleased to learn about less expensive equivalent therapies. They don't teach economics in medical school, and you should not expect doctors to know the price of the things they prescribe. Unlike you, they rarely see the inside of a pharmacy.

Doctors get many of their own prescriptions for free, as samples from pharmaceutical representatives.

Medical Tests

Unnecessary medical tests are another area where doctors can waste hundreds or thousands of your dollars. There are obviously some medical tests you should never skip—like having an annual mammogram or taking a biopsy of an unusual growth. But many tests are simply a waste of money. When doctors tell you they want to send you, or a sample of your fluids, for a medical test, here are some questions you should ask them:

- Why do you want this test?
- What are the likely results from the test, and what is the recommended action for each outcome?
- If the therapy is the same regardless of the result, could we skip the test and just begin the therapy?
- Are there any different tests that we should consider?
- How much does the test cost, and is there any way to get it done less expensively?
- If you were spending your own money, would you take this test?

You may be surprised by the responses you get, particularly to the last question. Many tests and medical procedures are not even sanctioned by the doctors who prescribe them—they are required to do so for liability reasons by their medical malpractice insurance carriers. Ask again, "Would you take this test with your own money?" If the candid answer is no, ask whether you can sign a waiver instead, stating that your doctor advised you to take the test but that you refused against medical advice (AMA).

Surgery

Check your wallet when a doctor starts talking about surgery—then get a second or third opinion. Make sure you receive advice from at least one doctor who is not a candidate to perform the surgery. Doctors often have a financial conflict of interest when it comes to recommending a surgery they might perform themselves. Be particularly careful when your doctor has already leased or purchased expensive equipment (e.g., LASIK tools) that they need to keep busy. Do not hesitate to ask, "What do you earn personally if I choose to do, or not to do, the surgery?" Doctors are not subject to the same conflict-of-interest standards that have become commonplace for lawyers, public officials, and other professionals.

In this section, we have explored only a few of the things you can do to save money and improve your health—which in itself should be an entire book. Each time you speak with your doctor about reducing your prescriptions, changing your lifestyle, getting wellness care, or spending your money more wisely, you and your doctor become better educated about the most important social and economic challenge facing us today—improving our health and reducing the cost of healthcare.

5. HOW TO SAVE 10 TO 75 PERCENT ON YOUR PRESCRIPTION DRUGS

Approximately 131 million people in the United States, about 66 percent of all adults, use prescription drugs. If you are like most people and have health insurance coverage with an annual deductible of more than a few hundred dollars, you have a big incentive to be smart about the way you buy prescription drugs. This is especially true if you have HSA-qualified high-deductible health insurance. All the money you save on prescription drugs stays in your pocket or keeps growing in your health savings account. If you begin at age 35, each $50 a month you save in healthcare expenses means an additional $20,000 a year in your HSA when you retire.

Here are the top three ways to save money on prescription drugs:

1. Get a drug discount card.
2. Substitute generic drugs.
3. Use a different drug that has similar effects.

Not so long ago, you didn't need to worry about the cost of your prescription drugs; your employer paid all your prescription drug costs, or you made a small copay of $5 or $10 per prescription. Doctors didn't worry about drug costs either, since their patients weren't paying much, if anything, for the drugs they prescribed. In fact, doctors often closely followed the advice of pharmaceutical sales representatives (who, by the way, typically rewarded them with trips to Hawaii and other perks).

Today, people are more aware of how expensive drugs are since they have to pay for them. They are so expensive that roughly 25 percent of the prescriptions written in the United States each year are not filled, primarily because of price.

Get a Drug Discount Card and Save 10 to 25 Percent

If you don't get a good discount card through your health insurance, you should get a drug discount card. For $0 to $50 a year you can obtain a drug discount card that will save you 10 to 25 percent on your prescriptions.

There are numerous drug discount cards on the market now; they typically required an annual fee when they were first introduced, but today most are free.

Tip: Watch the fine print when signing up for any drug discount card, particularly one that is free. Some charge high rates for shipping and handling, some charge extra fees to add family members, and some appear to be free, but when you try to use them you're charged an activation fee of $15 or more.

Tip: You should obtain every card you can that is free, and use the one that gives you the best discount for each individual prescription—different cards have different discounts for each drug, so no one card is universally the best. Always ask your pharmacist whether any rebates are associated with your prescription and whether you can get these rebates yourself instead of having the pharmacy or the drug discount card company keep them.

Most people think that when they use the drug discount card that comes with their health insurance, their insurance carrier or employer pays part of the cost of their prescription. Actually, the opposite is sometimes true. In many cases, the provider of the drug discount card is actually paid a $1 to $3 prescription fee from the pharmacy that accepted the card.

Drug discount cards are typically accepted at almost every retail pharmacy chain and at some mail-order pharmacies. The size of the discount, and the drug price itself, varies widely among different retail pharmacies and sometimes even among stores in the same retail chain.

Ask for Generic Drugs

A generic drug is a chemical copy of a brand-name drug. It has the same dosage, safety, and strength. It is intended for the same use as a brand-name drug, is taken the same way, is of the same quality, and has the same efficacy. Generic drugs are available for about 90 percent of all prescriptions, and you should almost always ask your doctor to prescribe a generic version if one is available.

In some cases, switching from a brand-name drug to a generic can actually be medically better for you—because many patients are taking outdated brand-name drugs prescribed years ago when they first developed a medical condition. When you ask your doctor for a generic prescription, you may actually receive a prescription for a better, newer version of the drug you have been taking, at a much lower cost.

 Tip: Generic drugs are sometimes safer or better than the brand-name products they replace because they have been prescribed more recently and thus contain improved formulas.

Generics are also made for over-the-counter medicines. For example, in most drugstores, Tylenol, a product to relieve pain and reduce fever, is sold in a generic form as acetaminophen. It costs much less, but is essentially the same. According to the Congressional Budget Office, generic drugs save consumers an estimated $8 to $10 billion a year at retail pharmacies.

Use a Different Drug That Has Similar Effects

If no generic version of your prescribed drug is available, you can still save money by asking your doctor to prescribe a cheaper drug that has the same or similar effect. This is known as therapeutic substitution, or category shifting. Before your doctor writes a prescription for you, ask the following questions:

- **If no generic version is available, are there other drugs in the same class?** For almost every condition that is treatable, there is more than one drug that can successfully be used to attack the problem. The second and third competing drugs put on the market are sometimes called *me-too* drugs, and they often sell at a lower price.
- **Are there older, cheaper drugs available that are just as effective?** Doctors often prescribe new drugs that are more expensive than older ones. You can also save by asking for an older version of your expensive prescription drug. Once a prescription drug goes off patent, drug companies usually change the formula slightly and heavily promote the new formula. Sometimes the older version is still on the market and is as effective, but available for a much lower price.

Other Ways to Save

There are plenty of other ways you can reduce your pharmacy bill. Here are a few more ideas for you to consider.

- **Shop around by phone.** Make a list of your medications, including strength and number taken daily, and call at least six pharmacies to compare prices, keeping in mind whether the pharmacies are on your plan.
- **Use a pill splitter (but do your research first).** Many drugs are cheaper if you buy them in higher doses, and then cut them in half. Ask your pharmacist or doctor first, though, since many drugs cannot be split without

reducing their effectiveness. Most pharmacists say you should split only pills that are scored (i.e., those with a predesigned breakoff line).

- **Save by buying a 90-day versus a 30-day supply.** Most pharmacies offer higher savings if you buy a larger supply. In addition, people with insurance prescription coverage may save even more by getting a larger supply.
- **Stop using drugs you no longer need.** You should review all your prescriptions with your doctor at each visit. You may be taking drugs you no longer need. Also, report any side effects and ask questions about possible drug interactions. Don't hesitate to ask your pharmacist questions; it's free and can often save you money.

One of the main reasons prescription drugs are so expensive is because, until now, consumers have had few incentives to make economic choices about which drugs to take and where to buy them. In most areas of our economy other than medical care, informed consumers increasingly demand and receive (1) better products for less money and (2) cheaper and more convenient methods of distribution for the products and services they have chosen. Medical care, starting with the prescription drugs you choose and how you obtain them, is about to join the rest of the U.S. economy.

6. CHANGE YOUR LIFESTYLE (DIET AND EXERCISE)

There's a lot you can do to improve your health and cut your healthcare costs, but let's look at why we spend so much on healthcare.

Why Americans Spend So Much on Healthcare

The United States spends far more per person on healthcare than any other country—about two to three times as much as other developed nations. Yet people in the United States don't appear to be getting their money's worth. The United States lags far behind other developed countries on almost every important medical statistic—life expectancy, infant mortality, cancer, diabetes, heart disease, and so forth. So, what is the problem with American healthcare?

- Is it our inefficient medical bureaucracy, where 2 to 3 million Americans are employed by medical providers and insurance carriers—not to deliver healthcare, but merely to pass the buck for that care to someone else?
- Is it the cost of medical malpractice insurance, which adds more than $27 billion a year to the cost of providing healthcare—enough to pay annually a high-deductible insurance premium for more than half of the 45 million Americans without health insurance?
- Is it our employer-based system, whereby the ultimate providers of healthcare for most people (employers) have little incentive to spend

even $1 today on wellness and preventive care in order to save $100 tomorrow—because the odds are that the employee will be long gone or receiving Medicare by the time serious diseases like cancer and heart disease develop?

The partial answer is yes to all of these questions, but the main reason Americans spend two times what they should on healthcare is not because of something wrong with American healthcare. The main reason Americans spend two times what they should on healthcare is because Americans (along with Australians and Britons) are two times more unhealthy than people in most other nations, primarily because of their diet and a lack of exercise.

Today, more than 63 percent of Americans are overweight or medically obese—a figure that has doubled since the 1980s. Being overweight is just one of the symptoms of having a terrible diet—most Americans are also deficient in the basic vitamins and minerals necessary to keep their minds sharp and avoid major diseases like cancer.

Proper diet and exercise is the key to a healthy lifestyle and will reduce you and your family's healthcare costs over time.

WHAT YOU LEARNED

- If you or your spouse is employed, you should ask your company to adopt a defined contribution healthcare program.
- With defined contribution, your company reimburses you for your individual health insurance costs up to a monthly healthcare allowance (or defined contribution) set by the company.
- During the annual enrollment period every year, you should revisit your state's Health Insurance Marketplace to get updated health insurance rates and coverage options for the upcoming year.
- Health savings accounts (HSAs) allow you to save hundreds of thousands of dollars, tax free, for your future medical expenses or retirement—while financially reforming the entire U.S. healthcare system.
- You should speak to your doctor about spending your money as if it were his or her own money—many doctors will immediately think of ways to save your family money on prescriptions, tests, and surgery.
- Switching to generic drugs can save you a lot of money, and they are sometimes safer or better than the brand-name products they replace because they have been prescribed more recently and thus contain improved formulas.
- Proper diet and exercise are the keys to a healthy lifestyle and will reduce you and your family's healthcare costs over time.

Part III

HOW TO SWITCH TO DEFINED CONTRIBUTION HEALTHCARE

T his section describes new ways that your company can save hundreds of thousands of dollars each year while providing better coverage than traditional employer-provided health insurance. This part is written for owners, CEOs, CFOs, HR managers, and accountants at small and medium-sized companies—as well as for anyone at your company involved in the health benefits decision-making process.

Chapter 13

WHAT IS DEFINED CONTRIBUTION HEALTHCARE?

I f you are reading this book, you have probably come to the conclusion that employer-provided health insurance may no longer be the best solution for your company and its employees. Or, perhaps you are being forced to cancel your company's employer-provided health insurance plan due to cost. Look no further—there is a new and better way for your company to provide employee health benefits. It's called defined contribution healthcare. With this approach, instead of providing a one-size-fits-all employer-provided health insurance plan (a defined benefit), your company (1) allows each employee to purchase his or her own individual health insurance plan independent of the company, and (2) reimburses each employee for their cost up to a monthly healthcare allowance (or defined contribution) set by the company. While this concept has been around for many years, employers have been hesitant, until now, to make the switch primarily due to limitations in the individual market—limitations that no longer exist.

Due to the advantages of the improved individual health insurance market, your company should now terminate employer-provided health insurance in favor of defined contribution healthcare and individual health insurance. Doing so will allow your company to save up to $12,000 per employee per year, while offering a better employee health benefit program for recruiting and retention purposes. If you have 10 or more employees, that is $100,000 or more in savings per year.

Tip: Transitioning to defined contribution healthcare and individual health insurance can save a 10-person company $100,000 or more per year.

THE PROBLEM—EMPLOYER-PROVIDED HEALTH INSURANCE COSTS ARE UNSUSTAINABLE

In the past, employer-provided health insurance was the best way to provide quality health insurance to employees. Today, as can be seen in Figure 13.1, this traditional approach has become a source of frustration and increased costs. Since 2000, the percentage of Americans covered by employer-provided health insurance has steadily declined. Facing double-digit growth in health insurance premiums, many businesses have either eliminated health benefits or redesigned plans to include higher deductibles, larger copayments, and greater premium sharing by employees.

From 1999 to 2013, the cost of employer-provided health insurance for families of four increased from $5,791 in 1999 to $16,351 in 2013—a more than 180 percent increase. Today, only half of small and medium-sized U.S. employers provide health insurance to employees. As shown in Figure 13.2, only 57 percent of small firms (3 to 199 employees) offer health insurance, while 99 percent of larger

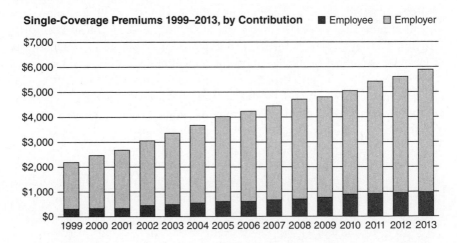

Figure 13.1   Cost to Cover a Single Employee with Employer-Provided Health Insurance

Source: Kaiser Family Foundation 2013.

Employer Size	1999	2013
3–9 employees	55%	45%
10–24 employees	74%	68%
25–49 employees	88%	85%
50–199 employees	97%	91%
All small and medium employers (3–199 workers)	65%	57%
All large employers (200+ workers)	99%	99%
All firms	66%	57%

Figure 13.2   Percentage of Employers Offering Health Benefits 1999 to 2013
Source: Kaiser Family Foundation 2013.

	Actual	Projected	
	2013	2014	2015
Single	$5,884/year	$6,472/year	$7,120/year
Family	$16,351/year	$17,986/year	$19,785/year

Figure 13.3   Projected Cost of Employer-Provided Health Insurance (2014 to 2015)

firms (200+ employees) offer health insurance—although most large employers do not cover their hourly workers.

Even worse, employer-provided health insurance costs are expected to continue to skyrocket. In 2014, the annual average cost of traditional employer-provided health insurance is expected to reach $17,986 per family and $6,472 per individual (see Figure 13.3).

This price pressure has created a paradigm shift in the way companies offer employee health benefits—a shift from an employer-provided defined benefit model to an employer-funded defined contribution model. While the transition from employer-provided health insurance to individual health insurance has been gradual since 2000, the post-2014 enhancements to the individual market have accelerated this shift.

THE SOLUTION—REIMBURSE EMPLOYEES FOR INDIVIDUAL HEALTH INSURANCE

If your company is among the 50 percent of employers with an employer-provided health insurance plan, you and your employees can save 20 to 60 percent by

Employer-Provided Health Insurance	Defined Contribution Healthcare
You provide your employees with a one-size-fits-all health insurance plan or defined benefit at uncertain annual cost.	You provide your employees with a monthly allowance or defined contribution to spend on their own individual health insurance at an annual cost you control.

Figure 13.4   Employer-Provided Health Insurance versus Defined Contribution Healthcare

switching to defined contribution healthcare. You can do this by canceling your existing employer-provided plan and giving the money you were spending to your employees so they can buy their own individual health insurance (see Figure 13.4). You will be relieved to be out of the health insurance business, and most of your employees will be able to buy better insurance on their own for half of what you are currently paying for your company plan. If your company is among the 50 percent of companies that have already terminated employer-provided health insurance due to costs, you can now re-establish an employee benefits program at a price you control.

THREE REASONS INDIVIDUAL HEALTH INSURANCE IS BETTER FOR YOUR COMPANY

You should not switch to a defined contribution program for just the obvious financial reasons. In addition to saving thousands of dollars, all of your employees will also receive the numerous benefits of individual policies described throughout this book. Unlike your company plan in which the premium will rise significantly in the year following any major medical claims from employees, your employees' individual health insurance premiums cannot be increased due to an individual major illness or expensive claim. Also, your employees' individual plans cannot be canceled for as long as they pay the premium—even if they no longer work for your company. And finally, as we'll examine in a moment, if your employees qualify for a premium tax credit (the subsidy) because they earn less than $100,000 a year, their monthly after-subsidy premium cost can only increase with their income regardless what happens to medical costs (for more on premium tax credits, see Chapter 6).

With defined contribution, you reimburse employees on payroll for approved health insurance premiums. Your company's expense is controlled, and employees shop for policies that best meet their health and financial preferences.

There are three reasons individual health insurance is better for your company than traditional employer-provided health insurance:

1. Individual health insurance costs 20 to 60 percent less.
2. Individual health insurance policies provide greater value to employees.
3. Defined contribution programs provide greater value to your company.

1. Individual Health Insurance Costs 20 to 60 Percent Less

Individual health insurance plans cost 20 to 60 percent less than traditional employer-provided health insurance on average, and special discounts are now available for plans purchased in the Health Insurance Marketplaces. If your employees qualify, these discounts, called premium tax credits, allow your employees to buy individual plans at significantly reduced prices beyond the 20 to 60 percent savings. Depending on your company's contribution, many employees will get 100 percent of their out-of-pocket costs reimbursed by your company.

 Tip: Employees are only eligible for tax credits if your business does not offer employer-provided health insurance.

Figure 13.5 shows a state-by-state cost comparison of individual health insurance premiums compared to employer-provided health insurance premiums. Per the chart, in all states, individual health insurance costs are less expensive than employer-provided health insurance on average even before one takes into account premium tax credits.

Once you factor in premium tax credits, many employees may save 80 to 90 percent. (See Figure 13.6.) Eligibility for the tax credits is based on income and household size. Households with income up to 400 percent above the federal poverty line (FPL) are eligible—that is up to $46,680 for an individual and $95,400 for a family of four in 2014. See Chapter 6 for more information on premium tax credits.

State	Single		Family	
	Employer Premiums	Individual Premiums	Employer Premiums	Individual Premiums
United States average	$539	$254	$1,499	$759
Alabama	$497	$234	$1,236	$702
Alaska	$743	$408	$1,734	$1,220
Arizona	$521	$168	$1,477	$504
Arkansas	$447	$271	$1,288	$811
California	$543	$267	$1,540	$805
Colorado	$528	$252	$1,553	$755
Connecticut	$594	$244	$1,636	$729
Delaware	$559	$289	$1,511	$866
District of Columbia	$559	$294	$1,667	$983
Florida	$519	$212	$1,499	$635
Georgia	$517	$239	$1,419	$714
Hawaii	$509	$183	$1,426	$548
Idaho	$445	$231	$1,362	$691
Illinois	$541	$202	$1,526	$604
Indiana	$551	$274	$1,498	$819
Iowa	$515	$208	$1,386	$623
Kansas	$498	$203	$1,332	$608
Kentucky	$541	$274	$1,524	$821
Louisiana	$539	$282	$1,462	$845
Maine	$570	$295	$1,570	$883
Maryland	$531	$214	$1,476	$642
Massachusetts	$613	$349	$1,659	$1,073
Michigan	$537	$200	$1,395	$573
Minnesota	$535	$154	$1,493	$524
Mississippi	$472	$276	$1,373	$825
Missouri	$516	$238	$1,452	$717
Montana	$560	$245	$1,424	$735
Nebraska	$511	$219	$1,402	$655
Nevada	$496	$246	$1,250	$524
New Hampshire	$570	$289	$1,586	$866
New Jersey	$585	$318	$1,642	$951
New Mexico	$504	$218	$1,538	$653
New York	$604	$418	$1,639	$1,190

Figure 13.5   Cost Comparison of Employer-Provided Health Insurance versus Individual Health Insurance

State	Single		Family	
	Employer Premiums	Individual Premiums	Employer Premiums	Individual Premiums
North Carolina	$564	$269	$1,512	$805
North Dakota	$539	$271	$1,390	$812
Ohio	$509	$228	$1,497	$684
Oklahoma	$486	$191	$1,313	$573
Oregon	$547	$214	$1,500	$640
Pennsylvania	$539	$170	$1,489	$509
Rhode Island	$588	$293	$1,537	$878
South Carolina	$511	$230	$1,384	$689
South Dakota	$542	$258	$1,453	$772
Tennessee	$508	$180	$1,442	$539
Texas	$513	$188	$1,416	$562
Utah	$517	$207	$1,410	$635
Vermont	$559	$426	$1,462	$1,198
Virginia	$532	$250	$1,489	$749
Washington	$538	$300	$1,578	$897
West Virginia	$589	$248	$1,515	$743
Wisconsin	$575	$244	$1,574	$731
Wyoming	$587	$395	$1,511	$1,181

Figure 13.5 (Continued)

Household Income (2014)	Employer Premiums	Individual Premiums (after tax credits)	Percent Savings
$50,000	$1,540/month	$281/month	82%
$75,000	$1,540/month	$594/month	61%
$90,000	$1,540/month	$713/month	54%

Figure 13.6 Sample 2014 Rates for Employer-Provided Health Insurance versus Individual Health Insurance with Premium Tax Credits, for a Family of Four (Two Adults Age 40 with Two Children)

Source: Covered California 2014.

2. Individual Health Insurance Policies Provide Greater Value to Employees

Once educated, employees prefer individual health policies to employer-provided plans due to three key advantages: choice, portability, and guaranteed acceptance. (See Figure 13.7.)

1. **Choice.** With individual health insurance, your employees choose the coverage and doctors that best fit their families' needs. Purchasing individual health insurance is now simple—employees will only be asked a few additional financial questions to see if they qualify for a premium tax credit. Four standard levels of coverage, called metallic tiers, are used to categorize the individual health plans. Within each tier, employees choose their coverage by insurance company, doctor network, and coverage provided by the plan.
2. **Portability.** With individual health insurance, your employees keep their health insurance when they switch jobs. Individual health policies are permanent and portable, independent of their employment. This is

	Employer-Provided Health Insurance	Individual Health Insurance
Keep your plan when you switch jobs.	No	Yes
You choose the coverage and doctors.	No	Yes
Premium tax credits available.	No	Yes
Coverage for pre-existing medical conditions.	Yes	Yes
Coverage for essential health benefits.	Yes	Yes
Average cost (2014)		
Single	$6,472/year	$3,048/year
Family	$17,986/year	$9,108/year
How is the plan paid for?	Your employer purchases the plan. You reimburse your employer via your paycheck.	You purchase the plan. Your employer reimburses you via your paycheck.

Figure 13.7 Employer-Provided Health Insurance versus Individual Health Insurance

especially valuable if an employee or a family member has pre-existing medical conditions. Also, ex-employees will no longer need COBRA since they will have permanent and portable health insurance.

3. **Guaranteed acceptance.** All individual market insurance companies must make individual health plans available on a guaranteed-issue basis. This means your employees cannot be denied coverage due to a pre-existing condition, or even asked embarrassing questions about their health.

3. Defined Contribution Programs Provide Greater Value to Your Company

Your company is also much better off with defined contribution programs. With a defined contribution program, you and your business associates are able to: save money, concentrate on your business, control costs, and offer better benefits for employees.

Save money. Your company will save up to 60 percent per employee by switching to defined contribution healthcare and individual health insurance—that's up to $12,000 per employee per year. The cost of employee health benefits now exceeds profits for most companies and is increasing faster than profits. If you don't do something now, you are walking away from hundreds of thousands of dollars in annual savings.

Concentrate on your business. With a defined contribution program, your company can concentrate on your business and your customers instead of managing the complexities and spiraling costs of your health insurance plan. The true cost of employer-provided health insurance is the immeasurable productivity toll it takes on management. Save time and resources by redirecting the time and inhouse personnel you now devote to health insurance to improving your products and service to customers.

Control costs. With defined contribution, your company can increase or decrease the contribution amount over time depending on business needs. Your company can also create employee classes that offer benefits tailored to the company's objectives, transforming a health benefit plan into a tool to find and keep great employees. Providing different levels of benefits to different types of employees is at the core of benefits compensation and is routinely done by major corporations. With salary and other types of compensation, employers compensate groups of employees differently. Field sales people are compensated differently than sales managers. Some employees get company cars, while others earn quarterly bonuses.

Offer better benefits for employees. With defined contribution, employees have a clear budget to spend on health insurance. All employees (regardless of health conditions) are now able to purchase an individual health insurance policy that is better for them than traditional employer-provided health insurance options. Lastly, employees value health benefits that are easy to understand and easy to use. Similar to the transition from defined benefit pensions to 401(k) retirement plans, defined contribution requires employees to take more control of their health benefits. It costs a typical company the equivalent of six to nine months in salary each time they have to replace a salaried employee—that's $20,000 to $30,000 for a $40,000 manager in recruiting and training expenses, along with the potential lost revenue from customers. You can save up to $15,000 or more per replaced employee with a health benefits plan that helps you better recruit new employees and retain existing employees.

 Tip: Once educated, your employees will thank you for helping them get individual policies for the rest of their lives—especially those employees with unhealthy family members who previously lived in fear of losing their employer-provided health insurance.

HOW DEFINED CONTRIBUTION WORKS

The concept of defined contribution is already familiar to most of your employees: Over the past 30 years, company retirement programs have moved away from defined benefit pension plans, in which workers are paid a given amount of retirement income based on their former salary, toward defined contribution 401(k) plans, where employees are given back only what they and their employer have collectively contributed for retirement savings.

Here is a basic overview of how your defined contribution program will work once it is implemented. As shown in Figure 13.8, the concept is simple. With a defined contribution program, your company offers employees a monthly healthcare allowance to use on individual health insurance. Employees purchase their own health plan, and are reimbursed up to the defined contributions you have made available.

THREE WAYS TO OFFER DEFINED CONTRIBUTION HEALTHCARE

There are three main approaches to defined contribution healthcare your company can consider (see Figure 13.9):

1. A taxable monthly stipend.
2. A taxable reimbursement program.
3. A tax-free reimbursement plan.

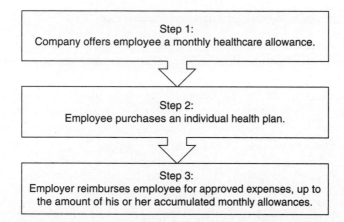

Figure 13.8 How Defined Contribution Works

	Stipend	Taxable Reimbursement	Tax-Free Reimbursement Plan
Expense deductible to business?	Yes	Yes	Yes
Payroll tax savings?	No	No	Yes
Tax-free to employee?	No	No	Yes
Company keeps unused contributions?	No	Yes	Yes
Classes allowed?	Yes	Yes	Yes
Administration software available?	Yes	Yes	Yes

Figure 13.9 Defined Contribution Program Options

1. A Taxable Stipend

With this approach, your company provides a taxable monthly stipend on employee paychecks. When offering a taxable stipend, employers will likely see the stipend as a health benefit, but your company has no way of ensuring employees use the dollars to purchase health insurance. As a result, some companies prefer to establish a formal reimbursement program that requires employees to purchase health insurance in order to receive the defined contribution.

2. A Taxable Reimbursement Program

With this approach, your company establishes a formal reimbursement program to reimburse employees for their substantiated individual health insurance costs on a post-tax basis—up to a healthcare allowance specified by the company. When offering a taxable reimbursement plan, your company ensures employees use the dollars on health insurance, and employees associate the arrangement with a health benefit. However, one limitation of this approach is the lack of tax advantage—employees are forced to pay taxes on the reimbursements they receive. It is no surprise that, given the choice, most employees would prefer their employers to establish a tax-free reimbursement plan.

3. Tax-Free Reimbursement Plan

With this approach, your company utilizes Section 105 of the Internal Revenue Code to establish a formal *self-insured medical reimbursement plan* to reimburse employees for their substantiated individual health insurance costs on a pretax basis. When providing tax-free reimbursement of individual health insurance policies, the company must ensure compliance with federal regulations, including but not limited to legal plan documents, summary plan descriptions, and the new market reforms required by the Affordable Care Act. Failing to comply with the applicable regulations could result in fines of up to $100 per day per employee if a failure is not corrected within 30 days once the failure is identified. In Chapter 3, we discussed how to design these arrangements to ensure compliance.

At Zane Benefits, many clients choose to set up a formal, tax-free reimbursement plan for the following reasons:

- **Control**. Reimbursement plans ensure employees use the money on health insurance. If employees do not purchase health insurance, they do not get your defined contribution.
- **Preferred employer tax treatment option**. Setting up a tax-free reimbursement plan will allow your company to save 7.65 percent in payroll taxes on your defined contributions.
- **Preferred employee tax treatment option**. Setting up a tax-free reimbursement plan will allow your employees to save 20 to 40 percent in state and federal income and payroll taxes.

 Tip: Regardless of which approach you decide to take, your company should utilize third-party administration software to ensure compliance. See Chapter 16 for help selecting a defined contribution vendor.

For simplicity, when we discuss defined contribution healthcare for the remainder of this book we will be referring to a reimbursement program. However, regardless of which approach you decide to take to help fund your employees' individual health insurance costs, the advantages to your company and your employees are virtually identical.

HOW MUCH WILL YOUR COMPANY SAVE WITH A DEFINED CONTRIBUTION PROGRAM?

The numbers used in this book are mostly national averages based on employees age 40. With health insurance, no one state, and no one employer-provided plan, is average—premiums vary among states and employee groups for the same coverage. Here's how to estimate how much you and your employees can save with a defined contribution healthcare program in your state.

Step 1: Calculate the Cost of Your Existing Employer-Provided Health Insurance Plan

First calculate the total cost of your existing employer-provided health benefits program—both the company-paid amount and the employee contribution amount. (See Figure 13.10 for a sample.) This will include your total employer-provided health insurance premium and administrative personnel costs.

Let's say that your company currently pays 100 percent of the annual cost for each employee, and 50 percent of the total additional cost for an employee to add their family to the plan. The total cost of your employer-provided plan is $1 million per year for 100 employees ($700,000 paid by your company and $300,000 paid by employees who have added their families to the plan).

Step 2: Estimate the Cost of a New Defined Contribution Program

Refer to Appendix A and locate sample health insurance premiums for individual policies in your state.

 Tip: The figures in Appendix A are for employees age 40 and families of four—premiums vary based on age, health, and family size. Visit the website for this book—www.healthinsurancerevolution.org—to get prices for individual health insurance based on the average age and family size of your employee group.

	Employee Contributions	Employer Contributions	Total Cost
100 employees	$0	$400,000	$400,000
60 families	$300,000	$300,000	$600,000
Total	**$300,000**	**$700,000**	**$1,000,000**

Figure 13.10 Sample Worksheet for Calculating the Annual Cost of Your Employer-Provided Health Insurance

Let's assume your employees live in Illinois where a typical employer-provided health insurance plan costs $18,312 per year ($1,526 per month) for a healthy family of four, and $6,492 per year ($541 per month) for a single employee (see Figures 13.11 and 13.12).

	Single	Family
Individual plan costs	$2,424/year	$7,248/year
Employer plan costs	$6,492/year	$18,312/year
Savings per employee	$4,068/year	$11,064/year
Percentage savings	62%	60%

Figure 13.11 Sample Worksheet for Estimating the Annual Cost Savings, per Employee, of a Defined Contribution Plan (Illinois)

	Employer-Provided Health Insurance		Defined Contribution Plan	
	Per Employee	Total	Per Employee	Total
40 single employees	$6,492	$259,680	$2,424	$96,960
60 families (incl. employee)	$18,312	$1,098,720	$7,248	$434,880
Total costs		**$1,358,400**		**$531,840**
Total employer plan cost (Employer pays 70%)		$950,880		$372,288
Annual savings with defined contribution plan				**$578,592**

Figure 13.12 Total Annual Cost Savings: Employer-Provided Health Insurance versus Defined Contribution Plan (Illinois)

As you can see, in Illinois, or virtually any other state, your company and your employees can save significant money and get better coverage by switching to a defined contribution plan.

These enormous savings on health benefits for each new employee are shared by your company and your existing employees. In the next chapter, we will walk you through how to conduct a detailed financial analysis for your company.

CLIENT CASE STUDY—51-PERSON DELIVERY AND LOGISTICS COMPANY

Problem: A courier company in Colorado was dependent on health benefits for recruiting and retaining its top employees, but had an employer-provided health insurance plan that exceeded their internal budgets. The company was in need of a health benefits solution that offered the same level of healthcare for employees while remaining within budget.

Solution: The company switched to a defined contribution program to give all full-time employees healthcare allowances of anywhere from $100 to $500 per month to spend on individual health insurance policies.

The company established three employee classes: management, dispatch, and drivers (see Figure 13.13). Employees in the management class were required to work a minimum of 40 hours per week, while the remaining classes were only required at least 30 hours per week; all three classes had a 90-day waiting period for new hires.

Employee Class Name	Eligibility Criteria	Waiting Period	Reimburse-ment Percentage	Monthly Healthcare Allowances			
				Single	Married	Single w/ Children	Married w/ Children
Management (3 of 51)	40+ Hours/ Week	90 Days	100%	$500	$500	$500	$500
Dispatch (3 of 51)	30+ Hours/ Week	90 Days	100%	$300	$300	$300	$300
Driver (45 of 51)	30+ Hours/ Week	90 Days	100%	$100	$100	$100	$100

Figure 13.13 Plan Design for Delivery and Logistics Company

(continued)

CLIENT CASE STUDY—51-PERSON DELIVERY AND LOGISTICS COMPANY (*Continued*)

Results: By setting up a defined contribution solution, the company was able to limit its health benefits liability to $1,200 to $6,000 per employee per year, depending on the employee class. In 2014, the company is projected to save $21,408 per month compared with projected 2014 employer-provided health insurance rates in Colorado—that's $256,896 (or 80%) in annual savings (see Figure 13.14).

Employer-provided health insurance cost (monthly coverage for 100% of premiums for 51 individuals in Colorado)	$26,928
Defined contribution program cost (monthly, 80% utilization)	$5,520
Monthly savings with defined contribution	**$21,408**
Annual savings	**$256,896**
Savings percent	**80%**

Figure 13.14 Cost Analysis for Delivery and Logistics Company

WHAT YOU LEARNED

- With a defined contribution program, your company offers employees a monthly healthcare allowance to use on individual health insurance. Employees purchase their own health plan, and are reimbursed up to the defined contributions you have made available.
- Due to the advantages of the improved individual health insurance market, your company should now terminate employer-provided health insurance in favor of defined contribution healthcare and individual health insurance.
- Transitioning to defined contribution healthcare and individual health insurance will allow your company to save up to $12,000 per employee per year.

- There are three main approaches to defined contribution healthcare your company can consider:
  1. A taxable monthly stipend.
  2. A taxable reimbursement program.
  3. A tax-free reimbursement plan.
- Regardless of the defined contribution approach you decide to take, your company should utilize third-party administration software to ensure compliance.

Chapter 14

HOW TO CONDUCT A DEFINED CONTRIBUTION FINANCIAL ANALYSIS

The cost of a defined contribution program is entirely in your company's control, and depends on two factors:

1. The total amount of allowances you are giving employees on a monthly (or annual) basis.
2. The total amount of shared responsibility payments you are required to pay on a monthly (or annual) basis if you have more than 50 full-time employees, starting in 2015 or 2016.

Before you switch to defined contribution healthcare, you should ensure it is the best financial decision for your company. (See Figure 14.1.) In this chapter, we will walk through how to conduct a defined contribution financial analysis.

 Tip: The implementation of the employer shared responsibility payments has been delayed twice while writing this book—so check out government websites or www.healthinsurancerevolution.org for the latest information before conducting your analysis. Currently, it is delayed until 2015 for employers with 100 or more employees and to 2016 for employers with between 50 and 99 employees.

---

1. Save employees and employers a combined 50% on health insurance costs.
2. Allow employees a full choice of health insurance plans.
3. Provide employees with better, more flexible health insurance options.

Figure 14.1   Three Reasons to Switch to Defined Contribution

CONDUCTING A FINANCIAL ANALYSIS—SIX STEPS

The following six steps will help you conduct a defined contribution financial analysis for your company.

1. Collect employee census information.
2. Gather estimated individual health insurance costs for each employee.
3. Estimate premium tax credits for each employee.
4. Collect group health insurance costs for each employee.
5. Estimate shared responsibility payments for the company if applicable.
6. Analyze the results.

We will use the census template in Figure 14.2 to organize the analysis. We recommend working through these steps with the health benefits decision-makers at your company.

Tip: A defined contribution solution provider, such as Zane Benefits (www.zanebenefits.com), will complete this cost analysis for you free of charge.

1. Collect Employee Census Information

First, you will use an employee census to obtain specific information about your employees. Throughout the next steps, we will use this census to compare the

Name	Age	Zip	Family Size	Household Income

Figure 14.2   Employee Census Sample

costs of a defined contribution program with the costs of traditional employer-provided coverage. The census form you use should include the following fields:

- Name
- Age
- Residential zip code
- Family size
- Projected annual household income

The census should not include discriminatory factors such as health status, race, or religion. See Figure 14.2 for a blank employee census.

 To download an electronic version of this census, go to www.health insurancerevolution.org/tools.

For example, as shown in Figure 14.3, ABC Manufacturing is a company based in San Diego, California with nine employees—four single employees and five employees with families of four.

2. Gather Estimated Individual Health Insurance Costs for Each Employee

Once you have collected the census information, you will use the information to estimate the costs for each individual health plan. Defined contribution

Name	Age	Zip	Family Size	Household Income
John Smith	27	92109	1	$25,000
Jennifer Wong	31	92037	1	$32,000
Scott Johnson	22	92117	1	$27,000
Wendy Stewart	40	92109	1	$27,000
Jason Hansen	26	92109	4	$40,000
Sylvia Nguyen	38	92037	4	$65,000
Lisa Jordon	51	92117	4	$80,000
Edward Kane	53	92140	4	$70,000
Karen Meyer	43	92037	4	$50,000

Figure 14.3 Sample Employee Census for a Nine-Person Company, ABC Manufacturing

solution providers, such as Zane Benefits (www.zanebenefits.com), will provide you with tools that automatically estimate the individual health insurance costs for each employee. If you are doing this on your own, you can either (1) use Appendix A in the back of this book to gather estimates or (2) use the tool we have created at www.healthinsurancerevolution.org/tools to automatically gather the quotes for you. We recommend using the premium for the second lowest-cost Silver plan available in the employee's state Health Insurance Marketplace—this will make estimating premium tax credits for each employee easier.

 Tip: We have created a calculator at www.healthinsurancerevolution .org/tools that will automatically estimate your employees' individual health insurance costs.

Continuing our earlier example, Figure 14.4 provides an example of estimated individual health insurance premiums for ABC Manufacturing's employees. The estimated monthly individual insurance premiums range from $256 to $1,218 per month before subsidies. For example, John Smith, who is single and 27 years old, has an estimated monthly premium of $256, while Edward Kane, who is 53 years old and has a family of four, has an estimated monthly premium of $981.

Name	Age	Zip	Family Size	Household Income	Individual Premium (monthly)
John Smith	27	92109	1	$25,000	$256
Jennifer Wong	31	92037	1	$32,000	$283
Scott Johnson	22	92117	1	$27,000	$244
Wendy Stewart	40	92109	1	$27,000	$312
Jason Hansen	26	92109	4	$40,000	$499
Sylvia Nguyen	38	92037	4	$65,000	$690
Lisa Jordon	51	92117	4	$80,000	$1,218
Edward Kane	53	92140	4	$70,000	$981
Karen Meyer	43	92037	4	$50,000	$661

Note: Individual premiums are based on the second lowest-cost Silver plan available (Covered California 2014).

Figure 14.4 Sample Employee Census with Estimated Individual Health Insurance Premiums

3. Estimate Premium Tax Credits for Each Employee

Depending on each employee's household size and income, some employees may be eligible for new federal subsidies—called premium tax credits—that cap the cost of health insurance as a percentage of the employee's household income (see Chapter 6 for more on premium tax credits). These tax credits will only be available for individual plans purchased through your state's Health Insurance Marketplace (see Chapter 8 for more on Health Insurance Marketplaces). To estimate the premium tax credits employees are eligible for, we recommend using a premium tax credit calculator like the one at www.healthinsurancerevolution .org/tools. Remember, your employees are only eligible for premium tax credits if you do not offer employer-provided health insurance.

 Tip: Your employees are only eligible for premium tax credits if you do not offer employer-provided health insurance.

In Figure 14.5, we have added estimated premium tax credits to our analysis for ABC Manufacturing employees. As you can see, John Smith will only pay $145 a month for health insurance after the premium tax credit is applied and Edward Kane will only pay $228 a month for his family of four after the premium tax credit is applied.

4. Collect Group Health Insurance Costs for Each Employee

Now, it is time to add the cost for employer-provided health insurance. If you have an existing employer-provided health insurance plan, use those rates. If you

Name	Age	Zip	Family Size	Household Income	Individual Premium	Premium Tax Credit	Adjusted Monthly Cost
John Smith	27	92109	1	$25,000	$256	$111	$145
Jennifer Wong	31	92037	1	$32,000	$283	$46	$237
Scott Johnson	22	92117	1	$27,000	$244	$74	$170
Wendy Stewart	40	92109	1	$27,000	$312	$142	$170
Jason Hansen	26	92109	4	$40,000	$499	$335	$164
Sylvia Nguyen	38	92037	4	$65,000	$690	$439	$251
Lisa Jordon	51	92117	4	$80,000	$1,218	$584	$634
Edward Kane	53	92140	4	$70,000	$981	$753	$228
Karen Meyer	43	92037	4	$50,000	$661	$380	$281

Figure 14.5 Sample Employee Census Chart with Estimated Premium Tax Credits

do not have an existing employer-provided health insurance plan, you can use the average employer-provided health insurance rates for your state. Defined contribution solution providers will provide you with tools that automatically estimate your employer-provided health insurance costs for each employee. If you are doing this on your own, you can either (1) use Appendix A in the back of this book to gather estimates or (2) use the tool we have created at www.healthinsurancerevolution.org/tools to automatically gather the rates for you.

 Tip: We have created a calculator at healthinsurancerevolution.org/tools that will automatically estimate your company's employer-provided health insurance costs.

Continuing our example, Figure 14.6 presents the employer-provided health insurance rates for ABC Manufacturing's employees. The cost of ABC Manufacturing's current employer-provided health insurance plan is $543 per month for single employees and $1,540 per month for employees with families. As you can see, John Smith is projected to save $398 per month ($543 minus $145) and Edward Kane is projected to save $1,312 ($1,540 minus $228).

5. Estimate Employer Shared Responsibility Payments for Company If Applicable

The Affordable Care Act includes an employer mandate for large employers (defined as companies with greater than 50 full-time equivalent employees or

Name	Age	Zip	Family Size	Household Income	Adjusted Individual Cost	Employer-Provided Cost
John Smith	27	92109	1	$25,000	$145	$543
Jennifer Wong	31	92037	1	$32,000	$237	$543
Scott Johnson	22	92117	1	$27,000	$170	$543
Wendy Stewart	40	92109	1	$27,000	$170	$543
Jason Hansen	26	92109	4	$40,000	$164	$1,540
Sylvia Nguyen	38	92037	4	$65,000	$251	$1,540
Lisa Jordon	51	92117	4	$80,000	$634	$1,540
Edward Kane	53	92140	4	$70,000	$228	$1,540
Karen Meyer	43	92037	4	$50,000	$281	$1,540

Figure 14.6 Employee Census with Average Employer-Provided Costs

FTEs) to either offer employer-provided health insurance or else make annual *employer shared responsibility payments*. Originally, the employer mandate and shared responsibility payments were scheduled to take effect January 1, 2014. However, in July 2013, the Administration announced the employer mandate would be delayed until 2015. See Appendix B for a guide that will help your company calculate its shared responsibility payments. If you are unsure whether the employer mandate applies to your company, check with your CPA. As a general rule, if you have less than 50 employees, you are not subject to the employer mandate. Since ABC Manufacturing only has nine employees, ABC Manufacturing is not subject to the mandate, and will not be required to make shared responsibility payments.

 If you have less than 50 employees, you are not subject to the employer mandate. If you have 50 or more employees, you may be subject to the employer mandate.

---

6. Analyze the Results

Now that you have collected all the information you need, it's time to analyze the results. If the total cost of your individual health insurance costs (plus any tax penalties from step 5) is equal to or less than the total cost of employer-provided health insurance, the switch to employer-funded individual health insurance is a no-brainer for your company.

Name	Age	Zip	Family Size	Household Income	Adjusted Individual Cost	Employer-Provided Cost	Monthly Savings
John Smith	27	92109	1	$25,000	$145	$543	$398
Jennifer Wong	31	92037	1	$32,000	$237	$543	$306
Scott Johnson	22	92117	1	$27,000	$170	$543	$373
Wendy Stewart	40	92109	1	$27,000	$170	$543	$373
Jason Hansen	26	92109	4	$40,000	$164	$1,540	$1,376
Sylvia Nguyen	38	92037	4	$65,000	$251	$1,540	$1,289
Lisa Jordon	51	92117	4	$80,000	$634	$1,540	$906
Edward Kane	53	92140	4	$70,000	$228	$1,540	$1,312
Karen Meyer	43	92037	4	$50,000	$281	$1,540	$1,259
TOTAL					$2,280	$9,872	$7,592 (77%)

Figure 14.7 Example—ABC Manufacturing Cost Analysis for Individual Health Insurance versus Employer-Provided Health Insurance

Employer-provided health insurance	$9,872
Individual health insurance	$2,280
Shared responsibility payments (<u>Only</u> for employers with 50+ full-time equivalent employees)	$0
Monthly savings	**$7,592**
Annual savings	**$91,104**
Savings percentage	**77%**

Figure 14.8 Cost Analysis Summary for ABC Manufacturing

Let's analyze our ABC Manufacturing example. See Figure 14.7 for a completed census. Please note that some columns have been removed for simplicity.

As you can see, ABC manufacturing employees will save from $306 per month (Jennifer Wong) to $1,376 per month (Jason Hansen) by switching to individual health insurance plans. When we compare the total cost of the employer-provided plan ($9,872) to the total cost of individual health plans ($2,280), the savings total $7,592 per month—that's $91,104 per year or 77 percent in hard-dollar savings. See Figure 14.8 for a summary.

CLIENT CASE STUDY—FIVE-PERSON HEALTHCARE RECRUITMENT FIRM

Problem: A national healthcare recruitment firm based in Texas was facing obstacles obtaining competitive healthcare benefits that remained within their annual budget. As head of a healthcare recruitment firm, the business owner understood how vital benefits were for employee recruitment and retention.

Solution: The firm implemented a defined contribution program to give all employees, full-time and part-time, monthly healthcare allowances ranging from $100 to $150 to spend on individual health insurance policies.

The company established two classes, called *full-time employees* and *part-time employees*, both of which required a 90-day waiting period for new hires. Full-time employees were required to work a minimum of 40 hours

(continued)

CLIENT CASE STUDY—FIVE-PERSON HEALTHCARE RECRUITMENT FIRM (*Continued*)

a week, while part-time employees were required to work a minimum of 15 hours a week. (See Figure 14.9.)

Results: By implementing a defined contribution program, the firm limited its health benefits to $1,200 to $1,800 per employee per year depending on the employee class. In 2014, the company is projected to save $2,085 per month compared to the projected 2014 employer-provided health insurance rates in Texas—that's $25,020 (or 81 percent) in annual savings. (See Figure 14.10.)

Employee Class Name	Eligibility Criteria	Waiting Period	Reimbursement Percentage	Monthly Healthcare Allowances			
				Single	Married	Single w/ Children	Married w/ Children
Full-time employees (2 of 5)	40 hours/ week	90 days	100%	$150	$150	$150	$150
Part-time employees (3 of 5)	15 hours/ week	90 days	100%	$100	$100	$100	$100

Figure 14.9   Plan Design for Five-Person Healthcare Recruitment Firm

Employer-provided health insurance cost (monthly) (monthly coverage for 100% of premiums for five individuals in Texas)	$2,565
Defined contribution program cost (monthly, 80% utilization)	$480
Monthly savings with defined contribution	**$2,085**
Annual savings	**$25,020**
Savings percentage	**81%**

Figure 14.10   Cost Analysis for Five-Person Healthcare Recruitment Firm

WHAT YOU LEARNED

- The cost of a defined contribution program is entirely in your company's control, and depends on two factors:
  1. The total amount of allowances you are giving employees on a monthly (or annual basis).
  2. If you have more than 50 full-time employees, the total amount of shared responsibility payments you are required to pay on a monthly (or annual basis), starting in 2015 or 2016.
- Before you switch to defined contribution healthcare, you should ensure it is the best financial decision for your company.
- The implementation of the employer mandate has been delayed twice while writing this book. Check government websites or www.health insurancerevolution.org for the latest information before conducting your analysis.
- For a defined contribution financial analysis, we recommend using the premium for the second lowest-cost Silver plan available in the employee's state Health Insurance Marketplace—this will make estimating premium tax credits for each employee easier.
- To estimate the premium tax credits employees are eligible for, we recommend using a premium tax credit calculator like the one at www .healthinsurancerevolution.org/tools.
- If you do not have an existing employer-provided health insurance plan, you can use the average employer-provided health insurance rates for your state.

Chapter 15

HOW TO IMPLEMENT A DEFINED CONTRIBUTION SOLUTION

Once you have conducted the in-depth financial analysis described in Chapter 14, you have all the information you need to implement a defined contribution solution. Keep in mind you want to utilize a defined contribution solution provider to help you implement your company's program and administer it on an ongoing basis. For help selecting a defined contribution provider, see Chapter 16. In this chapter, we will walk you through how to plan for and implement a defined contribution solution.

IS YOUR COMPANY READY FOR DEFINED CONTRIBUTION?

Regardless of your company's current health benefits offering, you should answer the following general questions before proceeding with a defined contribution solution. If you answer yes to these questions, then defined contribution is a terrific fit for your company.

- **Does your company have one or more employee(s)?** Defined contribution healthcare works for companies of any size. However, if you do not have any employees, defined contribution may not work for your company.
- **Do you have a budget to spend on employee healthcare?** You must have money available to spend on employee healthcare. If you are unwilling or unable to set aside money each month, defined contribution will not work for your company.

- **Are you looking to grow your company size or retain your existing staff?** The primary purpose of a defined contribution program is to recruit and retain staff. If you are looking to grow or maintain your existing staff, defined contribution is a terrific solution for your company. If not, why offer health benefits in the first place?

IMPLEMENTING A DEFINED CONTRIBUTION SOLUTION IN SIX STEPS

Follow these six steps to implement a defined contribution program for your company. We recommend working through these steps with the health benefits decision-makers at your company. We will use the planning worksheet in Figure 15.1 to organize the program details.

1. Pick a start date.
2. Set a cancelation date.
3. Decide who is eligible.

Start Date: _____	Cancelation Date: _____						
				Monthly Healthcare Allowances			
Employee Class Name	Eligibility Criteria	Waiting Period	Reimbursement %	Single	Married	Single w/ Children	Married w/ Children

- **Start Date:** When would you like the plan to start? This is your plan effective date.
- **Cancelation Date:** What date will you cancel your existing coverage?
- **Employee Classes:** Who will you offer the defined contribution program to? You can offer the benefit to all employees, or by class of employee. Classes need to be based on bona-fide job criteria such as job description, hours worked weekly, location, etc. You can offer different monthly amounts by class of employee.
- **Waiting Period:** How many days will the waiting period be? The maximum is 90 days. Waiting periods can vary by employee class.
- **Reimbursement Percentage:** What percentage of employees' approved expenses would you like to reimburse (up to the amount of employees' allowance)?
- **Monthly Healthcare Allowances:** How much would you like to allocate monthly, by class and family status (single, married, single with children, married with children)?

Figure 15.1 Defined Contribution Implementation Planning Worksheet

4. Allocate allowances.
5. Communicate your new program to employees.
6. Help employees buy individual health insurance.

 Tip: Work through these questions with the health benefits decision-makers at your company. To download a detailed worksheet, visit www.healthinsurancerevolution.org/tools.

---

1. PICK A START DATE

The first step is to pick a start date or plan effective date. This will be the date your new defined contribution program will begin. If you do not currently have an employer-provided health insurance plan in place, you should start your defined contribution program immediately. However, if you have an existing employer-provided health insurance plan that needs to be canceled, we recommend delaying the start date of your defined contribution program 30 to 60 days—this will give employees ample time to purchase new individual coverage.

For example, ABC Company learned about defined contribution on May 15th. Since ABC Company has an existing employer-provided health insurance plan, it picks a start date of July 1st for its defined contribution program (see Figure 15.2). This gives employees 45 days to purchase individual coverage.

2. SET A CANCELATION DATE

If you have an existing employer-provided health insurance plan, you will also need to set a *cancelation date* for existing coverage. We recommend setting a cancelation date equal to the day before your defined contribution *start date*. This will make it easy for employees to avoid a gap in coverage when they purchase their new individual health plans.

Start Date: July 1st	Cancelation Date: _____						
				Monthly Healthcare Allowances			
Employee Class Name	Eligibility Criteria	Waiting Period	Reimbursement %	Single	Married	Single w/ Children	Married w/ Children

Figure 15.2 Example Defined Contribution Implementation Planning Worksheet for ABC Company

Most employer-provided health insurance plans are unilateral contracts. This means you can cancel the policy at any time during the year. While some carriers request 30 days' notice, this is not always required—call a customer representative with the insurance company to confirm the exact steps required to cancel. Your health insurance broker can assist you; however, your business will be required to notify the insurance company directly. When you inform your existing health insurance broker of your intentions to cancel coverage, be prepared for the broker to be negative about defined contribution. Remember, your existing broker will no longer receive a commission on your canceled employer-provided health insurance plan. If you have hundreds of employees, this could mean a loss of tens of thousands of dollars in commissions—it's no wonder your current health insurance broker does not want you to know about defined contribution health benefits.

Tip: When you inform your existing health insurance broker of your intentions to cancel coverage, be prepared for the broker to be negative about defined contribution.

When you cancel your employer-provided plan, all employees who lose coverage will become eligible to purchase individual health insurance via a special enrollment period equal to 60 days—you are triggering a qualifying event which makes covered employees eligible to purchase new individual coverage. See Chapter 7 for more information on special enrollment periods.

Tip: Canceling your existing health insurance policy is surprisingly easy. Most health insurance policies are unilateral contracts, which means you can cancel your policy at any time with little or no notice.

For example, ABC Company is starting its defined contribution program on July 1st. Since ABC Company had an existing employer-provided health insurance plan, it set a cancelation date for June 30th (see Figure 15.3).

3. DECIDE WHO IS ELIGIBLE

With a defined contribution program, your company controls who is eligible for health benefits and who is not. Recruiting and retaining great employees is important to every company—from major global corporations to the smallest of

Start Date: July 1st		Cancelation Date: June 30th						
				Monthly Healthcare Allowances				
Employee Class Name	Eligibility Criteria	Waiting Period	Reimburse-ment %	Single	Married	Single w/ Children	Married w/ Children

Figure 15.3 Example Defined Contribution Implementation Planning Worksheet for ABC Company

businesses. Getting the best employees requires you to give them great compensation, and your health benefit plan is a key part of the compensation you offer. With salary and other types of compensation, employers routinely compensate groups of employees differently. Field sales people are compensated differently than sales managers. Some employees get company cars, while others earn quarterly bonuses. Because health benefits are such an important part of compensation, why not provide benefits that vary by class of employee?

With defined contribution, your company can create job-based employee classes that offer benefits tailored to your company's business objectives, transforming your health benefit program into a tool to find and keep great people. Job-based employee classes allow you to: (1) offer a defined contribution to some classes of employees and not to others, and (2) vary the monthly healthcare allowances between employee classes. In order to comply with federal regulations, the classes must be based on bona-fide business criteria and you must treat all employees within a class equally.

To illustrate how classes work, consider an electrical contracting company that struggles to hire and keep journeymen electricians in a very tight labor market. Instead of offering the same health plan to all employees, the company creates separate classes for apprentices and journeymen and gives journeymen $350 more per month to spend on health insurance. This large increase helps the company reduce attrition among journeymen. Plus, it creates a visible incentive for apprentices to complete the education required to become journeymen.

Federal regulations state that your company may treat employees as two or more distinct groups (or classes) of similarly situated individuals if the distinction between or among the employee classes is based on bona-fide employment-based criteria consistent with your company's usual business practices. To comply with these regulations, employee classes must:

- **Be based on bona-fide business differences**. These may include job categories, geographic location, part-time or full-time status, date of hire, and so on.

- **Treat all "similarly situated" employees equally.** By creating classes based on genuine job categories, all employees within a class will be "similarly situated."
- **Not discriminate against unhealthy people.** Your company cannot provide inferior benefits to specific individuals with adverse health conditions.

Waiting Periods and Minimum Hours Worked Requirements

Once you have determined your employee classes, you can further customize the eligibility requirements within each class by setting a waiting period for new hires and a minimum hours worked requirement.

The *waiting period* for new hires is the period of time that must pass before a new employee is eligible to participate in the defined contribution program. For each employee class, you will need to set a waiting period for new hires. You have four choices for your waiting period: 0 days, 30 days, 60 days, or 90 days. If you select a waiting period of 0 days, new hires will immediately become eligible for the defined contribution program on their start date. Alternatively, if you select a waiting period of 90 days, new hires will not become eligible for the defined contribution program until 90 days after their start date. Due to new rules under the Affordable Care Act, you may not establish a waiting period longer than 90 days.

 Tip: Unlike an employer-provided health insurance plan where some employees are denied coverage, ineligible employees—like those outside the waiting period—can still get individual health insurance coverage; they just may not get reimbursed for the cost.

The *minimum hours worked* requirement is the number of hours an employee must work per week on average in order to be eligible for the benefit. Typically, companies set the minimum hours worked requirement equal to 30 or 40 hours per week. However, you may want to reduce the hours worked requirement to incorporate benefits for employees who work part-time.

If an employee meets the job criteria for an employee class and satisfies the waiting period and hours worked requirements, then he or she is eligible to receive the defined contribution—or monthly healthcare allowance—associated with that class of employees.

For example, ABC Company has created two employee classes with varying waiting periods and hours worked per week requirements, as shown in Figure 15.4. Based on these eligibility requirements, all sales employees who work 40 or more hours per week and who have been employed for more than

Plan Start Date: July 1st			Cancelation Date: June 30th					
					Monthly Healthcare Allowances			
Employee Class Name	Eligibility Criteria	Waiting Period	Reim- burse- ment %	Single	Married	Single w/ Children	Married w/ Children
Sales employees	Sales, 40+ hours/week	30 days						
Service employees	Service, 30+ hours/week	90 days						

Figure 15.4 Example Defined Contribution Implementation Planning Worksheet for ABC Company

30 days are eligible for the Sales Employees class. Similarly, all service employees who work 30 or more hours per week and who have been employed for more than 90 days are eligible for the Service Employees class.

4. ALLOCATE ALLOWANCES

In this step, you will set a *monthly healthcare allowance* for each employee class. The monthly healthcare allowance is the amount eligible employees will receive each month to reimburse their individual health insurance costs. Within each employee class, you can customize the monthly healthcare allowance based on an employee's *family status* within the following categories:

- Single
- Married
- Single with children
- Married with children

 Tip: You can find a worksheet and our advanced calculator to design your defined contribution program and calculate your costs and savings at www.healthinsurancerevolution.org/tools.

With defined contribution, your company is in full control of costs. There are no minimum or maximum contribution requirements—the budget is up to you. When setting your monthly healthcare allowances, it is a best practice to calculate the allowances as a percentage of projected annual salary for a class of employees; while not required, this approach will make it easy to forecast and manage your healthcare costs as a function of company salaries. The strategy for setting this percentage depends on your company's financial goals.

The best place to start is to set an annual or monthly budget for your program. For illustration and analysis purposes, this section assumes that you are currently contributing $7,200 per year ($600 per month) per employee on average to your existing employer-provided health insurance.

Strategy 1: Ensure Company Savings

Some companies' employer-provided health insurance costs are currently so high that those costs threaten their very survival. Companies in this situation have to keep some of the savings from a defined contribution plan in order to stay in business. In this scenario, using our example, your company might set an annual budget per employee equal to $3,600 per year ($300 per month) per employee, guaranteeing an immediate 50 percent savings to the company.

Strategy 2: Pass the Savings to Employees

Many companies are so pleased to get rid of their employer-provided health insurance plan that they do not want to keep a dime of the savings—they give 100 percent of the former cost to their employees in new contributions towards individual health insurance premiums. In this scenario, using our example, your company would set an annual budget per employee equal to $7,200 per year ($600 per month). Many employees may be elated that you are giving them so much money to spend directly on their own healthcare because they likely had no idea how much you were spending on your employer-provided health plan.

Strategy 3: Customize the Program to Ensure Employee Happiness

The third option requires more analysis, but accomplishes two goals simultaneously—it maximizes the company's savings while ensuring employees are left in an equal or better financial situation. With this strategy, using our example, your company would estimate individual health insurance costs for each employee, and structure the monthly healthcare allowances to ensure every employee is the same or better off. As discussed in Chapter 16, your defined contribution solution provider can help you design the perfect program.

For example, ABC Company has created two employee classes with varying allowance amounts for each family status. According to Figure 15.5, all sales employees who are eligible for the Sales Employees class will receive a defined contribution ranging from $300 to $400 per month depending on their family statuses. Similarly, all service employees who are eligible for the Service Employees class will receive a defined contribution ranging from $200 to $250 per month.

Start Date: July 1st				Cancelation Date: June 30th			
				Monthly Healthcare Allowances			
Employee Class Name	Eligibility Criteria	Waiting Period	Reim- burse- ment %	Single	Married	Single w/ Children	Married w/ Children
Sales employees	Sales, 40+ hours/week	30 days	100%	$300	$350	$400	$400
Service employees	Service, 30+ hours/week	90 days	100%	$200	$225	$250	$250

Figure 15.5   Example Defined Contribution Implementation Worksheet for ABC Company

With a Defined Contribution Solution, Your Company Keeps What Your Employees Do Not Use

Remember, if you are utilizing a reimbursement plan for your defined contribution program, your company only incurs an expense if employees use the money to purchase health insurance coverage. As a result, the real annual cost of your defined contribution program will depend on how much of the money your employees actually use during the year. For example, if your company is making available $100,000 in healthcare allowances per year and only 80 percent of the allowances are utilized, your company's annual cost will only be $80,000—your company will keep the $20,000 that was not used.

One way to encourage employee consumerism, while also reducing your company's cost, is to add a *reimbursement percentage* restriction to the defined contribution program. By default, your company will reimburse 100 percent of employees' out-of-pocket insurance expenses up to the monthly healthcare allowance they are receiving. However, if you modify the reimbursement percentage to, for example, 50 percent, your company will only be required to reimburse 50 percent of employees' approved reimbursement requests up to the monthly healthcare allowances they are receiving. Taking this approach can drastically decrease the annual cost of your defined contribution program. In our example in Figure 15.5, ABC Company has decided to leave the reimbursement percentage at 100 percent.

5. COMMUNICATE YOUR NEW PROGRAM TO EMPLOYEES

Employees are happiest when they understand the what, how, when, and why of your health benefits program. Specifically, you need to educate employees on the following:

- What is defined contribution and what is individual health insurance?
- How does defined contribution work and how do employees purchase individual health insurance?
- When will the existing plan be canceled and when will the new defined contribution program start?
- Why is the company making this change?

In Chapter 17, we provide you with several example templates to help you effectively communicate these items to your employees.

6. HELP EMPLOYEES BUY INDIVIDUAL HEALTH INSURANCE

Applying for individual health insurance has never been easier. However, for some employees this is a new experience. As a result, we recommend providing employees with resources and services to help them research, apply for, and purchase new individual health insurance plans. This service will also be helpful for new employees you hire in the future. And, it sends a message to every employee that your company cares about its employees' healthcare.

CLIENT CASE STUDY—13-PERSON DENTAL OFFICE

Problem: A dental office in Texas wanted to provide health benefits that were affordable and offered quality coverage without a high deductible. However, the practice was unable to find an employer-provided health insurance plan that was affordable to the practice and employees.

Solution: The practice switched to a defined contribution program that gave employees more choice by selecting their own insurance plans tailored to their personal healthcare needs (see Figure 15.6).

The practice allocated employees monthly healthcare allowances of $50 to $100 per month to spend on individual health insurance. The practice established three employee classes, including Dental Assistant, Dental Hygienist, and Administrative. All three classes required the employee to work at least 32 hours a week and included a 30- to 60-day waiting period for new hires, depending on the employee class.

Results: By implementing a defined contribution program, the practice was able to limit its health benefits liability to anywhere from $600 to

(*continued*)

CLIENT CASE STUDY—13-PERSON DENTAL OFFICE (*Continued*)

$1,200 per employee per year, depending on the employee class. In 2014, the practice is projected to save $5,849 per month or $70,188 per year in comparison with projected 2014 employer-provided health insurance rates in Texas—a savings of 88 percent. (See Figure 15.7.)

Employee Class Name	Eligibility Criteria	Waiting Period	Reim-bursement Percentage	Monthly Healthcare Allowances			
				Single	Married	Single w/ Children	Married w/ Children
Dental Assistant (1 of 13)	32+ hours/ week	60 days	100%	$50	$50	$50	$50
Dental Hygienist (9 of 13)	32+ hours/ week	30 days	100%	$75	$75	$75	$75
Administrative (3 of 13)	32+ hours/ week	30 days	100%	$100	$100	$100	$100

Figure 15.6 Plan Design for 13-Person Dental Office

Employer-provided health insurance cost (monthly coverage for 100% of premiums for 13 individuals in Texas)	$6,669
Defined contribution program cost (monthly, 80% utilization)	$820
Monthly savings with defined contribution	$5,849
Annual savings	$70,188
Savings percentage	88%

Figure 15.7 Cost Analysis for 13-Person Dental Office

WHAT YOU LEARNED

- The first step is to pick a start date or plan effective date. This will be the date your new defined contribution program will begin.
- If you have an existing employer-provided health insurance plan, you will also need to set a cancelation date for existing coverage.
- When you cancel your employer-provided plan, all employees who lose coverage will become eligible to purchase individual health insurance via a special enrollment period equal to 60 days—you are triggering a qualifying event that makes covered employees eligible to purchase new individual coverage.
- With defined contribution, your company can create job-based employee classes that offer benefits tailored to your company's business objectives, transforming your health benefit program into a tool to find and keep great people.
- Once you have determined your employee classes, you can further customize the eligibility requirements within each class by setting a waiting period for new hires and a minimum hours worked requirement.
- Within each employee class, you can customize the monthly healthcare allowance based on an employee's family status.
- With defined contribution, your company is in full control of costs. There are no minimum or maximum contribution requirements—the budget is up to you.
- If you are utilizing a reimbursement plan for your defined contribution program, the real annual cost of your defined contribution program will depend on how much of the money your employees actually use during the year.

Chapter 16

HOW TO CHOOSE A DEFINED CONTRIBUTION SOLUTION PROVIDER

Y our company should utilize a third-party solution provider to help implement and administer the defined contribution program. The right provider will allow your company to administer your defined contribution programs online, easily add reimbursements (or stipends) to payroll, and change plan rules and documents at any time. Most importantly, your defined contribution solution provider will also help ensure your company stays in compliance by keeping your solution up to date with all current statutes and regulations including but not limited to Internal Revenue Service (IRS), Health Insurance Portability and Accountability Act (HIPAA), and Employee Retirement Income Security Act (ERISA) rules. This chapter will guide you through the process of choosing a defined contribution solution provider.

 Tip: You should establish a formal defined contribution program to ensure compliance, save time, and create a powerful recruiting and retention tool.

BEST PRACTICES FOR DEFINED CONTRIBUTION HEALTHCARE

Establish a Formal Defined Contribution Program

The first best practice is to set up a formal defined contribution program. This will establish a tangible health benefits program your company can use as a marketing tool for recruiting and retention purposes. Additionally, a defined contribution solution provider can help employees navigate the individual health insurance market via an add-on service, such as a health insurance concierge program. Some companies consider setting up healthcare allowances without a formal defined contribution program—this devalues the benefit and does not give your company a formal program to market to current and prospective employees. Also, in order to ensure compliance, your company should never reimburse an employee for his or her insurance premiums on a pretax basis without setting up legal plan documents—failing to do so will put your company out of compliance with IRS rules. You do not need to spend thousands or more for a lawyer to write these documents. A third-party provider should be able to provide you with the documents you need for a one-time fee of $1,000 or less.

 Tip: You do not need to spend thousands or more for a lawyer to write legal plan documents. A third-party provider should be able to provide you with the documents you need for a one-time fee of $1,000 or less.

Set Affordable Allowance Amounts

When you implement your defined contribution program, your company will be able to set any allowance amount it wants as long as the allowance amounts are the same within an employee class and do not discriminate in favor of highly compensated individuals. As a best practice, your company should set the allowance amount to a level that is competitive enough to attract talent, but also sustainable for the business over the long term. See Chapter 15 for more information about designing your program.

Provide a Health Insurance Concierge

Your company should work with a licensed health insurance broker or service provider to help employees select and purchase individual health insurance

Blue Advantage Silver HMO 003
HMO | Silver
Blue Cross Blue Shield of Texas
Details   Apply

Monthly premium	Deductible	Out-of-pocket Maximum	Copayments/Coinsurance:
$128/mo	**$5,000**/yr Per individual	**$5,000**/yr Per individual	Primary Doctor: $30 Specialist Doctor: $50 Generic Prescription: No Charge ER Visit: $500
One enrollee Premium before tax credit $181/mo			

Blue Advantage Silver HMO 004
HMO | Silver
Blue Cross Blue Shield of Texas
Details   Apply

Monthly premium	Deductible	Out-of-pocket Maximum	Copayments/Coinsurance:
$133/mo	**$2,500**/yr Per individual	**$5,200**/yr Per individual	Primary Doctor: $35 Specialist Doctor: $55 Generic Prescription: No Charge ER Visit: $500 Copay and 20% Coinsurance after deductible
One enrollee Premium before tax credit $186/mo			

Blue Cross Blue Shield Solution 4, a Multi-State Plan
PPO | Silver
Blue Cross Blue Shield of Texas
Details   Apply

Monthly premium	Deductible	Out-of-pocket Maximum	Copayments/Coinsurance:
$170/mo	**$5,000**/yr Per individual	**$5,000**/yr Per individual	Primary Doctor: $40 Specialist Doctor: $70 Generic Prescription: No Charge ER Visit: $500
One enrollee Premium before tax credit $223/mo			

Figure 16.1   Sample Comparison Tool from Healthcare.gov

plans. Be sure to select an insurance service provider who is familiar with the individual market, has experience working with defined contribution solutions, and is knowledgeable about healthcare reform. For example, at Zane Benefits, we partner with the top individual health insurance providers to ensure clients receive the best possible experience. The health insurance concierge program should include phone and web support. See Figure 16.1 for an example of a web comparison tool from www.healthcare.gov.

Never Pay for Individual Health Plans Directly

The federal government has guidelines for employers who want to contribute to an employee's individual health insurance premiums. To avoid endorsement of individual health insurance plans, your company must not be involved in employees' decisions to purchase individual health insurance, or their decision of which insurer or plan to use. With a defined contribution program, your company must limit its role to simply verifying that a health insurance premium expense was incurred, and then reimbursing the amount from the program.

FEATURES TO LOOK FOR IN A DEFINED CONTRIBUTION SOLUTION PROVIDER

Now that we have discussed a few best practices, let's move on to the key features. Your company's defined contribution provider should provide your company and your employees with the following services and features.

Free Savings Analysis

Your defined contribution provider should conduct a financial analysis (like the one described in Chapter 14) to ensure defined contribution is the best decision for your company and your employees. This financial analysis should project your employees' individual health insurance costs compared with your employer-provided health insurance costs, and it should also take into account any potential premium tax credits your employees may be eligible for.

Multiple Defined Contribution Options

As discussed earlier, there are three core defined contribution approaches your company can consider:

1. **A taxable monthly stipend.** With this approach, your company provides a taxable monthly stipend on employee paychecks.
2. **A taxable reimbursement program.** With this approach, your company establishes a formal reimbursement plan to reimburse employees for their substantiated individual health insurance costs on a post-tax basis up to a healthcare allowance specified by the company.
3. **A tax-free reimbursement plan.** With this approach, an employer utilizes Section 105 of the Internal Revenue Code to establish a formal *self-insured medical reimbursement plan* to reimburse employees for their substantiated individual health insurance costs on a pretax basis.

Your defined contribution provider should provide you with the ability to choose the option that best fits your company's needs. In addition, your provider should provide you with a full program design consultation, including suggestions on how best to structure your contributions based on your recruiting and retention goals. For example, as discussed in Chapter 15, your defined contribution provider should allow your company to specify classes of employees and produce customized plan documents for each class of employee, based on the benefits offered.

Compliance and Software Updates

Your provider should be committed to keeping your program up to date and compliant with applicable rules and regulations as they change, including but not limited to the following (see Figure 16.2):

- **IRS plan documents**. Most defined contribution programs are employee welfare plans under ERISA. ERISA requires that every welfare plan be established and maintained pursuant to a written instrument. The written instrument or *plan document* defines what expenses are eligible for reimbursement, the amount of employer contribution, and other plan details. For example, your provider should create custom plan documents that are automatically updated with plan changes at no additional cost. Your defined contribution provider should save you the time, hassle, and significant expense ($1,200 or more) needed to find and retain an ERISA-specialized attorney to draft customized documents.
- **HIPAA privacy rules**. Most defined contribution programs are governed by HIPAA privacy rules. In order to administer the reimbursement plan correctly, the entity processing employee reimbursement requests receives protected health information (PHI) that is required to be held confidentially under HIPAA. To comply, your defined contribution provider should review all reimbursement requests so your company does not come in contact with PHI.

✓ IRS plan documents
✓ HIPAA privacy rules
✓ ERISA compliance
✓ Internal and external claims appeal process
✓ Preventive care compliance
✓ Annual limit compliance
✓ Dependent coverage for adult children up to age 26
✓ Uniform explanation of coverage and definitions
✓ Integrated electronic plan documents, SPDs, and employee electronic signatures
✓ 60-day notice of material modification

Figure 16.2 Compliance Feature Checklist

- **ERISA compliance**. The U.S. federal government has specific regulations that your company must comply with in order to reimburse employees for individual health insurance premiums without triggering ERISA plan status for the individual health insurance policies. Your solution provider should enforce these rules through the administration software.
- **Internal and external claims appeal process**. The Affordable Care Act added new requirements to the internal and external appeal processes, including how and when procedures are communicated to participants. Your plan documents should include all required language, and the reimbursement request process should comply with these requirements.
- **Preventive care compliance**. Most defined contribution programs are required to cover basic preventive health services without cost sharing. Your plan documents should comply with this requirement.
- **Annual limit compliance**. No annual or lifetime limits may be placed on essential health benefits (EHB). These rules do not apply to benefits that are not essential health benefits, such as health insurance premiums. Your plan documents should comply with this requirement.
- **Dependent coverage for adult children up to age 26**. Most defined contribution programs must make coverage available for children until 26 years of age. Your plan documents should be structured to allow adult children up to age 26 to be enrolled as dependents.
- **Uniform explanation of coverage and definitions**. Most defined contribution programs require that participants and beneficiaries receive a standardized Summary of Benefits and Coverage (SBC) and a set of uniform definitions (Uniform Glossary), both of which must conform to requirements outlined in the ACA and the published regulations. Your provider should include all of the required documents, customized by each class of employee. The documents should be made available online at all times.
- **Integrated electronic plan documents, SPDs, and employee electronic signatures**. It is required that all plan participants are provided with the plan document, Summary of Benefits and Coverage (SBC), and summary plan description (SPD) when they elect coverage. Your defined contribution program should automatically create the required plan documents, SBCs, and SPDs. The solution should also be structured to automatically collect electronic signatures for employee enrollment.
- **60-day notice of material modification**. The ACA requires employers to provide 60-day advance notice to participants when making material modifications to the defined contribution program. Your defined contribution program should automatically monitor when material modifications are made midyear, and provide participants with updated SBCs when plan design changes are made midyear.

Employee Tools and Resources

Your provider should provide your employees with tools to make it easy for employees to purchase health insurance and request reimbursement for insurance premiums, including but not limited to the following (see Figure 16.3).

- **Online Portals and Ledgers.** Each employee should be provided with an online portal and unique login. These portals should allow employees to view their defined contribution amounts and balances as well as request reimbursements online. All reimbursement requests should be trackable, like FedEx packages, and stored for a minimum of 10 years with documentation on the employee's ledger. See Figure 16.4 for a sample employee dashboard.
- **Employee Welcome Kits.** When employees are added to the defined contribution program, your provider should automatically construct custom employee welcome kits that can be distributed via e-mail and printed out for in-person distribution. These welcome packets should contain instructions on how to use the defined contribution program, including their unique login and password information for their online portal. The welcome kit should also contain the required summary of plan documents (SPDs) and the Summary of Benefits and Coverage (SBC), customized for the correct employee class.
- **Health Insurance Concierge.** Your defined contribution solution should automatically provide employees with easy access to individual health insurance resources through their online portal and via a toll-free phone line. You should have the option of directing employees to a health insurance broker to find health insurance information, or to a website. And, employees should be allowed to purchase individual coverage via any source, whether that is through a broker, directly from an insurance company, or via the Health Insurance Marketplace.
- **HSA Compatibility.** Your defined contribution program should be compatible with health savings accounts (HSAs), allowing employees to

---

✓ Online portals and ledgers
✓ Employee welcome kits
✓ Health insurance concierge
✓ HSA compatibility
✓ Easy reimbursement requests
✓ Fast reimbursement request processing
✓ Unpaid claims tracking

Figure 16.3 Employee Feature Checklist

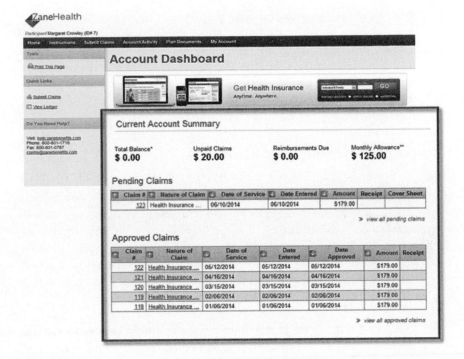

Figure 16.4 Sample ZaneHealth Employee Dashboard

contribute to an HSA while participating in your defined contribution program. Even better, your defined contribution provider should have relationships with the top HSA providers to help employees open the account online.

- **Easy Reimbursement Requests.** Employees should be allowed to submit requests for reimbursement online, by fax, or by mail, and immediately receive an e-mail acknowledging their request and providing an online link to monitor the status. All documentation should be made permanently available online for convenient access by employees.

- **Fast Reimbursement Request Processing.** The defined contribution solution provider should process employee reimbursement requests within one business day. Employees should be able to inquire about their request via their online portal, e-mail, fax, mail, or telephone. Requests should never be rejected for improper or incomplete submission without multiple contacts.

- **Unpaid Claims Tracking.** Your defined contribution provider should make it easy for employees to track reimbursement requests and balances.

If an employee's reimbursement request exceeds his or her balance, it should not be rejected. Rather, the software should track and carry forward unpaid balances until adequate funds have been accumulated. The approved request should then be paid off as allowances accrue. In other words, employees should continue to receive partial reimbursements until the entire reimbursement request has been reimbursed.

Company Tools and Resources

Someone at your company will need to be designated as a plan administrator for your defined contribution program. The plan administrator will be responsible for authorizing reimbursement for approved reimbursement requests, accessing reporting tools, and managing employee enrollment (see Figure 16.5). Your defined contribution provider should ensure that your company's plan administrator receives proper training. The provider should also offer access to a library of other resources such as whitepapers, e-books, webinars, and online tools, including but not limited to:

- **Online administrative portal**. Your company should be able to manage the entire defined contribution program via an online administrative portal. The online portal should allow your plan administrator to add and remove employees, modify plan rules, record reimbursements, and access reporting tools—all with the click of a button. Assistant accounts should also be available for team members with varying permission levels.
- **Real-time accounting**. Your defined contribution provider should automatically keep track of all defined contributions made available by your company to employees via ledgers. Specifically, the online portal should, in real time, provide access to a detailed accounting of the plan including total allowances given, total reimbursements approved, and outstanding liability to the company—in aggregate and on an employee-by-employee basis.
- **Streamlined employee enrollment**. Your plan administrator should be able to instantly enroll or remove employees on an individual or

---

✓ Online administrative portal
✓ Real-time accounting
✓ Streamlined employee enrollment
✓ Employee reimbursement and payroll integration
✓ Automated renewals

Figure 16.5 Employer Feature Checklist

batch basis. Your defined contribution solution should provide automatic e-mailing and printing of employee welcome kits and other plan administration information. For terminated employees, the system should automatically track a run-out period and notify the employee of removal from the plan.

- **Employee reimbursement and payroll integration**. Your defined contribution provider should make reimbursing employees easy—your plan administrator should be able to record reimbursements individually or on a periodic batch basis via check, payroll addition, or direct deposit. The system should leave a well-organized and permanently available audit trail. Additionally, employees should receive an e-mail notification when their reimbursement request is approved, and again confirming when (and how) it will be reimbursed.

- **Automated renewals**. One of the benefits of switching to defined contribution healthcare is eliminating the labor-intensive annual renewal process associated with traditional employer-provided health insurance plans. Your defined contribution provider should allow you to automatically renew your program online. There should be no paperwork required and no renewal fees. The process should be quick and easy for the plan administrator, and employees should be unaffected.

10 QUESTIONS TO ASK DEFINED CONTRIBUTION SOLUTION PROVIDERS

Here are 10 questions to ask defined contribution providers to help you evaluate and compare capabilities.

1. How Long Does It Take to Set Up and Generate the Defined Contribution Program Plan Documents?

Once you have made the decision to offer a defined contribution program, it should take less than an hour to design the program, enroll employees, and download the legal plan documents. Look for a defined contribution solution provider that offers paperless setup and paperless employee enrollment. Also, look for a defined contribution platform that allows you to administer the plan in less than 5 to 10 minutes per month.

2. What Are the Different Plan Options? Can We Set Up Different Allowances by Type of Employee?

Look for a defined contribution solution provider that offers plan design flexibility, such as designing different employee classes or setting a reimbursement percentage. The defined contribution platform should allow you to give employee allowances monthly or at any time on an exception basis—with automatic monitoring of HIPAA and ERISA discrimination compliance rules.

3. Where Will Employees Purchase Individual Health Insurance?

Find a defined contribution platform that makes it easy for employees to shop for and purchase individual health insurance policies, ideally directing employees to a designated broker for quotes. Your company should choose a provider that will allow your chosen health insurance broker to best serve your employees—including automatic notification to the broker when an employee's status changes due to family additions, job change, or premium increase.

4. How Do Employees Submit Reimbursement Requests? How Fast Are Those Requests Processed?

Employees should be able to submit requests for reimbursement online, by fax, or by mail, and immediately receive an e-mail acknowledging their request and providing an online link to monitor the approval status. Premium receipts should be permanently available online for convenient access by employees. Look for a defined contribution provider that offers online submission, has an easy-to-use employee portal, and processes the reimbursement requests within 24 hours. Employees should be able to inquire about their reimbursement request via online chat, e-mail, fax, mail, or telephone. All employee contact should leave clear audit trails and meet appropriate regulatory guidelines.

5. How Are the Reimbursements Handled? Is Prefunding Required, and How Is It Integrated with Our Payroll System?

With defined contribution programs, your company should be able to add employee stipends or reimbursements to an employee's paycheck via your existing payroll system. This way, funds stay with the company until the reimbursements are made and prefunding of third-party bank accounts is not required. When the reimbursements are recorded through the defined contribution platform, look for a provider that offers easy integration with your existing payroll system.

6. How Are Employees Notified of the Status of Their Reimbursement Requests? What Happens If They Submit a Claim Incorrectly?

As soon as employees submit a request for reimbursement, they should be notified by e-mail that the request has been received and is awaiting processing. Once the reimbursement request is processed they should again be notified by e-mail. Also, if there are any problems with the reimbursement request during processing, employees should receive communication describing what further documentation or information is required to approve the request. In other words, look for a defined contribution provider that offers responsive processing services, and provides 24/7 tracking of the status of reimbursement requests through the online employee portal.

7. Who Can an Employee Talk to If They Have Questions/Concerns about Their Reimbursements?

Look for a defined contribution provider that provides excellent and responsive employee support, available through multiple mediums—such as e-mail, telephone, and online chat.

8. How Can I Find Out about Other Companies' Experiences with Your Defined Contribution Solution?

Ask the defined contribution provider for case studies or client success stories that present return on investment (ROI) and payback period for the investment. This will help demonstrate how defined contribution works for real companies and nonprofits. Also, ask what the provider's client retention rate is—this will provide an indicator of client satisfaction.

9. What Are the Fees Associated with a Defined Contribution Program? What Is the Fee Structure?

Generally, defined contribution providers charge a one-time plan setup fee and a monthly per employee per month (PEPM) administration fee. There should not be an annual renewal fee.

10. Would We Have a Dedicated Defined Contribution Specialist to Assist Our Company?

In addition to setting up your defined contribution plan and processing the claims, look for a defined contribution provider that provides a dedicated account representative to support your business and a support team to help employees with their plan (see Figure 16.6). Defined contribution support teams should be accessible, responsive, and educated about defined contribution and health reform.

Defined Contribution Provider Evaluation Worksheet

✓ How long does it take to set up and generate the defined contribution program plan documents? _____

✓ What are the different plan options? Can we set up different allowances by type of employee? _____

✓ Where will employees purchase individual health insurance? _____

✓ How do employees submit reimbursement requests? How fast are those requests processed? _____

✓ How are the reimbursements handled? Is prefunding required, and how is it integrated with our payroll system? _____

✓ How are employees notified of the status of their reimbursement requests? What happens if they submit a claim incorrectly? _____

✓ Who can an employee talk to if they have questions/concerns about their reimbursements? _____

✓ How can I find out about other companies' experiences with your defined contribution solution? _____

✓ What are the fees associated with a defined contribution program? What is the fee structure? _____

✓ Would we have a dedicated defined contribution specialist to assist our company? _____

Figure 16.6 Defined Contribution Provider Evaluation Worksheet

CLIENT CASE STUDY—A 25-PERSON MEDICAL SUPPLY COMPANY

Problem: A leading medical supply company in Utah was offering employee health benefits through a health reimbursement arrangement (HRA). However, the company was facing challenges administering the reimbursement program in-house.

Solution: As a solution to the headaches and expense of self-administering their reimbursement plan, the company selected a defined contribution software provider to administer the plan online in five minutes per month.

With a software service, the company was able to offer more plan flexibility and easier access to the benefit of their employees.

The company allocated monthly healthcare allowances between $150 and $375 per month to spend on individual health insurance. The company established different allowances by employee class, which included entry level, mid-management, and upper-management. All three employee classes had a waiting period of 90 days and required eligible employees to work at least 40 hours per week. (See Figure 16.7.)

Results: By implementing a defined contribution program, this company was able to limit its health benefits liability to between $1,800 to $4,500 per employee per year, depending on the employee's class. In 2014, the company is projected to save $9,105 per month compared with projected 2014 employer-provided health insurance rates in Utah—that's $109,260 (or 70%) in annual savings. (See Figure 16.8.)

Employee Class Name	Eligibility Criteria	Waiting Period	Reimbursement Percentage	Single	Married	Single w/ Children	Married w/ Children
Entry Level (16 of 25)	40+ hours/ week	90 days	100%	$150	$150	$150	$150
Mid-Manager (5 of 25)	40+ hours/ week	90 days	100%	$175	$175	$175	$175
Upper-Manager (4 of 25)	40+ hours/ week	90 days	100%	$375	$375	$375	$375

(Monthly Healthcare Allowances)

Figure 16.7 Plan Design for 25-Person Medical Supply Company

Employer-provided health insurance cost (monthly coverage for 100% of premiums for 25 individuals in Utah)	$12,925
Defined contribution program cost (monthly, 80% utilization)	$3,820
Monthly savings with defined contribution	$9,105
Annual savings	$109,260
Savings percentage	70%

Figure 16.8 Cost Analysis for 25-Person Medical Supply Company

WHAT YOU LEARNED

- Your company should utilize a third-party solution provider to help implement and administer a defined contribution program.
- The right defined contribution provider will allow your company to administer your defined contribution programs online, easily add reimbursements (or stipends) to payroll, and change plan rules and documents at any time.
- Most importantly, your defined contribution solution will also help ensure that your company stays in compliance by keeping your solution up to date with all current statutes and regulations including but not limited to IRS, HIPAA, and ERISA rules.
- The federal government has guidelines for employers who want to contribute to an employee's individual health insurance premiums.
- To avoid endorsement of individual health insurance plans, your company must not be involved in any employees' decision to purchase individual health insurance, or their decision of which insurer or plan to use.
- Your defined contribution provider should conduct a financial analysis (as described in Chapter 14) to ensure defined contribution is the best decision for your company and your employees.
- Your provider should provide your employees with tools to make it easy for employees to purchase health insurance and request reimbursement for insurance premiums.
- Someone at your company will need to be designated as a plan administrator for your defined contribution program. Your defined contribution provider should ensure your company's plan administrator receives proper training.
- The provider should also offer access to a library of other resources such as whitepapers, e-books, webinars, and online tools.

Chapter 17

HOW TO COMMUNICATE DEFINED CONTRIBUTION TO EMPLOYEES

W hen your company makes the transition to defined contribution health-care, the change should be fully supported by employees. If your company does not properly communicate the advantages of individual health insurance and the financial benefits of your new defined contribution program, employees may incorrectly view the change as a benefit reduction. It is hard to blame employees—after all, most businesses have been reducing employee health benefits every year since 1999. As you transition to defined contribution, you are setting the foundation for a new approach to health benefits—one your employees should welcome. If you successfully communicate the benefits of individual health insurance to your employees, they will fully appreciate the new benefit your company is providing and they will know exactly how much your company contributes toward their healthcare.

COMMUNICATE EARLY AND FREQUENTLY

The first reaction any employee will have when you tell them your company is canceling employer-provided health insurance is panic. Therefore, it is vital for your company to be prepared to address all concerns quickly and transparently. During your initial communication, your company should make it clear you are not cutting health benefits; instead you are giving them access to better benefits by implementing a defined contribution program for individual health insurance plans that will lower costs for everyone.

The vast majority of employees have no idea how much their insurance costs your company or how much less expensive individual health insurance can be. We recommend that you share the cost analysis that you did in Chapter 14 with your employees as well as run an individual cost analysis of how much individual insurance will cost each employee.

There are numerous ways to educate employees, including:

- Benefit packets (the welcome kit or enrollment packet)
- Brochures or handouts
- E-mails
- All-staff presentations or trainings
- One-on-one meetings
- Webinars

How and what you communicate to employees varies by company. As a general rule, your company should make communication between HR and employees a two-way street. Many companies make assumptions about what employees prefer or understand when it comes to health benefits. By keeping communication open, you can address questions early on in the transition, and measure employees' overall satisfaction in the long term. Your defined contribution provider should provide you with all necessary employee communication materials.

 Tip: Your defined contribution provider should provide you with all necessary employee communication materials.

ANNOUNCING YOUR DEFINED CONTRIBUTION PROGRAM

Once you have made the decision to switch to defined contribution and you have selected a defined contribution provider, the first thing you should do is announce the new program. The best way to do this is to send a letter to the company 30 to 60 days prior to the start date of your program immediately accompanied by an in-person meeting. Figure 17.1 provides a sample general announcement letter for ABC Company. In addition, here are a few ways to simply explain the value of your defined contribution program to employees in a company meeting:

- "Our group health insurance costs have become unsustainable. Instead of cutting benefits or increasing your share of the costs, we have decided to reimburse you for your own individual health insurance."

- "Your new health insurance will be portable, which means you will not lose it if you leave the company, you will be able to choose from about 50 different plans, and it will be more affordable to both the company and yourself because of the premium tax credits that many of you will qualify for."
- "We are not cutting your health benefits. Instead, we are switching to a new health benefits program that will make you, your family, and our company all better off financially."

Dear ABC Company Employee,

After careful consideration and input from our employees, ABC Company is excited to announce a new and improved health benefits program.

As of the end of June, we will no longer offer the current employer-provided health insurance plan from Aetna. Instead, we are offering a new defined contribution healthcare program that will allow you to purchase an individual health insurance plan and be reimbursed by the company.

Starting July 1st, 2015, you will be provided with a monthly healthcare allowance you can spend on any health insurance plan available in the individual market. Specifically, you and your family will be allowed to purchase a health plan that best fits your needs from an insurance company of your choosing. The company will reimburse you for your cost up to your healthcare allowance each month. The benefits of this new program to you and your family are enormous. By offering health benefits in this way, ABC Company will be able to reduce costs both for our company and for you and your family.

There are several benefits to individual health insurance that we believe will better serve you and your family. With individual health insurance, you get to pick the plan that best fits your needs, including your doctor, and keep your same plan for as long as you want.

It is important to our company that you receive the best health insurance, at the lowest possible cost. On average, individual health plans cost 20 to 60 percent less than group health insurance for the same or better coverage, and there are new premium tax credits available to many families through the new Health Insurance Marketplaces. By making this transition away from employer-provided health insurance, we are giving you and your family access to the premium tax credits. Otherwise, you would not be eligible.

(continued)

Figure 17.1 ABC Company General Announcement Letter

We have contracted with ZaneHealth, the leader in defined contribution healthcare, to make this process easy for everyone. Over the coming weeks, we will provide you with more information on the reimbursement program, on your healthcare allowance, and on individual health insurance. We will also be providing you with resources, including a concierge service, to help you and your family purchase a new plan.

We look forward to helping you make the transition to individual health insurance and continuing to provide you with the best health benefits program available.

Sincerely,
Barbara Jones
President and CEO

Figure 17.1   *(Continued)*

In addition to your general announcement letter, you should also send each employee an individual announcement letter further describing the benefits of individual health insurance. Figure 17.2 provides a sample individual announcement letter for ABC Company.

Tip: Use these example communications to create an employee letter or presentation slides. Customize the reasons your company is transitioning to defined contribution, and the benefits most important to your unique workforce.

Dear [Employee Name],

As you may know, ABC Company will be offering you a new type of health benefit that gives you control over your health insurance. Instead of offering a one-size-fits-all health plan, we are providing you a monthly healthcare allowance you can spend on health insurance.

There are several benefits of individual health insurance that we believe will better serve you and your family:

✓   **Choice:** You choose how to spend your healthcare allowance. For example, you choose the health plan that best fits your family's

Figure 17.2   ABC Company Individual Announcement Letter

needs. This includes the insurance company, the coverage, and the doctors.

✓ **Flexibility:** You can keep the plan as long as you want. Or, plans can be modified to meet changing family medical needs. You are not tied in to one specific plan that the company chooses.

✓ **Lower Health Insurance Costs (Value!):** It's important to our company that you receive the best health insurance, at the lowest cost. On average, individual health plans cost less than traditional employer-provided plans for the same (or better) coverage, and there are new premium tax credits available to many families through our state's Health Insurance Marketplace. By not offering a traditional employer plan, we are giving you and your family access to the premium tax credits.

Contact information for a health insurance broker will be provided to help you understand plan options and enroll in a plan. You can also see options at HealthCare.gov, or purchase a plan online.

We look forward to launching ABC Company's new health benefits program. Please reach out with questions anytime.

Sincerely,
Barbara Jones
President and CEO

Figure 17.2 (Continued)

CUSTOM EMPLOYEE WELCOME PACKETS

Once you have announced the transition, you should be prepared to provide every employee with a custom welcome packet. A good employee welcome packet will provide employees with all the necessary information to answer the following questions:

- What is defined contribution and what is individual health insurance?
- How does defined contribution work and how do employees purchase individual health insurance?
- When will the existing plan be canceled and when will the new defined contribution program start?
- Why is the company making this change?

Tip: Your defined contribution provider should automatically generate these employee welcome letters for each employee.

Negative publicity and employee complaints about defined contribution stem from a lack of understanding about the program. Employee welcome packets should be used to provide a clear picture of why the change is being instituted. Depending on your approach, employee welcome packets can range from a simple one-page piece to a glossy booklet. Keep in mind that the employee welcome packet will become the primary document employees use to become familiar with individual health insurance and defined contribution. Figure 17.3 provides a sample description of the program that could be attached to an employee welcome packet.

Dear ABC Company Employee,

As you may know, ABC Company is offering a new type of health benefit that gives you (the employee) control over your health insurance. Instead of offering a one-size-fits-all health plan, we are providing you a monthly healthcare allowance you can spend on health insurance.

With this new defined contribution program, you get to purchase your own health insurance plan from any insurance company. As an employee, you will:

✓ **Choose an individual health plan.** Select and purchase a health plan with your own money. Contact information for a health insurance broker will be provided to help you understand plan options and enroll in a plan. You can also see options at HealthCare.gov.
✓ **Submit a reimbursement request.** Login to your online participant account to request reimbursement, or submit a paper form via fax or mail. You'll be given a welcome letter with your online login information.
✓ **Receive reimbursement.** Our defined contribution provider will review and approve all reimbursement requests. Then, our company

---

Figure 17.3 Sample Company Letter to an Individual Employee Explaining Reimbursement Program

is notified to reimburse you for your plan costs, up to the amount available to you. You'll receive reimbursements directly from our company on your paycheck.

We look forward to ABC Company's new health benefits program. Please reach out with questions anytime.

Sincerely,
Barbara Jones
President and CEO

Figure 17.3 (Continued)

HOW TO HELP EMPLOYEES PURCHASE INDIVIDUAL HEALTH INSURANCE PLANS

Applying for individual health insurance has never been easier, but for some employees this will be a new experience. Providing employees with the resources described below will help them choose plans that best fit their individual or family needs, such as keeping the same network of providers and balancing their premium with out-of-pocket costs. Providing these resources also highlights that the company cares about its employees' healthcare.

Ideal Solution—Health Insurance Concierge

The ideal way to help employees purchase individual health insurance plans is to provide a health insurance concierge service that is integrated with your defined contribution solution. Specifically, employees should be able to call an 800 number to speak with a licensed health insurance broker and receive assistance purchasing a plan. The health insurance concierge service should also allow employees to purchase plans via an online website without having to make a phone call.

 Tip: Your defined contribution provider should provide you with a health insurance concierge service that is integrated with the defined contribution platform.

USING YOUR DEFINED CONTRIBUTION PROGRAM TO RECRUIT NEW EMPLOYEES

Your company's new defined contribution program is one of the most powerful recruiting and retention tools at your disposal. Employee benefits play an important role in recruiting and keeping good employees—a top attraction driver for U.S. employees across all age groups is competitive health benefits. The cost savings alone will convince most of your employees of the merits of the new program. Keep in mind that money is not everything, and change can be hard (and scary) for some employees—especially when it comes to health insurance. It is important to point out the many advantages individual health insurance has over employer-provided health insurance including choice, portability, and guaranteed acceptance. See Figure 17.4 for a sample letter you can use for a prospective employee.

Dear [Prospective Employee Name],

Thank you for considering employment with ABC Company.

As part of ABC Company's compensation package, we are proud to offer competitive health benefits to all full-time employees.

Instead of offering a one-size-fits-all health insurance plan, ABC Company offers a monthly healthcare allowance that employees can spend on health insurance. Employees get to purchase any health plan and are reimbursed for their premium cost, up to their healthcare allowance. With this type of health benefits program employees have more choice, flexibility, and lower health insurance costs.

Enclosed you will find additional details about the health benefits offered with this position.

We look forward to you joining the ABC Company team.

Sincerely,
Barbara Jones
President and CEO

Figure 17.4   Sample Company Letter to Prospective Employee for Recruiting Purposes

CLIENT CASE STUDY—TWO-PERSON, FAITH-BASED NONPROFIT ORGANIZATION

Problem: A small, faith-based nonprofit organization in Washington wanted to provide health benefits to its two full-time employees. However, like many small nonprofits, the company was unable to find an employer-provided health insurance plan it could afford.

Solution: The nonprofit implemented a defined contribution program and gave all full-time employees monthly healthcare allowances of $300 to $400 per month to spend on individual health insurance. The nonprofit established one employee class, called Full-time Employees, requiring 30 hours' work per week and a 90-day waiting period for new hires. (See Figure 17.5.)

Results: By implementing a defined contribution program, the nonprofit limited its health benefits liability to $3,600 to $4,800 per employee per year, depending on the employee's family status.

In 2014, the nonprofit is projected to save $596 per month compared with projected 2014 employer-provided health insurance rates in Washington—that's $7,152 (or 55%) in annual savings. (See Figure 17.6.) Additionally, because the employees' individual health insurance premiums are less than the monthly allowance, employees effectively pay $0 for health insurance out-of-pocket.

Employee Class Name	Eligibility Criteria	Waiting Period	Reimbursement Percentage	Monthly Healthcare Allowances			
				Single	Married	Single w/ Children	Married w/ Children
Full-time Employees (2 of 2)	30 hours/ week	90 days	100%	$300	$300	$400	$400

Figure 17.5 Plan Design for Two-Person, Faith-Based Nonprofit Organization

(continued)

CLIENT CASE STUDY—TWO-PERSON, FAITH-BASED NONPROFIT ORGANIZATION (*Continued*)

Employer-provided health insurance cost (monthly coverage for 100% of premiums for two individuals in Washington)	$1,076
Defined contribution program cost (monthly, 80% utilization)	$480
Monthly savings with defined contribution	$596
Annual savings	$7,152
Savings percentage	55%

Figure 17.6   Cost Analysis for Two-Person Faith-Based Nonprofit Organization

WHAT YOU LEARNED

- When your company makes the transition to defined contribution health-care, the change should be fully supported by employees.
- If your company does not properly communicate the advantages of individual health insurance and the financial benefits of your new defined contribution program, employees may incorrectly view the change as a benefit reduction.
- It is vital for your company to be prepared to address all concerns quickly and transparently.
- During your initial communication, your company should make it clear you are not cutting health benefits; instead you are giving employees access to better benefits by implementing a defined contribution program for individual health insurance plans that will lower costs for everyone.
- How and what you communicate to employees varies by company. As a general rule, your company should make communication between HR and employees a two-way street.

- Once you have announced the transition, you should be prepared to provide every employee with a custom welcome packet.
- The ideal way to help employees purchase individual health insurance plans is to provide a health insurance concierge service that is integrated with your defined contribution solution.
- A defined contribution healthcare program is one of the most powerful recruiting and retention tools at your disposal.

STATE-BY-STATE GUIDE TO INDIVIDUAL/FAMILY HEALTH INSURANCE COSTS

This appendix shows the monthly cost, in each state, of representative individual/family health insurance policies for a single person (40-year-old male, nonsmoker), and a family of four (two 40-year-old adults and two children under 18, all nonsmokers). See each state for details.

METHODOLOGY

All employer-provided health insurance data is compiled from the U.S. Health and Human Services' MEPS 2012 report and the Kaiser Family Foundation's *2013 Employer Benefits Survey.* Deviations between state averages and the national average were computed based on MEPS 2012 numbers and were applied to the Kaiser Family Foundation's 2013 national average to arrive at 2013 state averages. The 2013 state averages were increased by 10 percent to arrive at the projected 2014 state-by-state, employer-provided health insurance cost averages. Individual health insurance data is sourced from the U.S. Health and Human Services' *QHP Landscape Market Medical* 2014 dataset or from eHealthinsurance.com for state-based marketplaces. When data was unavailable from either source, it was obtained directly from the state's Exchange website. All single data is based on a 40-year-old, nonsmoking male.

INDIVIDUAL SINGLE HEALTH INSURANCE

Monthly Cost in All States of a Silver Plan for a Single Person (2014)

Male, Age 40 Years Old, Nonsmoker

State	Silver Plan Premium	State	Silver Plan Premium
AL	$234	MT	$245
AK	$408	NE	$219
AZ	$168	NV	$246
AR	$271	NH	$289
CA	$267	NJ	$318
CO	$252	NM	$218
CT	$244	NY	$418
DE	$289	NC	$269
DC	$294	ND	$271
FL	$212	OH	$228
GA	$239	OK	$191
HI	$183	OR	$214
ID	$231	PA	$170
IL	$202	RI	$293
IN	$274	SC	$230
IA	$208	SD	$258
KS	$203	TN	$180
KY	$274	TX	$188
LA	$282	UT	$207
ME	$295	VT	$426
MD	$214	VA	$250
MA	$349	WA	$300
MI	$200	WV	$248
MN	$154	WI	$244
MS	$276	WY	$395
MO	$238	Average	$254

INDIVIDUAL FAMILY HEALTH INSURANCE

Monthly Cost in All States of a Silver Plan for a Family (2014)

Two Adults, Age 40 Years Old, Two Children under 18 Years Old, Nonsmokers

State	Silver Plan Premium	State	Silver Plan Premium
AL	$702	MT	$735
AK	$1,220	NE	$655
AZ	$504	NV	$524
AR	$811	NH	$866
CA	$805	NJ	$951
CO	$755	NM	$653
CT	$729	NY	$1,190
DE	$866	NC	$805
DC	$983	ND	$812
FL	$635	OH	$684
GA	$714	OK	$573
HI	$548	OR	$640
ID	$691	PA	$509
IL	$604	RI	$878
IN	$819	SC	$689
IA	$623	SD	$772
KS	$608	TN	$539
KY	$821	TX	$562
LA	$845	UT	$635
ME	$883	VT	$1,198
MD	$642	VA	$749
MA	$1,073	WA	$897
MI	$573	WV	$743
MN	$524	WI	$731
MS	$825	WY	$1,181
MO	$717	Average	$759

Exchange contact information:
www.healthcare.gov
Helpline: 1-800-318-2596

UNITED STATES

For more information see: www.healthinsurancerevolution.org/united-states.

Employer-Provided versus Individual Health Insurance Rates (2014)

	Family	Single
Employer-provided rate	$1,499	$539
Individual rate	$759	$254

Single Individual Health Insurance Costs by Metallic Tier (2014)

	Bronze	Silver	Gold
Premium	$209	$254	$305
Deductible	$5,145	$2,929	$1,425
Out-of-pocket limit	$6,253	$5,835	$4,191
Lifetime limit	Unlimited	Unlimited	Unlimited

Family Individual Health Insurance Costs by Metallic Tier (2014)

	Bronze	Silver	Gold
Premium	$623	$759	$913
Deductible	$10,374	$6,196	$3,076
Out-of-pocket limit	$12,393	$11,239	$8,526
Lifetime limit	Unlimited	Unlimited	Unlimited

Exchange contact information:
www.healthcare.gov
Helpline: 1-800-318-2596

ALABAMA

For more information see: www.healthinsurancerevolution.org/alabama.

Employer-Provided versus Individual Health Insurance Rates (2014)

	Family	Single
Employer-provided rate	$1,236	$497
Individual rate	$702	$253

Single Individual Health Insurance Costs by Metallic Tier (2014)

	Bronze	Silver	Gold
Premium	$209	$253	$305
Deductible	$5,145	$2,929	$1,425
Out-of-pocket limit	$6,253	$5,835	$4,191
Lifetime limit	Unlimited	Unlimited	Unlimited

Family Individual Health Insurance Costs by Metallic Tier (2014)

	Bronze	Silver	Gold
Premium	$623	$759	$913
Deductible	$10,374	$6,196	$3,076
Out-of-pocket limit	$12,393	$11,239	$8,526
Lifetime limit	Unlimited	Unlimited	Unlimited

Exchange contact information:
www.healthcare.gov
Helpline: 1-800-318-2596

ALASKA

For more information see: www.healthinsurancerevolution.org/alaska.

Employer-Provided versus Individual Health Insurance Rates (2014)

	Family	Single
Employer-provided rate	$1,734	$743
Individual rate	$1,220	$408

Single Individual Health Insurance Costs by Metallic Tier (2014)

	Bronze	Silver	Gold
Premium	$344	$408	$488
Deductible	$4,500	$2,500	$1,000
Out-of-pocket limit	$6,350	$4,500	$4,500
Lifetime limit	Unlimited	Unlimited	Unlimited

Family Individual Health Insurance Costs by Metallic Tier (2014)

	Bronze	Silver	Gold
Premium	$1,030	$1,220	$1,460
Deductible	$9,000	$5,000	$2,000
Out-of-pocket limit	$12,700	$9,000	$9,000
Lifetime limit	Unlimited	Unlimited	Unlimited

Exchange contact information:
www.healthcare.gov
Helpline: 1-800-318-2596

ARIZONA

For more information see: www.healthinsurancerevolution.org/arizona.

Employer-Provided versus Individual Health Insurance Rates (2014)

	Family	Single
Employer-provided rate	$1,477	$521
Individual rate	$504	$168

Single Individual Health Insurance Costs by Metallic Tier (2014)

	Bronze	Silver	Gold
Premium	$149	$168	$192
Deductible	$3,500	$1,500	$0
Out-of-pocket limit	$6,000	$6,350	$6,000
Lifetime limit	Unlimited	Unlimited	Unlimited

Family Individual Health Insurance Costs by Metallic Tier (2014)

	Bronze	Silver	Gold
Premium	$447	$504	$576
Deductible	$7,000	$3,000	$0
Out-of-pocket limit	$12,000	$12,700	$12,000
Lifetime limit	Unlimited	Unlimited	Unlimited

Exchange contact information:
www.healthcare.gov
Helpline: 1-800-318-2596

ARKANSAS

For more information see: www.healthinsurancerevolution.org/arkansas.

Employer-Provided versus Individual Health Insurance Rates (2014)

	Family	Single
Employer-provided rate	$1,288	$447
Individual rate	$811	$271

Single Individual Health Insurance Costs by Metallic Tier (2014)

	Bronze	Silver	Gold
Premium	$209	$271	$303
Deductible	$5,000	$3,500	$1,000
Out-of-pocket limit	$6,350	$6,000	$3,500
Lifetime limit	Unlimited	Unlimited	Unlimited

Family Individual Health Insurance Costs by Metallic Tier (2014)

	Bronze	Silver	Gold
Premium	$626	$811	$908
Deductible	$10,000	$7,000	$2,000
Out-of-pocket limit	$12,700	$12,000	$7,000
Lifetime limit	Unlimited	Unlimited	Unlimited

Exchange contact information:
www.healthcare.gov
Helpline: 1-800-318-2596

CALIFORNIA

For more information see: www.healthinsurancerevolution.org/california.

Employer-Provided versus Individual Health Insurance Rates (2014)

	Family	Single
Employer-provided rate	$1,540	$543
Individual rate	$805	$267

Single Individual Health Insurance Cost by Metallic Tier (2014)

	Bronze	Silver	Gold
Premium	$231	$267	$333
Deductible	$5,000	$2,000	$0
Out-of-pocket limit	$6,350	$6,350	$6,350
Lifetime limit	Unlimited	Unlimited	Unlimited

Family Individual Health Insurance Costs by Metallic Tier (2014)

	Bronze	Silver	Gold
Premium	$696	$805	$1,002
Deductible	$10,000	$4,000	$0
Out-of-pocket limit	$12,700	$12,700	$12,700
Lifetime limit	Unlimited	Unlimited	Unlimited

Exchange contact information:
www.coveredca.com
Helpline: 1-800-300-1506

COLORADO

For more information see: www.healthinsurancerevolution.org/colorado.

Employer-Provided versus Individual Health Insurance Rates (2014)

	Family	Single
Employer-provided rate	$1,553	$528
Individual rate	$755	$252

Single Individual Health Insurance Costs by Metallic Tier (2014)

	Bronze	Silver	Gold
Premium	$201	$252	$295
Deductible	$4,500	$1,750	$1,000
Out-of-pocket limit	$6,350	$5,000	$6,350
Lifetime limit	Unlimited	Unlimited	Unlimited

Family Individual Health Insurance Costs by Metallic Tier (2014)

	Bronze	Silver	Gold
Premium	$602	$755	$883
Deductible	$9,000	$3,500	$2,000
Out-of-pocket limit	$12,700	$10,000	$12,700
Lifetime limit	Unlimited	Unlimited	Unlimited

Exchange contact information:
www.connectforhealthco.com
Helpline: 855-752-6742

CONNECTICUT

For more information see: www.healthinsurancerevolution.org/connecticut.

Employer-Provided versus Individual Health Insurance Rates (2014)

	Family	Single
Employer-provided rate	$1,636	$594
Individual rate	$729	$244

Single Individual Health Insurance Costs by Metallic Tier (2014)

	Bronze	Silver	Gold
Premium	$281	$244	$430
Deductible	$5,500	$5,000	$1,500
Out-of-pocket limit	$6,350	$6,350	$3,000
Lifetime limit	Unlimited	Unlimited	Unlimited

Family Individual Health Insurance Costs by Metallic Tier (2014)

	Bronze	Silver	Gold
Premium	$842	$729	$1,286
Deductible	$11,000	$10,000	$3,000
Out-of-pocket limit	$12,700	$12,700	$6,000
Lifetime limit	Unlimited	Unlimited	Unlimited

Exchange contact information:
www.accesshealthct.com
Helpline: 1-855-805-4325

DELAWARE

For more information see: www.healthinsurancerevolution.org/delaware.

Employer-Provided versus Individual Health Insurance Rates (2014)

	Family	Single
Employer-provided rate	$1,511	$559
Individual rate	$866	$289

Single Individual Health Insurance Costs by Metallic Tier (2014)

	Bronze	Silver	Gold
Premium	$248	$289	$347
Deductible	$5,250	$3,000	$1,000
Out-of-pocket limit	$6,250	$5,000	$3,000
Lifetime limit	Unlimited	Unlimited	Unlimited

Family Individual Health Insurance Costs by Metallic Tier (2014)

	Bronze	Silver	Gold
Premium	$743	$866	$1,039
Deductible	$10,500	$6,000	$2,000
Out-of-pocket limit	$12,500	$10,000	$6,000
Lifetime limit	Unlimited	Unlimited	Unlimited

Exchange contact information:
www.healthcare.gov
Helpline: 1-800-318-2596

DISTRICT OF COLUMBIA

For more information see: www.healthinsurancerevolution.org/district-of-columbia.

Employer-Provided versus Individual Health Insurance Rates (2014)

	Family	Single
Employer-provided rate	$1,667	$559
Individual rate	$983	$242

Single Individual Health Insurance Costs by Metallic Tier (2014)

	Bronze	Silver	Gold
Premium	$268	$294	$367
Lifetime limit	Unlimited	Unlimited	Unlimited

Family Individual Health Insurance Costs by Metallic Tier (2014)

	Bronze	Silver	Gold
Premium	$894	$983	$1,224
Lifetime limit	Unlimited	Unlimited	Unlimited

Exchange contact information:
www.dchealthlink.com
Helpline: 1-855-532-5465

FLORIDA

For more information see: www.healthinsurancerevolution.org/florida.

Employer-Provided versus Individual Health Insurance Rates (2014)

	Family	Single
Employer-provided rate	$1,499	$519
Individual rate	$635	$212

Single Individual Health Insurance Costs by Metallic Tier (2014)

	Bronze	Silver	Gold
Premium	$167	$212	$235
Deductible	$5,600	$3,750	$2,500
Out-of-pocket limit	$6,350	$6,350	$3,500
Lifetime limit	Unlimited	Unlimited	Unlimited

Family Individual Health Insurance Costs by Metallic Tier (2014)

	Bronze	Silver	Gold
Premium	$500	$635	$703
Deductible	$11,200	$7,500	$5,000
Out-of-pocket limit	$12,700	$12,700	$7,000
Lifetime limit	Unlimited	Unlimited	Unlimited

Exchange contact information:
www.healthcare.gov
Helpline: 1-800-318-2596

GEORGIA

For more information see: www.healthinsurancerevolution.org/georgia.

Employer-Provided versus Individual Health Insurance Rates (2014)

	Family	Single
Employer-provided rate	$1,419	$517
Individual rate	$714	$239

Single Individual Health Insurance Costs by Metallic Tier (2014)

	Bronze	Silver	Gold
Premium	$202	$239	$274
Deductible	$6,300	$4,250	$2,500
Out-of-pocket limit	$6,300	$6,250	$3,500
Lifetime limit	Unlimited	Unlimited	Unlimited

Family Individual Health Insurance Costs by Metallic Tier (2014)

	Bronze	Silver	Gold
Premium	$605	$714	$820
Deductible	$12,600	$8,500	$5,000
Out-of-pocket limit	$12,600	$12,500	$7,000
Lifetime limit	Unlimited	Unlimited	Unlimited

Exchange contact information:
www.healthcare.gov
Helpline: 1-800-318-2596

HAWAII

For more information see: www.healthinsurancerevolution.org/hawaii.

Employer-Provided versus Individual Health Insurance Rates (2014)

	Family	Single
Employer-provided rate	$1,426	$509
Individual rate	$548	$183

Single Individual Health Insurance Costs by Metallic Tier (2014)

	Bronze	Silver	Gold
Premium	$148	$183	$207
Deductible	$5,000	$1,500	$1,000
Out-of-pocket limit	$6,350	$6,350	$6,350
Lifetime limit	Unlimited	Unlimited	Unlimited

Family Individual Health Insurance Costs by Metallic Tier (2014)

	Bronze	Silver	Gold
Premium	$443	$548	$620
Deductible	$10,000	$3,000	$2,000
Out-of-pocket limit	$12,700	$12,700	$12,700
Lifetime limit	Unlimited	Unlimited	Unlimited

Exchange contact information:
www.hawaiihealthconnector.com
Helpline: 877-628-5076

IDAHO

For more information see: www.healthinsurancerevolution.org/idaho.

Employer-Provided versus Individual Health Insurance Rates (2014)

	Family	Single
Employer-provided rate	$1,362	$445
Individual rate	$691	$231

Single Individual Health Insurance Costs by Metallic Tier (2014)

	Bronze	Silver	Gold
Premium	$192	$231	$264
Deductible	$5,000	$1,000	$1,000
Out-of-pocket limit	$6,350	$5,800	$2,900
Lifetime limit	Unlimited	Unlimited	Unlimited

Family Individual Health Insurance Costs by Metallic Tier (2014)

	Bronze	Silver	Gold
Premium	$573	$691	$791
Deductible	$10,000	$2,500	$2,500
Out-of-pocket limit	$12,700	$11,600	$5,800
Lifetime limit	Unlimited	Unlimited	Unlimited

Exchange contact information:
www.yourhealthidaho.org
Helpline: 1-855-944-3246

ILLINOIS

For more information see: www.healthinsurancerevolution.org/illinois.

Employer-Provided versus Individual Health Insurance Rates (2014)

	Family	Single
Employer-provided rate	$1,526	$541
Individual rate	$604	$202

Single Individual Health Insurance Costs by Metallic Tier (2014)

	Bronze	Silver	Gold
Premium	$139	$202	$241
Deductible	$5,000	$3,000	$3,250
Out-of-pocket limit	$6,250	$6,350	$3,250
Lifetime limit	Unlimited	Unlimited	Unlimited

Family Individual Health Insurance Costs by Metallic Tier (2014)

	Bronze	Silver	Gold
Premium	$415	$604	$722
Deductible	$12,700	$9,000	$9,750
Out-of-pocket limit	$12,700	$12,700	$9,750
Lifetime limit	Unlimited	Unlimited	Unlimited

Exchange contact information:
www.healthcare.gov
Helpline: 1-800-318-2596

INDIANA

For more information see: www.healthinsurancerevolution.org/indiana.

Employer-Provided versus Individual Health Insurance Rates (2014)

	Family	Single
Employer-provided rate	$1,498	$551
Individual rate	$819	$274

Single Individual Health Insurance Costs by Metallic Tier (2014)

	Bronze	Silver	Gold
Premium	$212	$274	$354
Deductible	$6,300	$2,500	$750
Out-of-pocket limit	$6,350	$6,350	$6,000
Lifetime limit	Unlimited	Unlimited	Unlimited

Family Individual Health Insurance Costs by Metallic Tier (2014)

	Bronze	Silver	Gold
Premium	$634	$819	$1,059
Deductible	$12,600	$5,000	$1,500
Out of pocket limit	$12,700	$12,700	$12,000
Lifetime limit	Unlimited	Unlimited	Unlimited

Exchange contact information:
www.healthcare.gov
Helpline: 1-800-318-2596

IOWA

For more information see: www.healthinsurancerevolution.org/iowa.

Employer-Provided versus Individual Health Insurance Rates (2014)

	Family	Single
Employer-provided rate	$1,386	$515
Individual rate	$623	$208

Single Individual Health Insurance Costs by Metallic Tier (2014)

	Bronze	Silver	Gold
Premium	$159	$208	$235
Deductible	$5,600	$3,750	$1,750
Out-of-pocket limit	$6,350	$6,350	$5,000
Lifetime limit	Unlimited	Unlimited	Unlimited

Family Individual Health Insurance Costs by Metallic Tier (2014)

	Bronze	Silver	Gold
Premium	$476	$623	$703
Deductible	$11,200	$7,500	$3,500
Out-of-pocket limit	$12,700	$12,700	$10,000
Lifetime limit	Unlimited	Unlimited	Unlimited

Exchange contact information:
www.healthcare.gov
Helpline: 1-800-318-2596

KANSAS

For more information see: www.healthinsurancerevolution.org/kansas.

Employer-Provided versus Individual Health Insurance Rates (2014)

	Family	Single
Employer-provided rate	$1,332	$498
Individual rate	$608	$203

Single Individual Health Insurance Costs by Metallic Tier (2014)

	Bronze	Silver	Gold
Premium	$153	$203	$228
Deductible	$6,300	$3,750	$1,250
Out-of-pocket limit	$6,300	$6,350	$5,000
Lifetime limit	Unlimited	Unlimited	Unlimited

Family Individual Health Insurance Costs by Metallic Tier (2014)

	Bronze	Silver	Gold
Premium	$458	$608	$683
Deductible	$12,600	$7,500	$2,500
Out-of-pocket limit	$12,600	$12,700	$10,000
Lifetime limit	Unlimited	Unlimited	Unlimited

Exchange contact information:
www.healthcare.gov
Helpline: 1-800-318-2596

KENTUCKY

For more information see: www.healthinsurancerevolution.org/kentucky.

Employer-Provided versus Individual Health Insurance Rates (2014)

	Family	Single
Employer-provided rate	$1,524	$541
Individual rate	$821	$274

Single Individual Health Insurance Costs by Metallic Tier (2014)

	Bronze	Silver	Gold
Premium	$222	$274	$373
Deductible	$6,300	$3,650	$750
Out-of-pocket limit	$6,350	$3,650	$6,000
Lifetime limit	Unlimited	Unlimited	Unlimited

Family Individual Health Insurance Costs by Metallic Tier (2014)

	Bronze	Silver	Gold
Premium	$664	$821	$1,116
Deductible	$12,600	$7,300	$1,500
Out-of-pocket limit	$12,700	$7,300	$12,000
Lifetime limit	Unlimited	Unlimited	Unlimited

Exchange contact information:
https://kynect.ky.gov
Helpline: 1-855-459-6328

LOUISIANA

For more information see: www.healthinsurancerevolution.org/louisiana.

Employer-Provided versus Individual Health Insurance Rates (2014)

	Family	Single
Employer-provided rate	$1,462	$539
Individual rate	$845	$282

Single Individual Health Insurance Costs by Metallic Tier (2014)

	Bronze	Silver	Gold
Premium	$205	$282	$292
Deductible	$4,500	$3,000	$1,500
Out-of-pocket limit	$6,350	$6,350	$3,000
Lifetime limit	Unlimited	Unlimited	Unlimited

Family Individual Health Insurance Costs by Metallic Tier (2014)

	Bronze	Silver	Gold
Premium	$615	$845	$873
Deductible	$12,700	$9,000	$3,000
Out-of-pocket limit	$12,700	$12,700	$6,000
Lifetime limit	Unlimited	Unlimited	Unlimited

Exchange contact information:
www.healthcare.gov
Helpline: 1-800-318-2596

MAINE

For more information see: www.healthinsurancerevolution.org/maine.

Employer-Provided versus Individual Health Insurance Rates (2014)

	Family	Single
Employer-provided rate	$1,570	$570
Individual rate	$883	$295

Single Individual Health Insurance Costs by Metallic Tier (2014)

	Bronze	Silver	Gold
Premium	$237	$295	$377
Deductible	$6,300	$2,000	$750
Out-of-pocket limit	$6,350	$6,350	$6,000
Lifetime limit	Unlimited	Unlimited	Unlimited

Family Individual Health Insurance Costs by Metallic Tier (2014)

	Bronze	Silver	Gold
Premium	$708	$883	$1,128
Deductible	$12,600	$4,000	$1,500
Out-of-pocket limit	$12,700	$12,700	$12,000
Lifetime limit	Unlimited	Unlimited	Unlimited

Exchange contact information:
www.healthcare.gov
Helpline: 1-800-318-2596

MARYLAND

For more information see: www.healthinsurancerevolution.org/maryland.

Employer-Provided versus Individual Health Insurance Rates (2014)

	Family	Single
Employer-provided rate	$1,476	$531
Individual rate	$642	$214

Single Individual Health Insurance Costs by Metallic Tier (2014)

	Bronze	Silver	Gold
Premium	$142	$214	$272
Deductible	$4,000	$2,000	$0
Out-of-pocket limit	$6,350	$6,350	$6,350
Lifetime limit	Unlimited	Unlimited	Unlimited

Family Individual Health Insurance Costs by Metallic Tier (2014)

	Bronze	Silver	Gold
Premium	$426	$642	$814
Deductible	$8,000	$4,000	$0
Out-of-pocket limit	$12,700	$12,700	$12,700
Lifetime limit	Unlimited	Unlimited	Unlimited

Exchange contact information:
www.marylandhealthconnection.gov
Helpline: 1-877-304-9934

MASSACHUSETTS

For more information see: www.healthinsurancerevolution.org/massachusetts.

Employer-Provided versus Individual Health Insurance Rates (2014)

	Family	Single
Employer-provided rate	$1,659	$613
Individual rate	$1,073	$349

Single Individual Health Insurance Costs by Metallic Tier (2014)

	Bronze	Silver	Gold
Premium	$311	$349	$399
Deductible	$2,000	$2,000	$2,000
Out-of-pocket limit	$6,350	$6,350	$4,000
Lifetime limit	Unlimited	Unlimited	Unlimited

Family Individual Health Insurance Costs by Metallic Tier (2014)

	Bronze	Silver	Gold
Premium	$957	$1,073	$1,230
Deductible	$4,000	$4,000	$4,000
Out-of-pocket limit	$12,700	$12,700	$8,000
Lifetime limit	Unlimited	Unlimited	Unlimited

Exchange contact information:
www.mahealthconnector.org
Helpline: 1-877-623-6765

MICHIGAN

For more information see: www.healthinsurancerevolution.org/michigan.

Employer-Provided versus Individual Health Insurance Rates (2014)

	Family	Single
Employer-provided rate	$1,395	$537
Individual rate	$573	$200

Single Individual Health Insurance Costs by Metallic Tier (2014)

	Bronze	Silver	Gold
Premium	$168	$200	$221
Deductible	$6,300	$1,650	$2,500
Out-of-pocket limit	$6,300	$6,350	$3,500
Lifetime limit	Unlimited	Unlimited	Unlimited

Family Individual Health Insurance Costs by Metallic Tier (2014)

	Bronze	Silver	Gold
Premium	$503	$573	$663
Deductible	$12,600	$9,200	$5,000
Out-of-pocket limit	$12,600	$12,600	$7,000
Lifetime limit	Unlimited	Unlimited	Unlimited

Exchange contact information:
www.healthcare.gov
Helpline: 1-800-318-2596

MINNESOTA

For more information see: www.healthinsurancerevolution.org/minnesota.

Employer-Provided versus Individual Health Insurance Rates (2014)

	Family	Single
Employer-provided rate	$1,493	$535
Individual rate	$524	$154

Single Individual Health Insurance Costs by Metallic Tier (2014)

	Bronze	Silver	Gold
Premium	$123	$154	$200
Deductible	$5,700	$4,400	$2,000
Out-of-pocket limit	$5,700	$4,400	$2,000
Lifetime limit	Unlimited	Unlimited	Unlimited

Family Individual Health Insurance Costs by Metallic Tier (2014)

	Bronze	Silver	Gold
Premium	$417	$524	$677
Deductible	$11,400	$7,000	$4,000
Out-of-pocket limit	$11,400	$7,000	$4,000
Lifetime limit	Unlimited	Unlimited	Unlimited

Exchange contact information:
www.mnsure.org
Helpline: 1-855-366-7873

MISSISSIPPI

For more information see: www.healthinsurancerevolution.org/mississippi.

Employer-Provided versus Individual Health Insurance Rates (2014)

	Family	Single
Employer-provided rate	$1,373	$472
Individual rate	$825	$276

Single Individual Health Insurance Costs by Metallic Tier (2014)

	Bronze	Silver	Gold
Premium	$243	$276	$314
Deductible	$6,300	$4,600	$2,500
Out-of-pocket limit	$6,300	$6,300	$3,500
Lifetime limit	Unlimited	Unlimited	Unlimited

Family Individual Health Insurance Costs by Metallic Tier (2014)

	Bronze	Silver	Gold
Premium	$727	$825	$941
Deductible	$12,600	$9,200	$5,000
Out-of-pocket limit	$12,600	$12,600	$7,000
Lifetime limit	Unlimited	Unlimited	Unlimited

Exchange contact information:
www.healthcare.gov
Helpline: 1-800-318-2596

MISSOURI

For more information see: www.healthinsurancerevolution.org/missouri.

Employer-Provided versus Individual Health Insurance Rates (2014)

	Family	Single
Employer-provided rate	$1,452	$516
Individual rate	$717	$238

Single Individual Health Insurance Costs by Metallic Tier (2014)

	Bronze	Silver	Gold
Premium	$183	$238	$270
Deductible	$6,300	$3,750	$1,750
Out-of-pocket limit	$6,300	$6,350	$5,000
Lifetime limit	Unlimited	Unlimited	Unlimited

Family Individual Health Insurance Costs by Metallic Tier (2014)

	Bronze	Silver	Gold
Premium	$549	$717	$809
Deductible	$12,600	$7,500	$3,500
Out-of-pocket limit	$12,600	$12,700	$10,000
Lifetime limit	Unlimited	Unlimited	Unlimited

Exchange contact information:
www.healthcare.gov
Helpline: 1-800-318-2596

MONTANA

For more information see: www.healthinsurancerevolution.org/montana.

Employer-Provided versus Individual Health Insurance Rates (2014)

	Family	Single
Employer-provided rate	$1,424	$560
Individual rate	$735	$245

Single Individual Health Insurance Costs by Metallic Tier (2014)

	Bronze	Silver	Gold
Premium	$205	$245	$277
Deductible	$6,000	$6,250	$700
Out-of-pocket limit	$6,000	$6,250	$4,500
Lifetime limit	Unlimited	Unlimited	Unlimited

Family Individual Health Insurance Costs by Metallic Tier (2014)

	Bronze	Silver	Gold
Premium	$613	$735	$829
Deductible	$12,000	$12,500	$1,400
Out-of-pocket limit	$12,000	$12,500	$9,000
Lifetime limit	Unlimited	Unlimited	Unlimited

Exchange contact information:
www.healthcare.gov
Helpline: 1-800-318-2596

NEBRASKA

For more information see: www.healthinsurancerevolution.org/nebraska.

Employer-Provided versus Individual Health Insurance Rates (2014)

	Family	Single
Employer-provided rate	$1,402	$511
Individual rate	$655	$219

Single Individual Health Insurance Costs by Metallic Tier (2014)

	Bronze	Silver	Gold
Premium	$192	$219	$255
Deductible	$6,350	$2,000	$1,500
Out-of-pocket limit	$6,350	$4,500	$2,000
Lifetime limit	Unlimited	Unlimited	Unlimited

Family Individual Health Insurance Costs by Metallic Tier (2014)

	Bronze	Silver	Gold
Premium	$574	$655	$763
Deductible	$12,700	$4,000	$3,000
Out-of-pocket limit	$12,700	$9,000	$4,000
Lifetime limit	Unlimited	Unlimited	Unlimited

Exchange contact information:
www.healthcare.gov
Helpline: 1-800-318-2596

NEVADA

For more information see: www.healthinsurancerevolution.org/nevada.

Employer-Provided versus Individual Health Insurance Rates (2014)

	Family	Single
Employer-provided rate	$1,250	$496
Individual rate	$524	$246

Single Individual Health Insurance Costs by Metallic Tier (2014)

	Bronze	Silver	Gold
Premium	$233	$246	$265
Deductible	$6,000	$2,250	$750
Out-of-pocket limit	$6,000	$6,000	$4,500
Lifetime limit	Unlimited	Unlimited	Unlimited

Family Individual Health Insurance Costs by Metallic Tier (2014)

	Bronze	Silver	Gold
Premium	$417	$524	$677
Deductible	$11,400	$8,800	$4,000
Out-of-pocket limit	$11,400	$8,800	$4,000
Lifetime limit	Unlimited	Unlimited	Unlimited

Exchange contact information:
www.nevadahealthlink.com
Helpline: 1-855-768-5465

NEW HAMPSHIRE

For more information see: www.healthinsurancerevolution.org/new-hampshire.

Employer-Provided versus Individual Health Insurance Rates (2014)

	Family	Single
Employer-provided rate	$1,586	$570
Individual rate	$866	$289

Single Individual Health Insurance Costs by Metallic Tier (2014)

	Bronze	Silver	Gold
Premium	$235	$289	$373
Deductible	$4,300	$1,500	$1,000
Out-of-pocket limit	$6,350	$6,000	$3,500
Lifetime limit	Unlimited	Unlimited	Unlimited

Family Individual Health Insurance Costs by Metallic Tier (2014)

	Bronze	Silver	Gold
Premium	$704	$866	$1,116
Deductible	$8,600	$3,000	$2,000
Out-of-pocket limit	$12,700	$12,000	$7,000
Lifetime limit	Unlimited	Unlimited	Unlimited

Exchange contact information:
www.healthcare.gov
Helpline: 1-800-318-2596

NEW JERSEY

For more information see: www.healthinsurancerevolution.org/new-jersey.

Employer-Provided versus Individual Health Insurance Rates (2014)

	Family	Single
Employer-provided rate	$1,642	$585
Individual rate	$951	$318

Single Individual Health Insurance Costs by Metallic Tier (2014)

	Bronze	Silver	Gold
Premium	$312	$318	$415
Deductible	$2,500	$1,350	$1,250
Out-of-pocket limit	$6,350	$5,100	$2,500
Lifetime limit	Unlimited	Unlimited	Unlimited

Family Individual Health Insurance Costs by Metallic Tier (2014)

	Bronze	Silver	Gold
Premium	$935	$951	$1,243
Deductible	$5,000	$2,700	$2,500
Out-of-pocket limit	$12,700	$10,700	$5,000
Lifetime limit	Unlimited	Unlimited	Unlimited

Exchange contact information:
www.healthcare.gov
Helpline: 1-800-318-2596

NEW MEXICO

For more information see: www.healthinsurancerevolution.org/new-mexico.

Employer-Provided versus Individual Health Insurance Rates (2014)

	Family	Single
Employer-provided rate	$1,538	$504
Individual rate	$653	$218

Single Individual Health Insurance Costs by Metallic Tier (2014)

	Bronze	Silver	Gold
Premium	$168	$218	$255
Deductible	$6,000	$2,000	$3,250
Out-of-pocket limit	$6,000	$6,350	$3,250
Lifetime limit	Unlimited	Unlimited	Unlimited

Family Individual Health Insurance Costs by Metallic Tier (2014)

	Bronze	Silver	Gold
Premium	$504	$653	$763
Deductible	$12,700	$4,000	$9,750
Out-of-pocket limit	$12,700	$12,700	$9,750
Lifetime limit	Unlimited	Unlimited	Unlimited

Exchange contact information:
www.bewellnm.com
Helpline: 1-855-996-6449

NEW YORK

For more information see: www.healthinsurancerevolution.org/new-york.

Employer-Provided versus Individual Health Insurance Rates (2014)

	Family	Single
Employer-provided rate	$1,639	$604
Individual rate	$1,190	$418

Single Individual Health Insurance Costs by Metallic Tier (2014)

	Bronze	Silver	Gold
Premium	$350	$418	$501
Deductible	$3,000	$2,450	$600
Out-of-pocket limit	$6,350	$6,350	$4,000
Lifetime limit	Unlimited	Unlimited	Unlimited

Family Individual Health Insurance Costs by Metallic Tier (2014)

	Bronze	Silver	Gold
Premium	$998	$1,190	$1,429
Deductible	$6,000	$4,900	$1,200
Out-of-pocket limit	$12,700	$12,700	$8,000
Lifetime limit	Unlimited	Unlimited	Unlimited

Exchange contact information:
https://nystateofhealth.ny.gov
Helpline: 1-855-355-5777

NORTH CAROLINA

For more information see: www.healthinsurancerevolution.org/north-carolina.

Employer-Provided versus Individual Health Insurance Rates (2014)

	Family	Single
Employer-provided rate	$1,512	$564
Individual rate	$805	$269

Single Individual Health Insurance Costs by Metallic Tier (2014)

	Bronze	Silver	Gold
Premium	$197	$269	$306
Deductible	$6,300	$3,750	$1,250
Out-of-pocket limit	$6,300	$6,350	$5,000
Lifetime limit	Unlimited	Unlimited	Unlimited

Family Individual Health Insurance Costs by Metallic Tier (2014)

	Bronze	Silver	Gold
Premium	$589	$805	$916
Deductible	$12,600	$7,500	$2,500
Out-of-pocket limit	$12,600	$12,700	$10,000
Lifetime limit	Unlimited	Unlimited	Unlimited

Exchange contact information:
www.healthcare.gov
Helpline: 1-800-318-2596

NORTH DAKOTA

For more information see: www.healthinsurancerevolution.org/north-dakota.

Employer-Provided versus Individual Health Insurance Rates (2014)

	Family	Single
Employer-provided rate	$1,390	$539
Individual rate	$812	$271

Single Individual Health Insurance Costs by Metallic Tier (2014)

	Bronze	Silver	Gold
Premium	$217	$271	$315
Deductible	$6,350	$1,300	$100
Out-of-pocket limit	$6,350	$5,450	$6,250
Lifetime limit	Unlimited	Unlimited	Unlimited

Family Individual Health Insurance Costs by Metallic Tier (2014)

	Bronze	Silver	Gold
Premium	$648	$812	$943
Deductible	$12,700	$3,900	$300
Out-of-pocket limit	$12,700	$12,700	$12,700
Lifetime limit	Unlimited	Unlimited	Unlimited

Exchange contact information:
www.healthcare.gov
Helpline: 1-800-318-2596

OHIO

For more information see: www.healthinsurancerevolution.org/ohio.

Employer-Provided versus Individual Health Insurance Rates (2014)

	Family	Single
Employer-provided rate	$1,497	$509
Individual rate	$684	$228

Single Individual Health Insurance Costs by Metallic Tier (2014)

	Bronze	Silver	Gold
Premium	$197	$228	$267
Deductible	$5,000	$3,500	$2,500
Out-of-pocket limit	$6,350	$4,850	$3,500
Lifetime limit	Unlimited	Unlimited	Unlimited

Family Individual Health Insurance Costs by Metallic Tier (2014)

	Bronze	Silver	Gold
Premium	$590	$684	$800
Deductible	$10,000	$7,000	$5,000
Out-of-pocket limit	$12,700	$9,700	$7,000
Lifetime limit	Unlimited	Unlimited	Unlimited

Exchange contact information:
www.healthcare.gov
Helpline: 1-800-318-2596

OKLAHOMA

For more information see: www.healthinsurancerevolution.org/oklahoma.

Employer-Provided versus Individual Health Insurance Rates (2014)

	Family	Single
Employer-provided rate	$1,313	$486
Individual rate	$573	$191

Single Individual Health Insurance Costs by Metallic Tier (2014)

	Bronze	Silver	Gold
Premium	$123	$191	$236
Deductible	$5,000	$3,000	$3,250
Out-of-pocket limit	$6,250	$6,350	$3,250
Lifetime limit	Unlimited	Unlimited	Unlimited

Family Individual Health Insurance Costs by Metallic Tier (2014)

	Bronze	Silver	Gold
Premium	$369	$573	$707
Deductible	$12,700	$9,000	$9,750
Out-of-pocket limit	$12,700	$12,700	$9,750
Lifetime limit	Unlimited	Unlimited	Unlimited

Exchange contact information:
www.healthcare.gov
Helpline: 1-800-318-2596

OREGON

For more information see: www.healthinsurancerevolution.org/oregon.

Employer-Provided versus Individual Health Insurance Rates (2014)

	Family	Single
Employer-provided rate	$1,500	$547
Individual rate	$640	$214

Single Individual Health Insurance Costs by Metallic Tier (2014)

	Bronze	Silver	Gold
Premium	$166	$214	$247
Deductible	$5,000	$3,000	$2,000
Out-of-pocket limit	$6,350	$6,000	$3,500
Lifetime limit	Unlimited	Unlimited	Unlimited

Family Individual Health Insurance Costs by Metallic Tier (2014)

	Bronze	Silver	Gold
Premium	$534	$640	$741
Deductible	$8,500	$6,000	$4,000
Out-of-pocket limit	$12,700	$12,000	$7,000
Lifetime limit	Unlimited	Unlimited	Unlimited

Exchange contact information:
www.coveroregon.com
Helpline: 1-855-268-3767

PENNSYLVANIA

For more information see: www.healthinsurancerevolution.org/pennsylvania.

Employer-Provided versus Individual Health Insurance Rates (2014)

	Family	Single
Employer-provided rate	$1,489	$539
Individual rate	$509	$170

Single Individual Health Insurance Costs by Metallic Tier (2014)

	Bronze	Silver	Gold
Premium	$156	$170	$216
Deductible	$5,500	$2,650	$1,000
Out-of-pocket limit	$6,350	$6,350	$4,500
Lifetime limit	Unlimited	Unlimited	Unlimited

Family Individual Health Insurance Costs by Metallic Tier (2014)

	Bronze	Silver	Gold
Premium	$468	$509	$646
Deductible	$11,000	$5,300	$2,000
Out-of-pocket limit	$12,700	$12,700	$9,000
Lifetime limit	Unlimited	Unlimited	Unlimited

Exchange contact information:
www.healthcare.gov
Helpline: 1-800-318-2596

RHODE ISLAND

For more information see: www.healthinsurancerevolution.org/rhode-island.

Employer-Provided versus Individual Health Insurance Rates (2014)

	Family	Single
Employer-provided rate	$1,537	$588
Individual rate	$878	$293

Single Individual Health Insurance Costs by Metallic Tier (2014)

	Bronze	Silver	Gold
Premium	$215	$293	$353
Deductible	$5,800	$3,000	$1,000
Out-of-pocket limit	$6,350	$6,350	$4,000
Lifetime limit	Unlimited	Unlimited	Unlimited

Family Individual Health Insurance Costs by Metallic Tier (2014)

	Bronze	Silver	Gold
Premium	$643	$878	$1,055
Deductible	$5,800	$3,000	$1,000
Out-of-pocket limit	$6,350	$6,350	$4,000
Lifetime limit	Unlimited	Unlimited	Unlimited

Exchange contact information:
www.healthsourceri.com
Helpline: 1-855-840-4774

SOUTH CAROLINA

For more information see: www.healthinsurancerevolution.org/south-carolina.

Employer-Provided versus Individual Health Insurance Rates (2014)

	Family	Single
Employer-provided rate	$1,384	$511
Individual rate	$689	$230

Single Individual Health Insurance Costs by Metallic Tier (2014)

	Bronze	Silver	Gold
Premium	$190	$230	$284
Deductible	$4,200	$3,500	$1,000
Out-of-pocket limit	$6,350	$3,500	$4,000
Lifetime limit	Unlimited	Unlimited	Unlimited

Family Individual Health Insurance Costs by Metallic Tier (2014)

	Bronze	Silver	Gold
Premium	$568	$689	$851
Deductible	$8,000	$7,000	$2,000
Out-of-pocket limit	$12,700	$7,000	$8,000
Lifetime limit	Unlimited	Unlimited	Unlimited

Exchange contact information:
www.healthcare.gov
Helpline: 1-800-318-2596

SOUTH DAKOTA

For more information see: www.healthinsurancerevolution.org/south-dakota.

Employer-Provided versus Individual Health Insurance Rates (2014)

	Family	Single
Employer-provided rate	$1,453	$542
Individual rate	$772	$258

Single Individual Health Insurance Costs by Metallic Tier (2014)

	Bronze	Silver	Gold
Premium	$249	$258	$313
Deductible	$5,000	$3,500	$1,500
Out-of-pocket limit	$6,350	$3,500	$3,000
Lifetime limit	Unlimited	Unlimited	Unlimited

Family Individual Health Insurance Costs by Metallic Tier (2014)

	Bronze	Silver	Gold
Premium	$745	$772	$937
Deductible	$10,000	$7,000	$3,000
Out-of-pocket limit	$12,700	$7,000	$6,000
Lifetime limit	Unlimited	Unlimited	Unlimited

Exchange contact information:
www.healthcare.gov
Helpline: 1-800-318-2596

TENNESSEE

For more information see: www.healthinsurancerevolution.org/tennessee.

Employer-Provided versus Individual Health Insurance Rates (2014)

	Family	Single
Employer-provided rate	$1,442	$508
Individual rate	$539	$180

Single Individual Health Insurance Costs by Metallic Tier (2014)

	Bronze	Silver	Gold
Premium	$138	$180	$238
Deductible	$4,000	$2,000	$2,100
Out-of-pocket limit	$6,350	$4,000	$2,100
Lifetime limit	Unlimited	Unlimited	Unlimited

Family Individual Health Insurance Costs by Metallic Tier (2014)

	Bronze	Silver	Gold
Premium	$414	$539	$714
Deductible	$8,000	$4,000	$4,200
Out-of-pocket limit	$12,700	$8,000	$4,200
Lifetime limit	Unlimited	Unlimited	Unlimited

Exchange contact information:
www.healthcare.gov
Helpline: 1-800-318-2596

TEXAS

For more information see: www.healthinsurancerevolution.org/texas.

Employer-Provided versus Individual Health Insurance Rates (2014)

	Family	Single
Employer-provided rate	$1,416	$513
Individual rate	$562	$188

Single Individual Health Insurance Costs by Metallic Tier (2014)

	Bronze	Silver	Gold
Premium	$132	$188	$230
Deductible	$5,000	$6,000	$3,250
Out-of-pocket limit	$6,250	$6,000	$3,250
Lifetime limit	Unlimited	Unlimited	Unlimited

Family Individual Health Insurance Costs by Metallic Tier (2014)

	Bronze	Silver	Gold
Premium	$396	$562	$690
Deductible	$12,700	$12,700	$9,750
Out-of-pocket limit	$12,700	$12,700	$9,750
Lifetime limit	Unlimited	Unlimited	Unlimited

Exchange contact information:
www.healthcare.gov
Helpline: 1-800-318-2596

UTAH

For more information see: www.healthinsurancerevolution.org/utah.

Employer-Provided versus Individual Health Insurance Rates (2014)

	Family	Single
Employer-provided rate	$1,410	$517
Individual rate	$635	$207

Single Individual Health Insurance Costs by Metallic Tier (2014)

	Bronze	Silver	Gold
Premium	$164	$207	$239
Deductible	$5,000	$3,000	$1,000
Out-of-pocket limit	$6,250	$4,900	$3,300
Lifetime limit	Unlimited	Unlimited	Unlimited

Family Individual Health Insurance Costs by Metallic Tier (2014)

	Bronze	Silver	Gold
Premium	$503	$635	$734
Deductible	$10,000	$6,000	$2,000
Out-of-pocket limit	$12,500	$9,800	$6,600
Lifetime limit	Unlimited	Unlimited	Unlimited

Exchange contact information:
www.healthcare.gov
Helpline: 1-800-318-2596

VERMONT

For more information see: www.healthinsurancerevolution.org/vermont.

Employer-Provided versus Individual Health Insurance Rates (2014)

	Family	Single
Employer-provided rate	$1,462	$559
Individual rate	$1,198	$426

Single Individual Health Insurance Costs by Metallic Tier (2014)

	Bronze	Silver	Gold
Premium	$348	$426	$505
Deductible	$3,500	$1,900	$750
Out-of-pocket limit	$6,350	$5,100	$4,250
Lifetime limit	Unlimited	Unlimited	Unlimited

Family Individual Health Insurance Costs by Metallic Tier (2014)

	Bronze	Silver	Gold
Premium	$977	$1,198	$1,420
Deductible	$7,000	$3,800	$1,500
Out-of-pocket limit	$12,700	$10,200	$8,500
Lifetime limit	Unlimited	Unlimited	Unlimited

Exchange contact information:
https://healthconnect.vermont.gov
Helpline: 1-800-899-9600

VIRGINIA

For more information see: www.healthinsurancerevolution.org/virginia.

Employer-Provided versus Individual Health Insurance Rates (2014)

	Family	Single
Employer-provided rate	$1,489	$532
Individual rate	$749	$250

Single Individual Health Insurance Costs by Metallic Tier (2014)

	Bronze	Silver	Gold
Premium	$176	$250	$294
Deductible	$6,000	$3,350	$1,750
Out-of-pocket limit	$6,000	$5,500	$5,000
Lifetime limit	Unlimited	Unlimited	Unlimited

Family Individual Health Insurance Costs by Metallic Tier (2014)

	Bronze	Silver	Gold
Premium	$527	$749	$881
Deductible	$12,000	$6,700	$3,500
Out-of-pocket limit	$12,000	$11,000	$10,000
Lifetime limit	Unlimited	Unlimited	Unlimited

Exchange contact information:
www.healthcare.gov
Helpline: 1-800-318-2596

WASHINGTON

For more information see: www.healthinsurancerevolution.org/washington.

Employer-Provided versus Individual Health Insurance Rates (2014)

	Family	Single
Employer-provided rate	$1,578	$538
Individual rate	$897	$300

Single Individual Health Insurance Costs by Metallic Tier (2014)

	Bronze	Silver	Gold
Premium	$230	$300	$352
Deductible	$5,250	$1,250	$1,500
Out-of-pocket limit	$5,250	$6,350	$4,500
Lifetime limit	Unlimited	Unlimited	Unlimited

Family Individual Health Insurance Costs by Metallic Tier (2014)

	Bronze	Silver	Gold
Premium	$687	$897	$1,054
Deductible	$10,500	$2,500	$3,000
Out-of-pocket limit	$10,500	$12,700	$9,000
Lifetime limit	Unlimited	Unlimited	Unlimited

Exchange contact information:
www.wahealthplanfinder.org
Helpline: 1-855-923-4633

WEST VIRGINIA

For more information see: www.healthinsurancerevolution.org/west-virginia.

Employer-Provided versus Individual Health Insurance Rates (2014)

	Family	Single
Employer-provided rate	$1,515	$589
Individual rate	$743	$248

Single Individual Health Insurance Costs by Metallic Tier (2014)

	Bronze	Silver	Gold
Premium	$203	$248	$295
Deductible	$4,000	$4,750	$1,000
Out-of-pocket limit	$6,350	$6,350	$3,500
Lifetime limit	Unlimited	Unlimited	Unlimited

Family Individual Health Insurance Costs by Metallic Tier (2014)

	Bronze	Silver	Gold
Premium	$607	$743	$884
Deductible	$8,000	$9,500	$2,000
Out-of-pocket limit	$12,700	$12,700	$7,000
Lifetime limit	Unlimited	Unlimited	Unlimited

Exchange contact information:
www.healthcare.gov
Helpline: 1-800-318-2596

WISCONSIN

For more information see: www.healthinsurancerevolution.org/wisconsin.

Employer-Provided versus Individual Health Insurance Rates (2014)

	Family	Single
Employer-provided rate	$1,574	$575
Individual rate	$731	$244

Single Individual Health Insurance Costs by Metallic Tier (2014)

	Bronze	Silver	Gold
Premium	$203	$244	$298
Deductible	$5,800	$4,500	$500
Out-of-pocket limit	$5,800	$4,500	$6,350
Lifetime limit	Unlimited	Unlimited	Unlimited

Family Individual Health Insurance Costs by Metallic Tie (2014)

	Bronze	Silver	Gold
Premium	$607	$731	$892
Deductible	$11,600	$9,000	$1,000
Out-of-pocket limit	$11,600	$9,000	$12,700
Lifetime limit	Unlimited	Unlimited	Unlimited

Exchange contact information:
www.healthcare.gov
Helpline: 1-800-318-2596

WYOMING

For more information see: www.healthinsurancerevolution.org/wyoming.

Employer-Provided versus Individual Health Insurance Rates (2014)

	Family	Single
Employer-provided rate	$1,511	$587
Individual rate	$1,181	$395

Single Individual Health Insurance Costs by Metallic Tier (2014)

	Bronze	Silver	Gold
Premium	$349	$395	$435
Deductible	$4,000	$2,500	$1,000
Out-of-pocket limit	$6,350	$5,000	$5,000
Lifetime limit	Unlimited	Unlimited	Unlimited

Family Individual Health Insurance Costs by Metallic Tier (2014)

	Bronze	Silver	Gold
Premium	$1,044	$1,181	$1,302
Deductible	$8,000	$5,000	$2,000
Out-of-pocket limit	$12,700	$10,000	$10,000
Lifetime limit	Unlimited	Unlimited	Unlimited

Exchange contact information:
www.healthcare.gov
Helpline: 1-800-318-2596

IS YOUR COMPANY REQUIRED TO OFFER EMPLOYER-PROVIDED HEALTH INSURANCE?

N o—your company is not required to offer employer-provided health insurance coverage. However, if your company has more than 50 employees you may be required to make a payment called the *employer shared responsibility payment* (or tax penalty). This is commonly referred to as the *employer mandate* or the play-or-pay requirement. This appendix will help you (1) determine if you are subject to the employer mandate, and (2) if you are subject to the mandate, calculate the amount of your shared responsibility payment.

IS YOUR COMPANY SUBJECT TO THE EMPLOYER MANDATE?

 Tip: If you have fewer than 50 full-time-equivalent employees, you are not subject to any employer shared responsibility payments for not offering employer-provided coverage.

A *full-time employee* is defined as working on average at least 30 hours per week in a given month. For purposes of determining whether your company is subject to the employer mandate, you must include all full-time employees plus the *full-time equivalent* of your *part-time employees*.

To calculate the full-time equivalent of part-time employees, add the number of hours worked by part-time employees in a given month and divide the total by 120. The sum of the full-time employees and the full-time equivalent of the part-time employees is the number (FTEs) you use to determine if you are subject to the employer mandate. If your company has less than 50 FTEs, you are not subject to the penalty.

See Figure B.1 for a worksheet you can use to complete this calculation. We've also provided an example for ABC Manufacturing (see Figure B.2).

A. Number of full-time workers (employees working 30+ hours per week for the month).	Total FT: _____	(A)
B. Add all hours in the month for part-time employees, then divide by 120 hours.	Total hours: _____ / 120 = _____	(B)
C. Add answers above to get the FTE for the month (A + B).	A + B = _____ (FTE for month)	(C)
D. Total all months for the year (if hours are variable each month, complete steps A–C for each month).	Total for all months: _____	(D)
E. Divide total months (D) by 12 to get average FTEs per month.	D / 12 = _____ (Average)	(E)*

*If (E) average is 50 or more, then you are considered an Applicable Large Employer.

Figure B.1   Worksheet—Calculating the Number of Full-Time Employees (FTEs)

A. Number of full-time workers	Total FT: _10_	(A)
B. Add all hours in the month for part-time employees, then divide by 120 hours.	Total hours: _0_ / 120 = _0_	(B)
C. Add answers above to get the FTE for the month (A + B).	A + B = _10_ (FTE for month)	(C)
D. Total all months for the year (if hours are variable each month, complete steps A–C for each month).	Total for all months: _120_	(D)
E. Divide total months (D) by 12 to get average FTEs per month.	D / 12 = _10_ (Average)	(E)

Figure B.2   Example Calculation of FTEs for ABC Manufacturing

Once you have calculated the number of FTEs for your company, you will know if you are subject to the tax penalty for not offering coverage. If you are subject to the employer mandate, you will need to calculate the size of your shared responsibility payment. ABC Manufacturing only has 10 full-time employees and no part-time employees. Therefore, ABC Manufacturing is not subject to any tax penalties for not offering coverage.

WHAT IS THE AMOUNT OF YOUR SHARED RESPONSIBILITY PAYMENT?

When calculating the amount of your company's shared responsibility payment, your company receives a credit of 30 full-time employees. For example, a company with 50 full-time employees only has to consider 20 employees for purposes of the penalty. The annual per employee payment is $2,000. (This fee is only charged if at least one employee purchases coverage through a Health Insurance Marketplace and receives a premium tax credit.) To get the monthly per employee payment, you simply divide the annual penalty by 12. To calculate the total monthly penalty, you multiply the number of full-time employees employed during the month, minus 30, by the monthly per employee payment. (See Figure B.3.)

For example, Bill's Plumbing employs 60 full-time employees and does not offer employer-provided health insurance coverage. If at least one employee receives a federal subsidy, Bill's Plumbing will be required to make a monthly shared responsibility payment of $5,000 for a total of $60,000 per year. (See Figure B.4.)

A. Number of full-time employees minus 30
   Note: Do *not* include part-time equivalents in   _____ FTs – 30 = _____
   this calculation.
B. Annual per employee shared responsibility $2,000
   payment.
C. Total annual shared responsibility payment. $2,000 × (A) = _____
D. Total monthly shared responsibility payment.   (C) ÷ 12 = _____

Note: 2015 is a phase-in year. See www.healthinsurancerevolution.org for how to calculate the penalty in 2015.

Figure B.3 Worksheet—Calculating Potential Shared Responsibility Payment

A. Number of full-time employees minus 30
   Note: Do *not* include full-time equivalents $60 - 30 = 30$
   in this calculation.
B. Annual per employee shared responsibility $2,000
   payment.
C. Total annual shared responsibility $2,000 \times 30 = \$60,000$
   payment.
D. Total monthly shared responsibility $60,000 \div 12 = \$5,000$
   payment.

Figure B.4   Example—Calculating Potential Shared Responsibility Payment for Bill's Plumbing

To estimate your shared responsibility payment, use the online tools at www.healthinsurancerevolution.org/tools.

REFERENCES

INTRODUCTION—THE END OF EMPLOYER-PROVIDED HEALTH INSURANCE

Kaiser Family Foundation. 2013. *2013 Employer Health Benefits Survey*. Retrieved from http://kff.org/private-insurance/report/2013-employer-health-benefits.

Mandelbaum, R. 2014. "Why Employers Will Stop Offering Health Insurance." *New York Times*, March 26. Retrieved from http://boss.blogs.nytimes.com/2014/03/26/why-employers-will-stop-offering-health-insurance.

U.S. Census. 2013. *Income, Poverty, and Health Insurance Coverage in the United States: 2012*. Retrieved from www.census.gov/prod/2013pubs/p60-245.pdf.

CHAPTER 1: THE DISADVANTAGES OF EMPLOYER-PROVIDED HEALTH INSURANCE

Covered California. 2014. *Shop and Compare Tool*. Retrieved from www.coveredca.com/shopandcompare/#calculator.

Kaiser Family Foundation. 2013. *2013 Employer Health Benefits Survey*. Retrieved from http://kff.org/private-insurance/report/2013-employer-health-benefits.

CHAPTER 2: THE ADVANTAGES OF INDIVIDUAL HEALTH INSURANCE

Kaiser Family Foundation. 2013. *2013 Employer Health Benefits Survey*. Retrieved from http://kff.org/private-insurance/report/2013-employer-health-benefits.

CHAPTER 3: THE SOLUTION—EMPLOYER-FUNDED INDIVIDUAL HEALTH INSURANCE

Goodman, J. 2010. "Goodbye, Employer-Sponsored Insurance." *Wall Street Journal*, May 21. Retrieved from http://online.wsj.com/news/articles/SB10001424052748703880304575236602943319816.

Internal Revenue Code (IRC) 105. 1954, August 16. *26 U.S. Code § 105— Amounts Received under Accident and Health Plans.* Retrieved from www.law .cornell.edu/uscode/text/26/105.

Kaiser Family Foundation. 2013. *2013 Employer Health Benefits Survey.* Retrieved from http://kff.org/private-insurance/report/2013-employer-health-benefits.

Terhune, C. 2007. "Employers Turn to Alternative for Insuring Staff." *Wall Street Journal,* July 30.

U.S. Department of Labor. 2013, September 13. *Technical Release No. 2013-03.* Retrieved from www.dol.gov/ebsa/newsroom/tr13-03.html.

CHAPTER 5: HOW MUCH DOES INDIVIDUAL HEALTH INSURANCE COST?

Covered California. 2014. *Shop and Compare Tool.* Retrieved from www.covered ca.com/shopandcompare/#calculator.

Kaiser Family Foundation. 2014, January 22. *Explaining Health Care Reform: Risk Adjustment, Reinsurance, and Risk Corridors.* Retrieved from http://kff .org/health-reform/issue-brief/explaining-healthcare-reform-risk-adjustment -reinsurance-and-risk-corridors/.

CHAPTER 7: WHEN CAN YOU BUY INDIVIDUAL HEALTH INSURANCE?

eHealthinsurance.com. 2014. *Shop Short-Term Plans.* Retrieved from www .ehealthinsurance.com/short-term-health-insurance.

CHAPTER 13: WHAT IS DEFINED CONTRIBUTION HEALTHCARE?

Kaiser Family Foundation. 2013. *2013 Employer Health Benefits Survey.* Retrieved June 30, 2014, from http://kff.org/private-insurance/report/2013-employer-health-benefits.

CHAPTER 14: HOW TO CONDUCT A DEFINED CONTRIBUTION FINANCIAL ANALYSIS

Covered California. 2014. *Shop and Compare Tool.* Retrieved from www.covered ca.com/shopandcompare/#calculator.

APPENDIX A: STATE-BY-STATE GUIDE TO INDIVIDUAL/FAMILY HEALTH INSURANCE COSTS

District of Columbia Health Exchange. 2014a. *DC Healthlink Shopping Tool*. Retrieved from www.dchealthlink.com/calculator.

District of Columbia Health Exchange. 2014b. *Second Lowest Cost Silver Plan Costs*. Retrieved from https://dchealthlink.com/sites/default/files/forms/2014_SLCSP_Listing(v3_2-28-14).pdf.

eHealthinsurance.com. 2014. *Health Insurance Shopping Tool*. Retrieved from www.ehealthinsurance.com.

Kaiser Family Foundation. 2013. *2013 Employer Benefits Survey*. Retrieved from kff.org/private-insurance/report/2013-employer-health-benefits/.

U.S. Health and Human Services. 2012. *Medical Expenditure Panel Survey*. Retrieved from meps.ahrq.gov/mepsweb/.

U.S. Health and Human Services. 2014. *QHP Landscape Market Medical*. Retrieved from data.healthcare.gov.

Vermont Health Connect. 2014. *Plan Comparison Brochures*. Retrieved from http://info.healthconnect.vermont.gov/healthplans#pcb.

ACKNOWLEDGMENTS

The first acknowledgment goes to Jim Tozer and Dave Eastman, members of the board of directors of Zane Benefits since 2007. Jim and Dave have provided us the support and guidance to challenge and change the conventional wisdom about health insurance. Jim became Paul's mentor at Citibank when Paul was 22 years old, just as Paul became Rick's mentor at Zane Benefits when Rick was 22. Jim has taught us that the most valuable reward from a successful business career is the lifelong friends you make along your journey.

We have also been inspired by the hundreds of employees at Zane Benefits from 2007 to today who have shared our dream of giving every American the right to choose the best health insurance policy for themselves and their families. We hope that Zane Benefits is making, and has made, a lifelong contribution to your life, both now at Zane Benefits and in whatever else you choose to pursue. We especially note Christina Merhar and Michael Dyer at Zanc Benefits, who helped us finish this manuscript.

Next are the thousands of independent Zane affiliates who have also shared our dream of helping American employers do the right thing when it comes to their employees' health insurance.

Then there are our tens of thousands of customers at Zane Benefits who have shared our dream of doing what is right—giving their employees their own hard-earned money, plus employer money, to spend on their own health insurance.

Last, but not least, are the hundreds of outside vendors, lawyers, consultants, and partners who are far too numerous to mention without leaving someone out.

The final acknowledgment goes to each of our respective families, especially Paul's wife Lisa and both of our respective parents, who have given us the support and unconditional love to do what is right even when it means challenging the status quo.

Paul Zane Pilzer
Rick Lindquist
Park City, Utah
September 2014

ABOUT THE AUTHORS

RICK LINDQUIST

Rick Lindquist is a writer, entrepreneur, and investor and the President of Zane Benefits, Inc. (see www.zanebenefits.com).

He earned his BS in Economics and his BA in computer science from Duke University in 2007. Lindquist joined Zane Benefits as its thirteenth employee in 2007, and became director of sales in 2009 and president in 2011.

Zane Benefits provides innovative healthcare solutions that save businesses time and money while ensuring employees have access to better health insurance options at a lower cost.

As president, Lindquist has been responsible for the development of the firm's flagship product, ZaneHealth, which helps employers ensure compliance with IRS, ERISA, and HIPAA regulations and the market reforms of the Affordable Care Act (ACA). Lindquist is a sought-after speaker and reference for his expertise on defined contribution health plans.

In June of 2014, Lindquist was featured in an article on the front page of *The New York Times* small business section explaining how Zane Benefits' software addresses the challenges small businesses face in offering compliant health insurance solutions. Zane Benefits has also been featured on the front page of *The Wall Street Journal* and USA *Today*.

PAUL ZANE PILZER

Paul Zane Pilzer is an economist, social entrepreneur, professor, public servant, and *The New York Times* bestselling author of 11 books and dozens of scholarly publications.

He earned his BA from Lehigh University in three years and received his MBA from Wharton Business School in 15 months at age 22. He became Citibank's youngest officer at age 22 and its youngest vice president at age 25. He was appointed an adjunct professor at New York University at age 24, where he taught for 21 years and was five times voted "best teacher." Since 1991, he has been a commencement speaker and/or visiting lecturer at the University of Pennsylvania, Lehigh University, the University of Utah, IIT (India), Moscow State University, Peking University, and the University of Hong Kong.

He has started, and/or taken public, six companies in healthcare and K–12 education with a total market capitalization exceeding $1 billion.

In healthcare, he is the founder of Extend Health (1999) and Zane Benefits (2006), suppliers of personalized health benefits to U.S. employees. Extend Health was acquired by Towers Watson in 2012. Zane Benefits, a software company, is the leading U.S. provider of online defined contribution platforms to employers who allow their employees to choose their own health benefits. Zane Benefits was featured on the front page of *The Wall Street Journal* (2007) and the front page of the business section of *The New York Times* (2014).

In education, he is the founder of CDROM publisher Zane Publishing (1989), which became publicly listed in 1995 on NASDAQ, The American Academy (2005), which provides online education and diplomas to former high school dropouts, and Zane Prep (2011), which leads our nation in K-8 STEM (Science, Technology, Engineering, and Math) education with Zaniac Learning Centers nationwide.

In public service, he was an appointed economic advisor in two U.S. presidential administrations (1983–1989) and today serves as a consultant to CEOs and government officials from China to Europe.

Pilzer's first book, *Other People's Money* (New York: Simon & Schuster, 1989), on the S&L financial crisis, was critically acclaimed by *The New York Times* and *The Economist* magazine and reviewed by John Kenneth Galbraith for *The New York Review of Books*.

Pilzer's next book, *Unlimited Wealth* (New York: Crown, 1991), explains how we live in a world of unlimited physical resources because of rapidly advancing technology. After reading *Unlimited Wealth*, the late Sam Walton, founder of Walmart, said that he was "amazed at Pilzer's business capacity" and his "ability to put it into layman's terms."

Pilzer's *God Wants You to Be Rich: The Theology of Economics* (New York: Simon & Schuster, 2007) explains how the foundation of our economic system is based on our Judeo-Christian heritage; this *New York Times* business best-seller was featured on the front page of *The Wall Street Journal* and on television shows ranging from *60 Minutes* to *First Person with Maria Shriver*.

In *The New Wellness Revolution* (New York: John Wiley & Sons, 2002), Pilzer identifies the newly emerging wellness business. For this book, he received an honorary doctorate in public service and was called a "wellness guru" by *The New York Times*. *The New Wellness Revolution* has been published in 25 languages and in 2009 Pilzer addressed the People's Republic of China from the Center Podium of the Great Hall of the People in Beijing.

The Next Millionaires (Cuyahoga Falls, OH: Momentum Media, 2006) explains why the number of U.S. millionaires doubled in the 1990s, how the economy is now creating 1 million millionaires a year from 2006 through 2016, and how ordinary people can become one of them. He lectured on this book in Hong Kong and spoke on social entrepreneurship at the University of Hong Kong in 2013.

The New Health Insurance Solution (Hoboken, NJ: John Wiley & Sons, 2005) sets forth a bold new direction for U.S. health insurance and explains how individuals can now get affordable health insurance independent of their employer. This book also explains how employers can end their health insurance nightmare while still being able to hire great employees.

A former commentator on National Public Radio and CNN, Pilzer was profiled on the front page of *The Wall Street Journal* in 2007 and has appeared three times on the *Larry King Live!* television program. He speaks live each year to approximately 200,000 people, and more than 20 million audiotapes of his speeches have been sold. He lives in Utah with his wife and four children, where they are all avid snowboarders, mountain bikers, and chess players.

INDEX